Digital Resilience

Dale Stephens · Matthew Stubbs · Samuel White
Editors

Digital Resilience

International and Domestic Legal Responses to Cyber Security and Artificial Intelligence

Springer

Editors
Dale Stephens
Adelaide Law School
University of Adelaide
Adelaide, SA, Australia

Matthew Stubbs
Adelaide Law School
University of Adelaide
Adelaide, SA, Australia

Samuel White
Adelaide Law School
University of Adelaide
Adelaide, SA, Australia

ISBN 978-981-97-9745-5 ISBN 978-981-97-9746-2 (eBook)
https://doi.org/10.1007/978-981-97-9746-2

This Springer imprint is published by the registered company Springer Nature Singapore Pte Ltd.
The registered company address is: 152 Beach Road, #21-01/04 Gateway East, Singapore 189721, Singapore

Contents

Editors and Contributors

About the Editors

Dale Stephens is Professor of the faculty of the Adelaide Law School at the University of Adelaide and Captain in the Royal Australian Navy Reserve who spent over 20 years as a permanent officer in the Royal Australian Navy before taking up his appointment at Adelaide Law School. He has occupied numerous staff officer positions throughout his career in the Australian Defence Force (ADF), including Fleet Legal Officer, Command Legal Officer (Naval Training Command), Chief Legal Officer of Strategic Operations Command, Director of Operational and International Law, Deputy Director of the Asia-Pacific Centre for Military Law (a joint venture with Melbourne University Law School), Director Navy Legal and Director of the Military Law Centre. He has deployed twice to East Timor (INTERFET and UNTAET) and twice to Iraq (Baghdad) in senior legal officer positions and has provided extensive advice to government at the strategic level. He is the recipient of the Conspicuous Service Medal and the (US) Bronze Star as well as ADF and UN commendations for his service. Dale.stephens@adelaide.edu.au

Matthew Stubbs is Professor of the faculty of the Adelaide Law School at the University of Adelaide, where he serves as Editor in Chief of the *Adelaide Law Review* and Program Coordinator of Postgraduate Coursework Programs and Military Law Programs. Professor Stubbs is involved with professional bodies in the law and academia and is a member and former Chair of the Space Law Committee and Human Rights Committee of the Law Society of South Australia and a member of the Law Council of Australia's National Human Rights Committee. Matthew was awarded the Law Society of South Australia President's Medal in 2023. Matthew.stubbs@adelaide.edu.au

Samuel White is Senior Lecturer of the faculty of the Adelaide Law School at the University of Adelaide. He is concurrently Visiting Fellow at the Australian Defence Force Academy and holds positions as Adjunct Associate Professor at the University of New England. In 2024, he was made Associate Fellow of the Royal Historical Society and the first Army Visiting Fellow at the Australian War Memorial. Samuel has also served as both a Royal Australian Infantry Corps and an Australian Army Legal Corps officer in a variety of tactical, operational and strategic level postings. His military experiences focussed his doctoral studies, which addressed the constitutional ambit and limitations of responding to foreign interference (both traditional and modern forms) via military responses. Samuel.white@adelaide.edu.au

Contributors

Deb Camden University of Queensland, Brisbane, Australia

Socrates Giatrakos The University of Adelaide, Adelaide, Australia

Joanna Jarose University of Adelaide Law School, Adelaide, Australia

Susanne L. Lloyd-Jones UNSW Faculty of Law and Justice, Sydney, Australia

Hamish Charles McNamara The University of Adelaide, Adelaide, Australia

Beth Nosworthy Adelaide Law School, The University of Adelaide, Adelaide, Australia

Aneta Peretko Adelaide, Australia

J. W. F. Small Directorate of Army Legal Services, Andover, United Kingdom

Dale Stephens The University of Adelaide, Adelaide, Australia; Adelaide Law School, Adelaide, Australia

Matthew Stubbs The University of Adelaide, Adelaide, Australia; Adelaide Law School, Adelaide, Australia

Elizabeth Watford The University of Adelaide, Adelaide, Australia

Samuel White The University of Adelaide, Adelaide, Australia; Adelaide Law School, Adelaide, Australia

Introduction

Dale Stephens, Matthew Stubbs, and Samuel White

This edited collection arises from the proceedings of the inaugural Research Unit on Military Law and Ethics (RUMLAE) Cyber Resilience Conference, held at the University of Adelaide on 4 September 2023. Individual contributors have developed their papers for this volume from the starting point of their presentations and the discussions held at the conference. Together, the papers in this volume seek to provide workable, pragmatic responses and options to promote resilience in cyberspace. This collection reflects perspectives from both Australian and international audiences; and across the spectrum of government, academia and industry.

Why resilience? Increasingly States are accepting that they will not be able to completely deter cybercrime and cyber security incidents and must instead focus on means of responding to cyber issues in such a way as to reduce disruptions and remain functional. There is no one definition of cyber resilience that commands universal assent. In their study of the concept, Vasiliki Tzavara and Savvas Vassiliadis define cyber resilience as

> the capability of an organization or system to endure and adjust to unfavorable cyber events, such as cyber attacks, data breaches, and system failures. It is a holistic approach to cyber security that recognizes that security incidents are inevitable, and focuses on building the organization's ability to withstand and bounce back from these incidents, rather than solely preventing them. … Cyber resilience involves not just defending against attacks, but also being able to recover, learn, and evolve from them.[1]

The contributions in this volume respond to these themes and others.[2]

D. Stephens · M. Stubbs · S. White (✉)
Adelaide Law School, Adelaide 5000, Australia
e-mail: Samuel.white@adelaide.edu.au

D. Stephens
e-mail: Dale.stephens@adelaide.edu.au

M. Stubbs
e-mail: Matthew.stubbs@adelaide.edu.au

D. Stephens et al. (eds.), *Digital Resilience*,
https://doi.org/10.1007/978-981-97-9746-2_1

The focus on resilience is driven by acceptance of two primary factors: that cyberthreats pose an existential economic threat, and that cyber and information operations are a means for strategic adversaries to advance their agendas at relatively low cost. First, the shift in strategic frameworks is clearly linked to the increase in the effectiveness of cyber-related incidents (due to the increasing connectivity and ubiquity of cyberspace). This trend is not set to reverse. In 2022, 65% of global gross domestic product (GDP) is expected to be digitised, illustrating the breadth of economic opportunity and necessity of data crossing borders.[3] Enhancing access to data has also been identified as a top five priority for the digital economy amongst Organisation for Economic Cooperation and Development ('OECD') countries.[4] Increasing digital connectivity can open an economy due to attractiveness in data and digital-related investment[5] and help reduce loss of talent overseas.[6] Yet it also comes with costs. From mid-2022 to mid-2023, the cost of cybercrime for Australian businesses rose by 14%.[7] The average cost of cybercrime for small businesses is now $46,000; for medium businesses $97,000; and for large businesses $71,600.[8] This is a threat that is accelerating but is not new. In 2015, the Australian Securities and Investments Commission ('ASIC') in its *Report 429 Cyber Resilience: Health Check* indicated that it expects businesses to: 'address cyberrisks as part of their legal and compliance obligations—including risk management and disclosure requirements'.[9] Australian Institute of Company Directors ('AICD') surveys consistently report that cyber security is the number one issue keeping directors awake at night;[10] KWM reports cyber security to be the one of three critical issues in the short and medium term for directors.[11]

Equally, the ubiquity of cyberspace has had strategic consequences. Within the cybercontext, offensive actions often cost less than defensive ones.[12] For 25 years, death and disruption from cyberattacks has been hypothesised but generally not eventuated.[13] The real risk has arisen from the ability to weaponise data to perform more pinpointed shaping operations, through the historically unique ability to connect to individuals in high cost, low impact operations.[14] In 2017, then-Australian Director-General of Security, Duncan Lewis, categorised espionage and foreign interference operations[15] as 'an insidious threat' and stated that 'foreign powers are clandestinely seeking to shape the opinions of members of the Australian public, of our media organisations and our government officials in order to advance their country's own political objectives'[16] on a scale and intensity that 'exceeds any similar operations launched against the country during the Cold War, or in any other period'.[17] Two years later, in late 2019, Lewis declared that foreign interference operations ('IOs') posed an 'existential threat to Australia' and are 'by far the most serious issue going forward' for Australian security.[18] No vulnerabilities in Australian society were publicly discussed, nor any steps suggested on countering the increasing IOs. Recently, the *2020 Defence Strategic Update*[19] to the *2016 Defence White Paper*[20] highlighted the risk IOs pose to Australia. This is important, for such operations are not common in the Western, and particularly Anglo-Saxon, approach to warfare. A lack of cultural experience with 'short of war' measures (sometimes called political warfare,[21] sometimes called information warfare[22]) has resulted in strategic blindness to their potential.

These two limbs requiring cyber resilience—one of economic drivers in cybercrime, and the other of the relative cheapness of information in a digital age for military operations—jointly together form the problem this book seeks to respond to. Broadly, the contributions in this volume suggest that the answer lies in means to build resilience and trust.

The recently released Australian Government *2023-2030 Australia Cyber Security Strategy* stated that: 'a digital economy relies on the ability to trust that our personal data, infrastructure, and underpinning systems are secure'. This statement highlights that before Australia can contribute to an open data economy, the critical infrastructure and foundations for cyber security must be laid first, in both government and industry.[23]. The strategy promotes six shields to incentivise and ensure resilience in Australia and the near-region: indeed, in 63 pages it references resilience 38 times.

Signalling the importance of business to cyber resilience, Shield 1 of the *Strategy* seeks to ensure 'citizens and businesses are better protected from cyberthreats and can bounce back quickly following a cyberattack'.[24] Central to this is that

> responsibility for cyber security is shared across the community, with more cyber risk allocated to those who are more capable of addressing them ... Larger businesses will play a central role in strengthening the security of the economy by helping those less able to do so.[25]

This volume draws together contributions focussing on both corporate, government and strategic issues relating to cyber resilience.

This edited collection is based around resilience. Whilst we have accepted Tzavara and Vassiliadis' definition of cyber resilience as a starting point above, our particular focus is to identify two aspects of resilience. Importantly, resilience does not suggest failure cannot occur. Instead, we emphasise two forms of resilience:

- **Engineering resilience**—the capacity of a system to suffer disturbances, whilst still retaining its ability to refer to an earlier stable state
- **Ecological resilience**—the capacity to absorb the effects of disturbances through adaption.

Both forms of resilience describe the ability of a system to retain its original functionality and identity in response to disturbance, but one focuses on static coping mechanisms (resistance and recovery) and the other on dynamic strategies (adaptation).[26] In our view, engineering and ecological resilience capture the dual nature of resilience. To use the generative metaphor[27] of a tree, can the branch bend and bounce back (engineering) or if it breaks, can a new branch grow in its place (ecological)? If yes to either, it is resilient. It is only by considering both forms of resilience—engineering and ecological—that we can build a comprehensive picture of what cyber resilience is, and how it can be promoted.

With this foundation of what resilience is, and the various tests for it, the book comprises the following chapters. The first three chapters all address (through various lenses) one of the more logical aspects of digital resilience: cyber security. Samuel White advocates to look away from international law and towards domestic law remedies through the case study of information operations, whilst Dale Stephens and Joanna Jarose argue that international law is indeed resilient enough to adapt and grow to the ubiquity of cyberspace. The edited work then moves towards data and the importance of data protection—the unseen yet invaluable 'fuel' for modern economics and national security. John Small offers insights from the European Union, whilst Aneta Peretko shows how Australia is catching up with data protection. Susanne Lloyd-Jones, also from an Australian perspective, then illuminates how wider systems of national significance (not just data) need to be looked to in order to promote resilience.

The work then turns to alternate and novel approaches to resilience. It first argues that 'People Power' should be tapped in order to both harden the population and to provide States with the ability to control the narrative—through so-called Internet Referral Units. In this vein, two of the editors offer in the subsequent chapter some reflections upon building overall social resilience through education. Hamish McNamara takes a separate view of utilising the judiciary to declare 'Truth', whilst Samuel White continues to suggest that domestic legal remedies are more than sufficient when addressing new threats within the Anglo-Saxon world by relying upon the Royal Prerogative. Yet, digital resilience is not just about crime. It is also about money. The edited work accordingly shows how corporate regulation is a key factor in any resilience assessment. To that end, Beth Nosworthy addresses how director's duties could be approached to promote resilient corporate cultures. Being central to the recent data hacks, corporations are particularly concerned with the legal and market reactions to their vulnerabilities. Stepping away from the law then, Debra Camden offers insights into how resilience can be signalled and communicated in a crisis.

It remains then to be seen *how* emerging technology will shape, test, break and re-make legal frameworks. It is the hope of this work to try engage—even just a little—with this evolving and critical area.

Notes

1. Vasiliki Tzavara and Savvas Vassiliadis, 'Tracing the evolution of cyber resilience: a historical and conceptual review' (2024) 23 *International Journal of Information Security* 1695, 1715.
2. There are a range of alternative definitions and explorations of cyber resilience in the literature. See, eg: Myriam Dunn Cavelty, Christine Eriksen and Benjamin Scharte, 'Making cyber security more resilient: adding social considerations to technological fixes' (2023) 26(7) *Journal of Risk Research* 801; Kjell Hausken, 'Cyber resilience in firms, organizations and societies' (2020) 11 *Internet of Things* 100204; Benoît Dupont et al, 'The tensions of cyber-resilience: From sensemaking to practice' (2023) 132 *Computers and Security* 103372.
3. Daniel S Hamilton and Joseph Quinlan, *Transatlantic Economy 2022* (Publication, 2022), 44.
4. Craig Gibson et al.'Leaked Today, Exploited for Life' (White Paper, Trend Micro Research, 18 October 2022), 3.
5. Marcel Boer, 'Open-Source Data Platforms', *Medium* (Website, 24 May 2020), <https://medium.com/swlh/open-source-data-platforms-b3b4768f9e3e>.
6. Marcel Boer, 'Open-Source Data Platforms', *Medium* (Website, 24 May 2020), <https://medium.com/swlh/open-source-data-platforms-b3b4768f9e3e>.

7. Australian Signals Directorate, *ASD Cyber Threat Report 2022-2023* (report, 14 November 2023), ch 4.
8. Australian Signals Directorate (n 2) '*Year in Review*'.
9. Australian Securities and Investments Commission, *Cyber Resilience: Health Check* (Report No 429, March 2015), 38.
10. Australian Institute of Company Directors, *Boards and Cyber Resilience* (Survey Findings June 2022), 5.
11. Meredith Paynter et al, *Directions 2023: Leading in turbulent times—is it time to swim hard or tread water?* (Publication, 4 September 2023) <www.kwm.com/au/en/insights/latest-thinking/publication/directions-2023.html>.
12. Trevor Thrall and Andrew Armstrong, 'Bear Market? Grizzly Steppe and the American Marketplace of Ideas' in Christopher Whyte, Trevor Thrall and Brian M Mazanec (eds), *Information Warfare in the Age of Cyber Conflict* (Routledge, 2020) 73.
13. Alvin Toffler, *The Third Wave* (William Morrow, 1980); Edward Waltz, *Information Warfare - Principles and Operations* (Artech House, 1st ed, 1998). There are only two known instances of physical destruction from a cyber attack—the destruction caused by Stuxnet, and apparent damage caused to a Germany blast furnace would appear the only two. Several major cyber-attacks, most notably at Saudi Aramco and Sony, have rendered computers inoperable, but that was as a result of hard-to-reverse changes in software, not damaged hardware.
14. The use of information as resource, environment and weapon within the 21st century is an emergent capability 'still seeking both language and concepts to become normative for discussions of warfare. See generally Edward Morgan and Marcus Thompson, 'Information Warfare - An Emergent Australian Defence Force Capability' (Discussion Paper No 3, Centre for Strategic and International Studies, October 2018) 6; See Elizabeth Watford & Samuel White, 'I Know Who You Are' (2023) 97 *Australian Law Journal* 766–786.
15. Foreign interference operations are 'covert, coercive or corrupt activities' against a State for the purpose of advancing the actor's interests—see Attorney-General's Department 2019, *Foreign Influence Transparency Scheme: Factsheet 2*, Australian Government. Accessed on 10 Oct 20 at https://www.ag.gov.au/sites/default/files/2020-03/influence-versus-interference.pdf.
16. Evidence to the Senate Legal and Constitutional Affairs Legislation Committee, Parliament of Australia, Canberra, 24 October 2017, 128 (Duncan Lewis).
17. Ibid.
18. Duncan Lewis, Address to the Lowy Institute (Speech, Lowy Institute, 4 September 2019).
19. Department of Defence (2020), 25.
20. Department of Defence, *2016 White Paper*, 9 at [1.19].
21. Angus Campbell, "War in 2025," (Keynote, Australian Strategic Policy Institute, 13 June 2019); Samuel White, 'Digital Payback' (2022) 4(2) *Australian Defence Journal of Strategic Studies* 235–258.
22. Dale Stephens, 'Influence Operations and International Law' (2020) 19(4) *Journal of Information Warfare* 1 ('Influence Operations & International Law'); Ducan Hollis, 'The Influence of War; The War for Influence' (2018) 32(1) *Temple International & Comparitive Law Journal* 32 ('The Influence of War; The War for Influence'). Michael Schmitt, 'Virtual Disenfranchisement: Cyber Election Meddling in the Grey Zones of International Law' in Trevor Thrall and Brian M. Mazanec Christopher Whyte (ed), *Information Warfare in the Age of Cyber Conflict* (Routledge, 1st ed, 2020) 186.
23. 2023-2030 Australian Cyber Security Strategy Discussion Paper, 10.
24. Department of Home Affairs, *2023-2030 Australian Cyber Security Strategy* (Report, 22 November 2023), 16.
25. Ibid 6.
26. Ibid, 848.
27. Julia Slupska, 'War, Health, and Ecosystem: Generative Metaphors in Cybersecurity Governance' (2020) 34 *Philosophy and Technology*, 469; see Samuel White 'Virus, Weapon, Litter, Industry: Generative Metaphors for Information Operations' (2024) 49(3) *Alternate Law Journal* 1–7.

Dale Stephens is a Professor of the faculty of the Adelaide Law School at the University of Adelaide and a Captain in the Royal Australian Navy Reserve who spent over 20 years as a permanent officer in the Royal Australian Navy before taking up his appointment at Adelaide Law School. He has occupied numerous staff officer positions throughout his career in the Australian Defence Force (ADF), including Fleet Legal Officer, Command Legal Officer (Naval Training Command), Chief Legal Officer Strategic Operations Command, Director of Operational and International Law, Deputy Director of the Asia-Pacific Centre for Military Law (a joint venture with Melbourne University Law School), Director Navy Legal and Director of the Military Law Centre. He has deployed twice to East Timor (INTERFET & UNTAET) and twice to Iraq (Baghdad) in senior legal officer positions and has provided extensive advice to Government at the strategic level. He is the recipient of the Conspicuous Service Medal and the (US) Bronze Star as well as ADF and UN commendations for his service.

Matthew Stubbs is a Professor of the faculty of the Adelaide Law School at the University of Adelaide, where he serves as Editor in Chief of the *Adelaide Law Review* and Program Coordinator of Postgraduate Coursework Programs and Military Law Programs. Professor Stubbs is involved with professional bodies in the law and academia, and is a member and former Chair of the Space Law Committee and Human Rights Committee of the Law Society of South Australia and a member of the Law Council of Australia's National Human Rights Committee. Matthew was awarded the Law Society of South Australia President's Medal in 2023.

Samuel White is a Senior Lecturer of the faculty of the Adelaide Law School at the University of Adelaide. He is concurrently a Visiting Fellow at the Australian Defence Force Academy and holds positions as an Adjunct Associate Professor at the University of New England. In 2024, he was made an Associate Fellow of the Royal Historical Society and the first Army Visiting Fellow at the Australian War Memorial. Samuel has also served as both a Royal Australian Infantry Corps and an Australian Army Legal Corps officer in a variety of tactical, operational and strategic level postings. His military experiences focused his doctoral studies, which addressed the constitutional ambit and limitations of responding to foreign interference (both traditional and modern forms) via military responses.

The Usefulness of International Law

Samuel White

Abstract This chapter delves into the intricate world of international law and its applicability in the realm of cybersecurity. This chapter serves as a critical examination of whether international legal frameworks are equipped to effectively regulate and respond to the ever-evolving challenges posed by cyber threats. The author navigates through the complexities of international treaties, conventions, and norms, dissecting their strengths and limitations in addressing the dynamic nature of cyberattacks. Readers will be exposed to a nuanced analysis of the evolving threat landscape and the role that international law plays in promoting digital resilience on a global scale. As they journey through this chapter, they will gain valuable insights into the legal intricacies that underpin the fight against cyber threats.

Introduction

Noting the dual limbs of cybercrime and cybersecurity identified in the introduction, it is important to highlight how international legal remedies (outside of treaty negotiation or norm development) are wholly inadequate in responding. To that extent, it can be claimed that international law lacks the resilience (engineering or environmental) to adapt to the threat of cyberspace. That proposition is against the backdrop of the author's own personal beliefs and experience, particularly with respect to trying to utilise international legal remedies to the threat of cyber security incidents (even outside the difficulties of technical, legal and political attribution!).

This chapter uses the threat of interference operations (IOs) to highlight that international law lacks the ability to respond properly.[1] It does so both to demonstrate the limitations of international law in this area and also to provide a more solid foundation for the following chapters which discuss domestic legal remedies.

S. White (✉)
Adelaide Law School at the University of Adelaide, Adelaide city centre, Australia
e-mail: Samuel.white@adelaide.edu.au

D. Stephens et al. (eds.), *Digital Resilience*,
https://doi.org/10.1007/978-981-97-9746-2_2

Can IOs Amount to a Breach of Sovereignty?

Beyond the use of force, international law may treat IOs as a breach of sovereignty. Sovereignty has been subject to heavy academic debate and criticism—is it a rule (to be enforced)[2] or a principle (that should be abided by)? The position is presently 'unclear'[3] although states are slowly starting to take public positions and cement their interests. These positions, however, often relate to cyber intrusions rather than IOs. States have said very little about the interrelation between IOs and sovereignty. The Netherlands has opined that 'the precise boundaries of what is and is not permissible have yet to fully crystallise',[4] whilst New Zealand believes 'further state practice is required for the precise boundaries of its application to crystallise'.[5]

No state has accused another, to date, of violating the principle of sovereignty through IOs. Accordingly, any examples are merely speculative as in practice claims of breach of sovereignty have not arisen. If sovereignty is a principle, it is not a freestanding rule capable of being breached. Even if sovereignty is accepted as a rule, there is still great uncertainty as to its content and the circumstances that would amount to a breach.[6] Existing precedent centres on physical effects, and territorial limits. IOs, centred on cognitive effects, would not currently seem to breach sovereignty.[7]

Can IOs Amount to a Prohibited Intervention?

There can be instances where a breach of sovereignty can amount to a prohibited intervention under international law. International law prohibits intervention by a State in the internal or external affairs of another State.[8] The prohibition on intervention, which forms 'part and parcel of customary international law',[9] is the 'corollary of every State's right to sovereignty, territorial integrity and political independence'.[10] It is widely accepted that the prohibition on intervention forms customary international law. On the customary status of the prohibition, the ICJ found that:

> [T]hough examples of trespass against this principle are not infrequent, the Court considers that it is part and parcel of customary international law...Expressions of an *opinio juris* regarding the existence of the principle of non-intervention in customary international law are numerous and not difficult to find...The existence in the *opinio juris* of States of the principle of non-intervention is backed by established and substantial practice.[11]

The question is whether, given only the most extreme IOs might ever amount to a use of force, any greater range of IOs might breach the obligation of non-intervention.

The prohibition is reflected in the UN *General Assembly Declaration on Friendly Relations*:

> [e]very State has an inalienable right to choose its own political, economic, social and cultural systems, without interference in any form by another State. No State or group of States has the right to intervene, directly or indirectly for any reason whatsoever, in the internal or external affairs of any other State.[12]

The leading case in this area is *Nicaragua v United States of America* (*Nicaragua*).[13] In *Nicaragua*, the International Court of Justice found that US funding of the *contras* in Nicaragua constituted a violation of the principle.[14] The Court relevantly held that:

> A prohibited intervention must ... be one bearing on matters in which each State is permitted, by the principle of State sovereignty, to decide freely. One of these is the choice of a political, economic, social and cultural system, and the formulation of foreign policy. Intervention is wrongful when it uses methods of coercion in regard to such choices, which must remain free ones. The element of coercion, which defines, and indeed forms the very essence of, prohibited intervention, is particularly obvious in the case of an intervention which uses force, either in the direct form of military action, or in the indirect form of support for subversive or terrorist armed activities within another State.[15]

Thus, in order for an act to qualify as a prohibited intervention, the activity does not need to have the element of force as is necessary under Article 2(4).[16] But it must have some element of coercion, which 'indeed forms the very essence of prohibited intervention'.[17]

What is coercion for the purposes of non-intervention? The term 'coercion' is not defined for the purpose of prohibited intervention or more generally in international law. Ordinarily, 'coercion' is defined as:

- the action of making someone do something that they do not want to do, using force or threatening to use force[18]
- to restrain or constrain by force, law, or authority; force or compel, as to do something[19]
- the use of force to persuade someone to do something they are unwilling to do[20]
- to compel an act or choice.[21]

Most of these definitions refer to the threat or use of force which is not required for the element of coercion under the prohibition on intervention. In other areas of international law, the term 'coercion' has similar but distinct meanings. For example, the International Law Commission (ILC) defined coercion in the context of Article 51 of the *Vienna Convention on the Law of Treaties* (VCLT) as 'any form of constraint or of threat' against a State representative seeking to consent to be bound by a treaty.[22] The ILC considered that there must be a causal link between the threat, the fear felt afterwards by the State representative, and the expression of consent to be bound to the treaty.[23] However, it is not necessary that the coercion is alone in determining the expression of the State representative and that forms of pressure that do not contain an element of fear do not fall within the scope of Article 51 of the VCLT.[24]

For the purpose of prohibited intervention, coercion can be generally understood as conduct which deprives, or is intended to deprive, another State of its ability to control, decide upon, or govern its internal or external affairs, either by compelling it to act, or refrain from acting, in a particular way.[25] In other words, to be coercive, the intervention must seek to compel or force a State to change its position, or to otherwise prevent a State from taking a particular course of action, thereby depriving the State of its sovereign will.[26] The *Tallinn Manual* offers that the term should 'not [be] limited to physical force, but rather refers to an affirmative act designed to deprive another

State of its freedom of choice, that is, to force that State to act in an involuntary manner or involuntarily refrain from acting in a particular way'.[27] The manual goes on to state: 'coercion must be distinguished from persuasion, criticism, public diplomacy, propaganda, retribution, mere maliciousness and the like in the sense that, unlike coercion, such activities merely involve ... influencing the voluntary actions of the target State'.[28]

The Australian Department of Foreign Affairs and Trade in 2019 provided an international law supplement, updating its interpretation of legal rules and their application.[29] Australia held that coercion means a targeted state is effectively deprived 'of the ability to control, decide upon or govern matters',[30] which can result from cyber operations that 'manipulate the electoral system to alter the results of an election in another State, intervention in the fundamental operation of Parliament, or in the stability of States' financial systems'.[31] In 2021, the Australian Government stated:

> The use by a State of cyber activities to prevent another State from holding an election, or manipulate the electoral system to alter the results of an election in another State, intervene in the fundamental operation of Parliament, or significantly disrupt the functioning of a States' financial systems would constitute a violation of the principle of non-intervention.[32]

This is a position Germany[33] and the United States have taken,[34] as well as some of Australia's Indo-Pacific neighbours.[35] New Zealand[36] and the Netherlands[37] have advocated a lower threshold. Importantly, for this thesis, Australia's definition, whilst encapsulating IOs against voting infrastructure, does not encapsulate IOs against the information environment more broadly. If coercion is to be understood as implying some form of compulsion, which leads the target state to act in a way it would not have done otherwise *or* to take a decision it would not have taken,[38] then by their very nature IOs cannot amount to prohibited interventions. How can covert operations that aim to have a target adopt or change certain behaviours willingly even be measured?[39]

It is for this reason that some scholars argue that coercion should be reinterpreted through a lens of deception—and accordingly advocate that IOs that manipulate 'the capacity to reason' are therefore coercive, as 'the projection of a different set of facts constrains one's freedom to act by making certain options and conclusions no longer seem viable or making others seem mandatory'.[40] Yet, Australia's Department of Foreign Affairs and Trade has been clear in its international law supplement that that would not constitute coercion.

Can IOs Amount to a Use of Force?

The *United Nations* (UN) *Charter* holds under Article 2(4): 'All Members shall refrain in their international relations from the threat or use of force against the territorial integrity or political independence of any State'. Accordingly, any activity that would amount to a use of force is prohibited under international law (unless conducted in self-defence under Article 51 of the *UN Charter*, or with Security Council authorisation).

A review of the drafting history of the *UN Charter* makes clear that the intended interpretation and meaning of 'use of force' was kinetic, physical damage. It was on this basis that it was accepted that economic sanctions do not constitute a use of force against a member state.[41] Extrapolating from this position, scholars have also noted that political pressure per se also does not fall within the prohibition of article 2(4) as constituting a use of force.[42] Yet the International Court of Justice has held that the training and arming of rebels, intent on overthrowing the incumbent government, would fall within the doctrinal concept of use of force under Article 2(4).[43] This mirrors the non-binding definition of the *Tallinn Manual* which focuses on effects rather than means or methods of warfare.[44]

As Stephens notes, it is improbable but not impossible that IOs might fall within this prohibition. He cites a scenario of 'an IO campaign that clearly manipulated individuals to organize into armed groups and to undertake physical attacks against another government (in the absence of an armed conflict against that State)'.[45] Continuing, however, Stephens notes that no parties asserted that the call to Kurdish arms, in Iraq, by the US President in 1991 violated article 2(4).[46] Further, Stephens' example is an extreme case—in the vast majority of instances, IOs are likely to have no demonstrable connection to any physical violence; indeed, the point of IOs is that they can achieve their aims without the need for physical violence. Given words alone cannot constitute a use of force, and most IOs cannot be responded to under the use of force paradigm of international law.

Can Countermeasures Work?

The above has outlined the difficulties of demonstrating both the legal attribution of an IO to a state and also identifying the breach of a relevant rule of international law even if an IO can be attributed. Even if those barriers can be overcome, however, there are difficulties in applying the remedy of countermeasures to an IO.

Countermeasures require attribution. In order to take legally justified countermeasures, the target state must have sufficient factual certainty of the source of the malign activity.[47] The difficulties with attributing IOs were covered above. The speed at which attribution would need to occur, in order to take countermeasures, means that this international legal remedy might be too slow for cyberspace. The delay in attribution is partly technological and partly political. Whilst advances in technology will of course increase the speed at which IOs can be attributed, there still remains the issue that an IO campaign may have ceased months earlier, but the consequences are only starting to manifest. Countermeasures must be proportionate,[48] temporary[49] and preceded by a demand that the offending state comply with its international obligations (unless the circumstances are urgent),[50] which all result in delays. Accordingly, even if the challenges of attribution and demonstrating a breach of international law can be overcome, there are some further difficulties in identifying how effective and legal countermeasures could be taken.

Conclusion as to International Law

This chapter has sought to demonstrate that domestic legal remedies and authorities are more likely to be useful in responding and promoting cyber resilience. It has done so through the lens of cybersecurity, but cybercrime falls within the same limitations (although cybercrime is much more regulated through treaty law—see, for example, the *Budapest Convention*).

Professor Duncan Hollis argues that international law is not well suited to regulate operations 'primarily defined by their connection to the cognitive dimension'.[51] This would seem reflected in the above legal analysis. Others disagree and walk a middle line. Professor Stephens opines:

> Influence Operations are generally permitted under international law. While it is possible to conceive of circumstances where an IO can violate Art 2(4), the principle of non-intervention and possibly even sovereignty (if that comprises a stand-alone rule under international law), such circumstances are very unique. Similarly, while due regard must be afforded the right to privacy under international human rights law (IHRL), it is clear that the equally applicable IHRL right to freedom of expression strongly underpins the capacity to undertake IO, especially where the narrative is credible.[52]

Accordingly, Stephens argues, it is likely that only the most extreme IOs such as those 'that clearly manipulated individuals to organise into armed groups and to undertake physical attacks against another government (in the absence of an armed conflict against that State)'[53] would breach international law. But these scenarios are extreme and, whilst possible, are less than plausible. They are also outside the scope of this thesis, which focuses on grey zone operations (and thus below the threshold of the use of force).

However, just because most IOs are probably legal under international law does not mean that Australia must remain a victim to them. The UN has consistently emphasised the importance of domestic legal remedies in the 1976 *Resolution on Non-interference in the Internal Affairs of States*[54] and the 1981 *Declaration on the Inadmissibility of Intervention and Interference in the Internal Affairs of States.*[55] Both made clear, explicit references to information operations conducted through the technology of the time, such as broadcast media, that attempted 'campaigns of vilification' and 'subversion and defamation'[56] in 1976, as well as 'any defamatory campaign, vilification or hostile propaganda for the purpose of intervening or interfering in the internal affairs of other States'[57] in 1981. The latter declaration, importantly, confirmed 'the right and duty of States to combat, within their constitutional prerogatives, the dissemination of false or distorted news which can be interpreted as interference in the internal affairs of other States'.[58]

Although this is not Australia's current interpretation of interference (and coercion), it is clear that domestic law (the so-called constitutional prerogatives) provides a degree of flexibility and power that international law simply does not have.

Notes

1. See Elizabeth Watford and Samuel White, 'I Know Who You Are' (2023) 97 *Australian Law Journal* 766.
2. Milton L Mueller, 'Against Sovereignty in Cyberspace' (2019) *International Studies Review* 1 provides a good summary of the general arguments about sovereignty. See also Michael Schmitt (ed), *Tallinn Manual 2.0* (Cambridge University Press, 2020) 14 [41] ('Rule 4: A State must not conduct cyber operations that violate the sovereignty of another State').
3. Harriet Moynihan, 'The Application of International Law to State Cyberattacks: Sovereignty and Non-intervention' (Research Paper, Chatham House, December 2019) 51 ('In due course, as further state practice and *opinio juris* emerge, a cyber-specific understanding of sovereignty may develop, much like that developed for other domains of international law. In the meantime, because it is unclear whether there is a limit or threshold to violations of sovereignty, states may prefer to use the more clearly established framework of non-intervention where that is possible').
4. UN General Assembly, *Official Compendium of Voluntary National Contributions on the Subject of How International Law Applies to the Use of Information and Communications Technologies by States Submitted by Participating Governmental Experts in the Group of Governmental Experts on Advancing Responsible State Behaviour in Cyberspace in the Context of International Security Established Pursuant to General Assembly Resolution 73/266*, UN Doc A/76/136 (13 July 2021) 5 ('*Official Compendium*').
5. New Zealand Ministry of Foreign Affairs and Trade, 'The Application of International Law to State Activity in Cyberspace' (Position Paper, 1 December 2020).
6. Dutch Minister of Foreign Affairs, 'Letter to the Parliament on the International Legal Order in Cyberspace' (Letter, 5 July 2019).
7. Duncan Hollis, 'Why States Need an International Law for Information Operations' (2007) 11 *Lewis and Clark Law Review* 1023; Duncan Hollis, 'An e-SOS for Cyberspace' (2011) 52 *Harvard International Law Journal* 373; Duncan Hollis, 'The Influence of War: The War for Influence' (2018) 32(1) *Temple International and Comparative Law Journal* 31.
8. *Case Concerning Military and Paramilitary Activities in an Against Nicaragua (Nicaragua v United States of America) (Merits)* [1986] ICJ Rep ('Nicaragua Case') [202]; *Declaration on Principles of International Law concerning Friendly Relations and Cooperation among States in accordance with the Charter of the United Nations*, GA Res 2625(XXV), 25th sess, 183rd plen mtg, UN Doc A/RES/2625(XXV) (24 October 1970) ('Friendly Relations Declaration') Principle 3.
9. Nicaragua Case [202].
10. Robert Jennings and Arthur Watts (eds), *Oppenheim's International Law (9th Edition): Volume 1 Peace* (1996) ('Oppenheim's International Law') 428; Nicaragua Case [202].
11. Nicaragua Case [202].
12. *Concerning Friendly Relations and Co-Operation Amongst States in Accordance with the Charter of the United Nations*, UN Doc A/RES/2625 (XXIV) (24 October 1970).
13. *Nicaragua Case* (n vii) [228].
14. Ibid.
15. Ibid [205].
16. Nicholas Tsagourias, 'Electoral Cyber Interference, Self-Determination and the Principle of Non-intervention in Cyberspace' (Speech, EJIL, 26 August 2019).
17. *Nicaragua Case* (n 106) [205]. See further Russel Buchan, 'Cyber Attacks: Unlawful Use of Force or Prohibited Intervention?' (2012) 17(2) *Journal of Conflict and Security Law* 211, 212.
18. Oxford dictionary.
19. Macquarie dictionary.
20. Cambridge dictionary.
21. Merriam-Webster dictionary.

22. Article 51.
23. Ibid.
24. Ibid.
25. Harriet Moynihan, 'The Application of International Law to State Cyberattacks: Sovereignty and Non-intervention' (Research Paper, Chatham House, December 2019) 51 ('In due course, as further state practice and *opinio juris* emerge, a cyber-specific understanding of sovereignty may develop, much like that developed for other domains of international law. In the meantime, because it is unclear whether there is a limit or threshold to violations of sovereignty, states may prefer to use the more clearly established framework of non-intervention where that is possible').
26. Schmitt (n ii).
27. Schmitt (n ii) 315 [18].
28. Ibid 318 [21].
29. Department of Foreign Affairs and Trade, *Australia's International Cyber Engagement Strategy: 2019 International Law Supplement* (2019).
30. Ibid 2.
31. Ibid.
32. UN General Assembly, *Official Compendium of Voluntary National Contributions on the Subject of How International Law Applies to the Use of Information and Communications Technologies by States Submitted by Participating Governmental Experts in the Group of Governmental Experts on Advancing Responsible State Behaviour in Cyberspace in the Context of International Security Established Pursuant to General Assembly Resolution 73/266*, UN Doc A/76/136 (13 July 2021) 5 ('*Official Compendium*').
33. Ibid.
34. Dale Stephens, 'Influence Operations and International Law' (2020) 19(4) *Journal of Information Warfare* 1, citing Brian Egan, 'International Law and Stability in Cyberspace' (Speech, University of California, Berkeley School of Law, 10 November 2016): 'a cyber operation by a State that interferes with another country's ability to hold an election or that manipulates another country's election results would be a clear violation of the rule of non-intervention'. See also Schmitt (n ii) 313.
35. Eric Corthay, 'The ASEAN Doctrine of Non-interference in Light of the Fundamental Principle of Non-intervention' (2016) 17(2) *Asian-Pacific Law and Policy Journal* 1, 14.
36. New Zealand Ministry of Foreign Affairs and Trade, 'The Application of International Law to State Activity in Cyberspace' (Position Paper, 1 December 2020).
37. UN General Assembly, *Official Compendium* (n iv).
38. Michael Schmitt, 'Virtual Disenfranchisement: Cyber Election Meddling in the Grey Zones of International Law' in Christopher Whyte, A Trevor Thrall and Brian M Mazanec (eds), *Information Warfare in the Age of Cyber Conflict* (Routledge, 2020) 186.
39. Hollis, 'The Influence of War' (n vii) 41.
40. Björnstjern Baade, 'Fake News and International Law' (2019) 29 *European Journal of International Law* 1357.
41. Summary Report of Eleventh Meeting of Comm I, Doc 784, I/1/XXVII UNCIO Docs 335 (4 June 1945); this mirrors Australia's understanding – see Explanatory Memorandum to the *Autonomous Sanctions Bill 2010,* 1.
42. DW Bowett, *Self Defense in International Law* (Praeger, 1958) 148 ('Taking the words in their plain, common-sense meaning, it is clear that, since the prohibition is of the "use or threat of force", they will not apply to economic or political pressure but only to physical, armed force').
43. *Nicaragua Case* (n 106) [228].
44. Schmitt (n ii) 328.
45. Stephens (n xxxiv) 1, 8.
46. Ibid.
47. Ibid.

48. International Law Commission, *Responsibility of States for Internationally Wrongful Acts* (Report, 2001) art 51.
49. Ibid arts 49(2), 53.
50. Ibid arts 43, 52.
51. Hollis, 'The Influence of War' (n vii) 44.
52. Stephens (n xxxiv) 9.
53. Ibid.
54. *UN General Assembly Resolution on Non-interference in the Internal Affairs of States*, GA Res 31/91, UN Doc A/RES/31/91 (14 December 1976) ('*Non-interference*').
55. *United Nations Declaration on the Inadmissibility of Intervention and Interference in the Internal Affairs of States*, GA Res 36/103, UN Doc A/RES/36/103 (9 December 1981).
56. *UN General Assembly Resolution on Non-interference in the Internal Affairs of States*, GA Res 31/91, UN Doc A/RES/31/91 (14 December 1976) ('*Non-interference*') preambular para 6.
57. *United Nations Declaration on the Inadmissibility of Intervention and Interference in the Internal Affairs of States*, GA Res 36/103, UN Doc A/RES/36/103 (9 December 1981) para II(j).
58. Ibid para III(d).

Samuel White is a Senior Lecturer of the faculty of the Adelaide Law School at the University of Adelaide. He is concurrently a Visiting Fellow at the Australian Defence Force Academy and holds positions as an Adjunct Associate Professor at the University of New England. In 2024, he was made an Associate Fellow of the Royal Historical Society and the first Army Visiting Fellow at the Australian War Memorial. Samuel has also served as both a Royal Australian Infantry Corps and an Australian Army Legal Corps officer in a variety of tactical, operational and strategic level postings. His military experiences focused his doctoral studies, which addressed the constitutional ambit and limitations of responding to foreign interference (both traditional and modern forms) via military responses.

Grey Zone Operations and Digital Resilience

Dale Stephens

Abstract This chapter takes readers into the heart of contemporary military operations, exploring the concept of the 'militarization of the grey zone'. This chapter provides a comprehensive analysis of how military operations have adapted and grown more resilient in an era marked by hybrid warfare, ambiguous conflict zones and unconventional tactics. The author offers readers an insider's perspective on the strategic considerations, adaptive tactics and technological innovations employed by armed forces to navigate the complexities of modern conflicts. As readers delve into this chapter, they will gain a profound understanding of the multifaceted challenges faced by military practitioners in the evolving landscape of warfare, shedding light on the resilience and adaptability of today's armed forces.

Introduction

A grey zone operation seeks to advance a State's interests through the deployment of coercive and assertive means beyond what is deemed acceptable statecraft.[1] Such an operation relies upon latent ambiguities and uncertainties in the law that cause a target State to hesitate in its response. States, like Australia, that are liberal democracies are particularly vulnerable to grey area operations, given the correlative need to ensure that reactions are legitimate and are perceived as such by public opinion in support of any kind of response. Within the realm of influence and cyber operations, grey zone operations have particular effectiveness. By design such operations are usually covert and undertaken 'behind the scenes' with issues of attribution often difficult, thus rendering the risk of public overreach by a victim State to be uncomfortably high.

This chapter will review the phenomenon of grey area operations within the context of influence and cyber operations. Both of these types of operations have been publicly acknowledged as representing a security threat to Australia, specifically in the grey area context.[2] It will be argued that the existing international law applicable in the *jus ad bellum* and *jus in bello* contexts doesn't easily provide a

D. Stephens (✉)
Adelaide Law School of The University of Adelaide, Adelaide, Australia
e-mail: Dale.stephens@adelaide.edu.au

D. Stephens et al. (eds.), *Digital Resilience*,
https://doi.org/10.1007/978-981-97-9746-2_3

ready foundation for redressing grey area operations in these contexts. Despite this, it will also be argued that States are all too well aware of their vulnerabilities and that a number of States are either augmenting their legal capacity to respond or otherwise developing the law to enable greater rights of response. Ultimately, it will be argued that there is sufficient evidence to conclude that there is, or will soon be, an adequate legal foundation to ensure effective digital resilience in the face of grey area operations.

Grey Zone Operations—What Are They?

Grey zone operations are a phenomenon of contemporary military and geo-strategic activity. A grey zone operation is not a legal term and these operations do not have legal significance per se, but they are intricately connected to the law. In the most recent *2020 Defence Strategic Update,* they are described as follows:

The conduct of 'grey-zone' activities has also expanded in the Indo-Pacific. These activities involve military and non-military forms of assertiveness and coercion aimed at achieving strategic goals without provoking conflict. In the Indo-Pacific, these activities have ranged from militarisation of the South China Sea to active interference, disinformation campaigns and economic coercion.[3]

Hicks provides a similar description as follows:

> An effort or series of efforts intended to advance one's security objectives at the expense of a rival using means beyond those associated with routine statecraft and below means associated with direct military conflict between rivals. In engaging in a grey zone approach, an actor seeks to avoid crossing a threshold that results in open war.[4]

Additionally, with more legal focus, McLaughlin describes their purposes as:

> [leveraging] legal categories and relationships—such as the threshold for the application of the law of armed conflict (LOAC)—to advance strategic objectives'[5] and that they are 'designed to exploit or create legal (and other) uncertainties for a military or strategic advantage.[6]

The phenomenon of grey zone operations has been subject to considerable analytical review over the past decade. Distinctions are sometimes drawn between this form of operation as against concepts of lawfare and hybrid warfare.[7] Whether the described distinctions actually add to any more reliable characterisation and modes of response, it can be safely concluded that all three concepts rely upon exploiting a sense of propriety concerning appropriate legal compliance and legitimacy of action.

Expanding upon this sense of self-perceived propriety, it is helpful to appreciate that the conduct of military operations occurs within a normative world of (actual and perceived) legitimacy.[8] The law itself provides a firm foundation for such legitimacy, though of course is, by its very nature, never completely certain and is rarely definitive. Hence it is a feature of normal statecraft to rely upon ambiguities and/or gaps in the law to advance a State's national objectives.[9] Critically though, this manoeuvring is normally undertaken against the backdrop of the 'invisible college' of international legal scrutiny.[10] Inside this geo-political environment, there is a basic sense of commitment to compliance with international law to ensure that key lines of behaviour are not crossed and armed conflict is not unwittingly initiated. Such actions are usually explained within the International Relations/International Law inter-disciplinary framework through the concept of constructivism. Hence constructivism is argued to shape a sense of national identity through a sense of compliance with, and internalisation of, legal values.[11] Accordingly, a logic of appropriateness comes to shape decision making, in contrast to a logic of consequence, which is more instrumentalist in its focus.[12]

Against this backdrop are the ‘red line’ thresholds of international law concerning the use of force and the initiation of the armed conflict. These thresholds contain numerous ambiguities and hence are very carefully parsed and given sufficient latitude. Initiating an international armed conflict when not intended rarely offers much to rationalist strategic planning. Despite the legal construction of these lines, it is also evident that a relatively high level of physical force is usually tolerated before a State deems an action a violation of international law let alone worthy of a forceful response that might initiate armed conflict. As is well understood, under Article 2(4) of the UN Charter[13] international law prohibits the use or threat of use of force and sets a relatively low threshold for when this line is crossed. Violation of this *jus ad bellum* prohibition does allow a State resort to countermeasures, but these cannot include an element of force.[14] Beyond a ‘mere’ use of force is an ‘armed attack’. According to the International Court of Justice, that is an egregious use of force that has sufficient ‘scale and effect’ and is to be contrasted to a mere ‘frontier incident’.[15] An armed attack gives rise to a right of individual or collective national self-defence under Article 51 of the UN Charter.[16] An exercise of national and/or collective self-defence can include the use of force (provided it is necessary and proportionate).[17] While some States view the ‘distance’ between a mere use of force and an armed attack as being so close as to be effectively non-existent,[18] others will regard the gap to be quantitively and qualitatively significant.[19] Hence, in this latter view, a use of force that may be particularly damaging is still not an ‘armed attack’ and can only give rise to a right of (non-forceful) countermeasures. Moreover, in the context of armed conflict, while common Article 2 of the 1949 Geneva Conventions[20] and the decisive *Tadic* case[21] require only the ‘mere’ use of force between sovereign nations to initiate armed conflict,[22] States tend to tolerate a relatively high degree of force before determining that they are in a state of armed conflict.[23]

Accordingly, when initiating a grey area operation, there are sufficient legal and policy leeways for coercive and forceful actions to achieve desired ends without risk of crossing a significant legal or normative threshold. As a result of underlying ambiguities, victim States can never be certain that a threshold has been crossed when some force is applied. Acting in accordance with an underlying ‘logic of appropriateness’ they will usually tolerate such actions. This is especially the case in a liberal democracy where military actions can be subject to significant political consequences.[24] While these enduring small-scale actions themselves do not cross a legal or policy threshold, their cumulative weight may nonetheless have a strategically corrosive impact. One that is desired as a medium- or long-term goal of an initiating State.

A. **Influence Operations and Grey Area Operations**

The *2020 Defence Strategic Update* expressly identified Influence Operations (IO) as a means to undertake grey area operations.[25] IOs are actions that seek to employ misinformation,[26] disinformation[27] and distorted news,[28] through electronic and traditional media gateways of distribution in order to achieve an instrumental goal. While Australia and other Western liberal democracies are committed to the exchange of ideas (as reflected in Article 19 of the 1966 *International Covenant on Civil and Political Rights*)[29] and recognise that States will often seek to persuade relevant audiences of a particular narrative,[30] IOs are different. Unlike cyber warfare that seeks to degrade cyber infrastructure, an IO actually relies upon the effective functioning of such infrastructure to convey instrumentalised messaging to sway belief and opinion. It has been described a 'net war' as opposed to 'cyber war.'[31] While an IO is not restricted to using social media or other digital sources of distribution, it is here that such an operation can have a particular reach and amplified effect. As described by ASIO, IOs become malevolent 'foreign interference' when an attempt at exerting influence is 'conducted covertly by, or on behalf, of a foreign actor; when it is clandestine, deceptive, corrupting or threatening in nature and when it is contrary to Australia's sovereignty and interests'.[32] Such actions may, *inter alia*, seek to erode confidence in the political system,[33] or seek to undermine financial stability,[34] or undermine confidence in a public health system[35] to advance a competing political agenda or narrative.

In the context of armed conflict, an influence operation will ordinarily accompany kinetic action in the battle space or even the initiation of armed conflict itself. As Kilcullen has observed that:

'By the time the first tank rolls, an adversary has already won. In fact, if they have not won through social media and electronic propaganda and all the shaping activity, they do not even roll the tanks.[36]

A well-tailored and targeted influence operation can also have a decisive military impact during an armed conflict. As is well documented,[37] during the non-international armed conflict between Iraq and ISIS in 2014, ISIS undertook an extremely effective influence operation that resulted in 1500 ISIS fighters capturing Mosul causing 25,000 Iraqi Army soldiers to flee. This was achieved through conveying a (false) perception of superior arms and capability.

In the peacetime context, international law does not impose very significant barriers to combat IOs. Short of an IO that directly motivates a population to engage in active armed rebellion against their Government, it is hard to imagine a circumstance where an IO would ever violate the Art 2(4) prohibition on the use of force, let alone constitute an 'armed attack'. More likely is the prospect that an IO will violate the prohibition on intervention in the internal or external affairs of a State and/or Sovereignty.

With respect to the prohibition on intervention, it is an established rule of international law that 'No State or group of States has the right to intervene, directly or indirectly for any reason whatsoever, in the internal or external affairs of any other State'[38] and this was similarly described by the International Court of Justice in the *Nicaragua* case as follows:

> '[i]ntervention is wrongful when it uses methods of coercion in regard to such choices, which must remain free ones. The element of coercion, which defines, and indeed forms the very essence of, prohibited intervention, is particularly obvious in the case of an intervention which uses force, either in the direct form of military action, or in the indirect form of support for subversive or terrorist armed activities within another State'.[39]

The Australian Government has addressed this question in the context of cyber by prescribing the threshold for violation. While addressed to the context of cyber, the set of criteria have equal application to an influence operation. They are as follows:

The use by a State of cyber activities to prevent another State from holding an election or manipulate the electoral system to alter the results of an election in another State, intervene in the fundamental operation of Parliament, or significantly disrupt the functioning of a States' financial systems would constitute a violation of the principle of non-intervention'.[40]

Germany has specifically addressed the violation of the principle of non-intervention in the context of influence operations as follows:

> … the element of coercion must not be assumed prematurely. Even harsher forms of communication such as pointed commentary and sharp criticism as well as (persistent) attempts to obtain, through discussion, a certain reaction or the performance of a certain measure from another State do not as such qualify as coercion.[41]

New Zealand has also addressed this principle specifically in the context of an influence operation as follows:

> 'a prolonged and coordinated cyber disinformation operation that significantly undermines a state's public health efforts during a pandemic'[42]

In all instances, there is a consensus that an IO can breach this principle, but States set extremely high thresholds for violation.

Finally, with respect to the principle of sovereignty, many States also agree that an IO can violate this principle, yet (to date) are not able to identify circumstances where this would be manifested. The Netherlands notes specifically that 'the precise boundaries of what is and is not permissible have yet to fully crystallise'[43] and New Zealand notes that 'further state practice is required for the precise boundaries of its application to crystallise'.[44] There have, to date, been no concrete examples of a State alleging violation of the principle of sovereignty as a result of an influence operation.

In summary, while international law does contain a number of thresholds that can amount to a violation, they are all particularly high and allow for significant freedom of action by a malevolent actor. Accordingly, devising a strategy of digital resilience needs to rely upon its own 'grey zone' criteria to ensure that sovereign interests, especially those that underpin a liberal democracy, are protected and preserved. These will be discussed below in Part 3.

B. Cyber Operations and Grey Area Operations

As mentioned above, Cyber operations differ from influence operations in that they are usually directed towards degrading digital capability to affect an advantageous result.[45] In the past 30 years cyber operations (previously referred as, inter alia, computer network attack[46] and network attack),[47]have become a dominant form of military engagement. Australia, like many other States has declared cyber to be a dedicated operational environment.[48] Given this focus, there has been a corresponding increase in public international attention upon identifying and articulating the law applicable to such an operational area.[49] One private initiative was the development of the *Tallin Manual* [50] that brought together a number of legal experts who sought to articulate the law applicable to cyber. The *Tallinn Manual 2.0* identified that the principles of sovereignty, due diligence, attribution and non-intervention all applied to govern cyber operations.[51]

More controversially, it also determined that Article 2(4) regarding the use of force and the issues of 'armed attack' for the purposes of national and collective self-defence similarly applied.[52] While the attraction of these prohibitions is straightforward, it was the criteria for their application that was the cause of subsequent State reaction.

In the course of their deliberations, the *Tallinn Manual* experts applied a very orthodox view of what constitutes an attack for both *jus ad bellum* and *jus in bello* purposes. The terms 'armed attack' (jus ad bellum) and 'attack'(jus in bello) have traditionally required a manifestation of physical force. In this context, the *Tallinn Manual* formula did adopt what may be termed an 'effects based' taxonomy. Hence, where cyber operations result in physical damage—notwithstanding that the cyber means themselves (the 'ones and zeros') do not themselves manifest such kinetic force—then the experts concluded it may qualify as an 'armed attack' (*jus ad bellum*) and 'attack' (*jus in bello*).[53]

Despite this innovation in thinking concerning 'effects based' targeting, the majority of experts in the Tallinn project were agreed that an actual physical consequence was a necessary requirement for an 'attack' (*jus in bello*). In this regard, there was a split of views, the majority determining that actual physical damage requiring replacement of parts satisfied the test. [54] In contrast, a minority view was that the removal of data resulting in an inability to 'perform it intended function' thus requiring an actual physical reinstallation of an operating systems or data was sufficient. [55] Finally, it was noted in the *Tallinn Manual* that 'a few experts' considered that any loss of functionality was sufficient.[56]

As a result of this conclusion, there would appear to be a sufficient opportunity for a State to undertake cyber operations of a kind that does not result in physical damage per se, but does destroy the functionality of a computer/IT system. Such an operation that does not result in actual physical damage nor replacement of any parts or software would not fall foul of the prohibition on attack—as articulated in the *Tallinn Manual 2.0*—because it was not, by definition, an attack. There are multiple examples of where personal data, banking systems, health records, transport systems and the like could be compromised and/or become dysfunctional and this would not give rise to a right of response, at least one using force. Such an outcome manifested in 2007 in Estonia where the Government was subject to mass cyber-attacks from an outside source (Russia was identified as the likely source). At that time, Government computer systems were profoundly affected (though not physically damaged) and the Estonian Defence Minister, Jaak Aaviksoo called for a NATO self-defence response which was not forthcoming. Indeed, the Defence Minister stated that '[n]ot a single NATO defence minister would define a cyber-attack as a clear military action at present'.[57]

Such a position taken by the drafters of the *Tallinn Manual* does therefore reflect a conventional understanding of what is a use of force. However, it leaves open a significant vulnerability that offers considerable 'grey zone' operation opportunity for an opposing side.

Digital Resilience

a. *Influence Operations and Digital Resilience*

Despite the incapacity of existing international law to redress tailored malevolent influence operations, especially those of a digital nature, there is much that can be done to resist and respond to such operations. McLaughlin offers a solution of States co-ordinating a response and publicly 'calling out' such aberrant behaviour.[58] This is certainly a key element of any response. However, the very open nature of the international legal regime, one that does not offer ready barriers, can also afford a foundation and freedom for response.

Undertaking a counter IO is an open response option under the existing international legal framework. The very values that may make liberal democratic States so vulnerable in this sphere, also afford a sound basis for a response. Mounting a digitally based counter response that extols the values of an open society and utilising virtual private networks to convey such ideas, especially within authoritarian States, are an obvious option. Current Australian Defence Force doctrine observes that the most effective influence operations is one that relies upon verifiable truth.[59] There is much that can be effectively proselytised in such a counter IO. Provided that such messaging and digital targeting do not violate the high thresholds of the principle of non-intervention nor the more nebulous criteria of sovereignty, then such an action is lawful and appropriate. Article 17 of the 1966 *International Covenant of Civil and Political Rights*[60] does provide for prohibitions on 'arbitrary or unlawful interference with … privacy, family, home or correspondence, [and] …unlawful attacks on [a person's] honour and reputation', hence (assuming extra territorial application in any instance) care must be taken in the content of a counter IO where personal details are disclosed. However, it is also notable that such a prohibition may also be waived where necessary in pursuit of a 'legitimate aim'.[61] Preserving national security and countering a foreign initiated IO would likely satisfy that criterion. In this regard, as will be discussed below there does exist a formidable array of national legislation that expressly provides powers to Australian Intelligence Agencies to mount counter-influence operations where in Australia's national interest.

Under existing Australian Commonwealth law, a number of Government Agencies, including Australian Security Intelligence Organisation (ASIO), Australian Secret Intelligence Service (AIS) and the Australian Signals Directorate (ASD), all have powers to detect, defend and respond to foreign influence operations where they constitute unlawful foreign interference in the form of a crime.

The Commonwealth Criminal Code creates an offence of 'intentional foreign interference'[62] that is, inter alia, directed at criminalising foreign influence operations that seek to covertly or deceptively undermine Australian democratic or political rights. The law applies extraterritorially[63] and permits Australian intelligence agencies under their respective legislation capacities to undertake (with civil and criminal immunity) a number of actions. These actions include intelligence collection, investigation, prevention and disruption.[64] Moreover, when undertaking these tasks, the *Telecommunications Act 1977*,[65] permits these agencies to request voluntary technical assistance from providers of digital platforms in countering 'foreign interference'[66] or, in certain circumstances, to compel such assistance.[67]

The extent of these powers theoretically allows for the lawful manipulation of the technical means of distribution and cyber activities that can degrade source capability. As has been acknowledged by the Australian Government, ASD acted very successfully (in coalition with US agencies) throughout the 2010s against the ISIS Propaganda unit by manipulating and degrading servers and other electronic means of communication to counter that activity.[68] These operations rendered ISIS communications degraded within seconds, therefore allowing coalitions troops to recapture a critical strategic zone along the Tigris River in Iraq.[69] Utilising such cyber means in this armed context was considered revolutionary to modern armed conflict with Mike Burgess the former Director-General of the ASD describing the operations as.

> .... the first time that an offensive cyber operation had been conducted so closely synchronised with the movements of military personnel in theatre.[70]

These actions occurred in the context of an armed conflict that likely enabled broader executive power of the Commonwealth to be relied upon by ASD in addition to existing legislative authority. Nonetheless, these actions also demonstrate the capacity for counter action and an example of digital resilience to this pernicious threat.

b. *Cyber and Digital Resilience*

The *Tallinn Manual 2.0* provides an accurate and conventional account of the legal characterisation of cyber operations. In so doing, it leaves open the possibility for significant pernicious and malevolent activity that would not amount to a breach of international law. Significant loss, disruption and national security compromise might be suffered with tradition forms of forceful redress because of the lack of physical damage occasioned by a cyber operation.[71]

As a result of this conclusion, a number of States have reacted to the findings and conclusions reached by the experts involved in the *Tallinn Manual* project.

In 2021 the Group of Government Experts finally began publishing their views on how to lawfully characterise cyber operations in the *jus ad bellum* and *jus in bello* fields.[72]

In the context of the *jus ad bellum*, States have started providing examples of when a cyber operation violates principles of sovereignty (Brazil has provided an example of intercepting communications,[73] The Netherlands has cited undertaking cyber investigations beyond borders without permission,[74] and Norway has cited blocking digital communications[75]). Similarly, a number of States have opined that there is a positive duty of 'due diligence' that must be exercised by States within their own territory where private actors are engaging in nefarious cyber operations against other States (i.e. Germany,[76] Japan,[77] Norway[78] and The Netherlands[79]). As stated above, States have also ventured opinions on when a cyber operation can constitute a prohibited intervention, albeit they have set high thresholds. As to the use of force, a growing number of States are declaring that direct physical damage is not necessary for a cyber operation to violate Article 2(4) (i.e. France,[80] Ireland,[81] Singapore,[82] Norway,[83] the Netherlands[84]). In this regard that statement by Ireland is representative of the sentiments shared by these other States when it stated that a cyber operation that caused 'significant impairment of the functionality of critical infrastructure' could be classed as a use of force, even in the absence of actual physical damage.[85] Despite these views, it is also clear that a number of other States have not committed to a position yet on this point. Nonetheless, it is evident that some States are willing to be more definitive as to the unique alignment of the existing law and the capacities of cyber operations and to that extent demonstrate a level of resilience in combating the threat posed by cyber grey area operations.

In the context of International Humanitarian Law (IHL) (otherwise known as the Law of Armed Conflict (LOAC)) much attention has been devoted to whether physical damage is a necessary element of an attack. Such an issue is critical given that an attack is a necessary criterion to attract many other protective obligations under IOHL/LOAC. Hence, when discussing the requirements of damage before an attack may be properly characterised as such, France has declared that:

Contrary to the *Tallinn Manual*, France considers that an attack within the meaning of Article 49 of AP I may occur **even if there is no human injury or loss of life, or physical damage to goods**. Thus, a cyberoperation constitutes an attack if the targeted equipment or systems can **no longer provide the service for which they were implemented, including temporarily or reversibly**, where action by the adversary is required in order to restore the infrastructure or the system.[86]

Similarly, Germany has determined as follows:

> Germany defines a cyberattack in the context of IHL as an act or action initiated in or through cyberspace to cause harmful effects on communication, information or other electronic systems, on the information that is stored, processed or transmitted on these systems or on physical objects or persons. **The occurrence of physical damage, injury or death to persons or damage or destruction to objects comparable to the effects of conventional weapons is not required for an attack in the sense of art. 49 para. 1 Additional Protocol**

> **I to the Geneva Conventions.** However, the mere intrusion into foreign networks and the copying of data does not constitute an attack under IHL.[87]

These views respond to the overall conclusions reached by the *Tallinn Manual* experts regarding the necessity of the element of physical damage, but also go further and imply a greater clarity as to the definition of the concept of data. The *Tallinn Manual* experts implicitly concluded that data was not an object that could be attacked per se under the Law of Armed Conflict. According to the *Tallinn Manual* experts, objects must be 'visible and tangible' before they can be attacked.[88] Such a view does accord with traditional thinking (hence an 'idea' cannot be kinetically attacked) and also some State practice specifically in the cyber realm,[89] but is nonetheless problematic. As the International Committee of the Red Cross notes, 'excluding essential civilian data from the protection afforded by IHL to civilian objects would result in an important protection gap',[90] and while the *Tallinn Manual* does make an exception for medical data,[91] the foundation for such an exception is not fully explained and cannot be reconciled with other, equally significant, data.

The minority view as expressed in the *Tallinn Manual 2.0* commentary does note that:

> for the purposes of targeting, **certain data should be regarded as an object**. In their view, the majority position is under inclusive in the sense that failure to include cyber operations targeting data per se in the scope of the term 'attack' would mean that even the deletion of essential civilian datasets such as social security data, tax records and bank accounts would potentially escape the regulatory reach of the law of armed conflict, thereby running counter to the principle (reflected in Article 48 of Additional Protocol I) that the civilian population enjoys general protection from the effects of hostilities.[92]

However, this was not the conclusion reached by the majority of the experts in the Manual.

As mentioned previously, whether data can be an object capable of being attacked and hence attracting the Law of Armed Conflict may not be a critical issue anymore. As France and Germany have declared, if a systems network becomes dysfunctional as a result of a cyber operation, then this alone may be sufficient to constitute an attack for the purposes of attracting the Law of Armed Conflict.

Moreover, even if this idea of dysfunction (while not suffering actual physical damage) is not yet the predominant view, it is possible to revisit the specific question of whether data is in fact an object. The *Tallinn Manual's* emphasis on physical properties may have led the experts to conflate this idea with what is visible. Data within a computer system comprise of magnetic reference points.[93] Hence to that end, the destruction of data will involve the physical destruction of such magnetic data points and thus comprise requisite physical damage.

In any event, an increasing majority of States have declared that in the context of any armed conflict civilian population must be independently protected.[94] From such a perspective, it would seem inevitable that further thinking will lead to a revised sense of legal characterisation. Hence it seems likely given the prevailing trend that a 'cyber attack' will increasingly be expanded in definition to be a form of a more traditional attack thus necessitating greater protections within the law. Such a development serves to better enhance the capacity of digital resilience even within grey zone operations.

Conclusion

This chapter is devoted to an assessment of the phenomenon of grey area operations and the capacity of digital resilience in the face of such operations when dealing with influence and cyber actions. It has been argued that the existing legal framework in both the traditional *jus ad bellum* and *jus in bello* contexts, is not well suited, or at least optimised, to addressing influence operations nor cyber operations in a decisive manner. Accordingly, the ability of an opposing actor (State or otherwise) to perniciously manipulate a set of circumstances to advance their own interests through the coercive and covert means that underpin a grey area operation is high.

Despite this, it is also equally evident that States are all too aware of the legal and policy context that provides the opportunities for grey area operations and are capable of responding. In the case of Influence Operations, this is manifested through the very openness of the international legal system that permits a counter campaign. In the case of Australia, this will be also founded upon some very clear domestic legal authority. It is within the capacity of a country like Australia to mount an effective and well-targeted counter Influence Operation that meets the grey area operation head-on. When it comes to cyber operations, it is also evident that States are similarly undertaking a slow but steady re-calibration of how cyber fits within the *jus ad bellum* and *jus in bello* contexts. While this is still an evolving area, it is clear that States are generally creating an 'effects based' non-physical damage exception to their traditional views as to what may constitute a use of force/armed attack under a *jus ad bellum* framework and what is an 'attack' under the IHL/LOAC/*jus in bello* framework.

In terms of viewing these developments through the lens of digital resilience, it is safe to conclude that there is a clear identification of the legal vagaries and ambiguities that are exploited by grey area operations. In turn, there is much evidence of an active commitment towards strengthening State capacity—under the law and its re-working—to resiliently respond to such digital threats.

Notes

1. Department of Defence, *Defence Strategic Update* (Report, 1 July 2020) 12 ('DSU').
2. Ibid.
3. Ibid 5.
4. Kathleen H Hicks et al., *By Other Means—Part I: Campaigning in the Gray Zone* (Report of the CSIS International Security Program, CSIS, 8 July 2019) 4.
5. Rob McLaughlin, 'The Law of the Sea and PRC Grey-Zone Operations in the South China Sea' (2022) 116(4) *American Journal of international Law* 821, 825.

6. Ibid 821.
7. Aurel Sari, 'Legal resilience in an Era of Grey Zone Conflicts and Hybrid Threats' (Working Paper Series 2019/1, Exeter Centre for International Law, University of Exeter (24 January 2019) 8–12.
8. Department of the Army, Marine Corporations, *Counterinsurgency Field Manual*, ed David H. Petraeus et al., (University of Chicago Press, Chicago, IL, No. 3 33–5 2007) 252.
9. See generally, Martti Koskenniemi, 'The Place of Law in Collective Security' (1996) 17(2) *Michigan.Journal of International Law* 455.
10. Oscar Schachter, 'Invisible College of International Lawyers' (1977–1978) 72(2) *Northwestern University Law Review* 217, 217.
11. Jack Goldsmith and Daryl Levinson, 'Law for States: International Law, Constitutional Law, Public Law' (2009) 122(7) *Harvard Law Review* 1791, 1828.
12. Jeffrey T. Checkel, 'The Constructivist Turn in International Relations Theory', (1998) 50(2) *World Politics*, 324, 326.
13. *Charter of the United Nations,* opened for signature 26 June 1945, 1 UNTS XVI (entered into force 24 October 1945) ('UN Charter').
14. International Law Commission, *Articles on State Responsibility*, (Report, A/56/10 August 2001) art 50 <https://casebook.icrc.org/case-study/international-law-commission-articles-state-responsibility> ('ILC Articles on State Responsibility').
15. *Military and Paramilitary Activities in and against Nicaragua* (*Nicaragua v U.S.A*) (Judgement), [1986] ICJ Rep 14 205 [93] ('*Nicaragua*').
16. UN Charter (n 13) art 51.
17. International Law Association, *Final Report on Aggression and Use of Force* (Report, April 2018) 3 ('ILA Report').
18. See, eg, The US position is that potentially any use of illegal force is an armed attack as discussed by the Office of General Counsel, Department of Defence, *Department of Defence Law of War Manual*, (Report, Washington DC) 47, 1.11.5.2.
19. ILA Report (n 17) 6.
20. *Geneva Convention for the Amelioration of the Condition of the Wounded and Sick in Armed Forces in the Field*, opened for signature 12 August 1949, 75 UNTS 31 (entered into force 21 October 1950) art II ('Geneva Convention I').
21. *Prosecutor v Tadic* (*Judgement*) (International Criminal Tribunal for the Former Yugoslavia, Appeals Chamber, Case No IT-941-A, 15 July 1999 34–35 ('*Tadic*').
22. International Committee of the Red Cross 'Common Article II: Commentary from 2016' (ICRC Commentary, 2016) <https://ihl-databases.icrc.org/en/ihl-treaties/gci-1949/article-2/commentary/2016?activeTab=1949GCs-APs-and-commentaries#148> .
23. See eg, the 'pinging' of RAN divers from HMAS Toowoomba by PLA-N vessel in Nov 2023 which caused personal injury was declared 'unsafe and unprofessional' by the Australian Government and not a use of force as described in Matt D. Montazzoli, John C. Tramazzo, 'International Law and Acoustic Antagonism in East Asian Waters' (2014) 103(4) *Stockton Center for International Law* 112, 127; Similarly in May 2022, the release of a bundle of chaff in front of a RAAF P-8A aircraft was described as a dangerous act and not a use in force as reported by Australian Government, Department of Defence, Chinese interception of P-8A Poseidon on 26 May 2022 (media release, 05 June 2022) (28 March 2024) <https://www.defence.gov.au/news-events/releases/2022-06-05/chinese-interception-p-8a-poseidon-26-may-2022> .
24. See generally, Margaret E. Keck, Kathryn Sikkink *Activists Beyond Borders: Advocacy Networks in International Politics* (Cornell University Press, 1998).
25. DSU (n 1) 11–12.
26. Catherine Theohary, 'Information Warfare: Issues for Congress' (Report, Congressional Research Service, 5 March 2018) 5.
27. Harriet Moynihan, 'The Application of International Law to State Cyberattacks: Sovereignty and Non-intervention' (Research Paper, Chatham House, December 2019), 41.

28. Jennifer Kavanagh, Michael Rich, ‘Truth Decay: An Initial Exploration of the Diminishing Role of Facts and Analysis in American Public Life’, *RAND Corporation* (webpage, 16 January 2018) (date accessed 27 March 2024), <https://www.rand.org/pubs/research_reports/RR2314.html>.
29. Article 19(2) protects the right to freedom of expression including seeking, receiving, and imparting information in a range of expressions as enshrined through the *International Covenant on Civil and Political Rights (1966)* opened for signature ATS 23 (entered into force 23 March 1976) art 19(2) *(‘ICCPR*’).
30. Department of Foreign Affairs and Trade, *Australia’s International Cyber and Critical Technology Engagement Strategy* (Report, April 2021) 12.
31. M. Sartonnen, A-M Huhtinen, M. Lehto, ‘Rhizomatic Target Audiences of the Cyber Domain’ 15(4) *Journal of Information Warfare* (2016) 1, 2.
32. Australian Government, Australian Security and Intelligence Operations, ‘Counter-Intelligence and Espionage’ (media release, 20 March 2024) <https://www.asio.gov.au/counter-espionage.html)> .
33. *Official Compendium of Voluntary National Contributions on the Subject of How International Law Applies to the Use of Information and Communications Technologies by States Submitted by Participating Governmental Experts in the Group of Governmental Experts on Advancing Responsible State Behaviour in Cyberspace in the Context of International Security Established Pursuant to General Assembly Resolution* 73/266, UN Doc A/76/136 (13 July 2021) 5 (submission of Australia) (‘*GGE Compendium 2021*’).
34. *GGE Compendium 2021* 5 (n 33).
35. *GGE Compendium 2021* 5 (submission of Australia) (n 33); New Zealand Foreign Affairs and Trade, *The Application of International Law to State Activity in Cyberspace* (Position Paper, 1 December 2020) 10 (‘*NZ Position on Cyberspace*’).
36. Max Blenkin, ‘Australia Could Lose the Next War’, *Australian Defence Magazine* (Webpage, 12 April 2019) (date accessed 25 March 2024) <https://www.australiandefence.com.au/defence/general/australia-could-lose-the-next-war> <https://www.australiandefence.com.au/defence/general/australia-could-lose-the-next-war>.
37. See Haroro J. Ingram, ‘The strategic logic of Islamic State information operations’ (2015) 69(6) *Journal of International Affairs* 729, 731; See generally Emerson T Brooking, P W Singer, ‘War Goes Viral’, *The Atlantic* (Web Page, November 2016).
38. *United Nations Declaration on the Inadmissibility of Intervention in the Domestic Affairs of States and the Protection of Their Independence and Sovereignty*, GA Res 2131 XX, UN Doc A/RES/2131, 20th sess, agenda item 107, (adopted 21 December 1965) (‘Friendly Relations Declaration’).
39. *Nicaragua* 98 (n 15).
40. *2021 GGE Compendium* 5 (submission of Australia) (n 33).
41. *GGE Compendium 2021* 34 (submission made by Germany) (n 33).
42. *NZ Position on Cyberspace* 10 (n 35).
43. *GGE Compendium 2021* 54–64 (statement from The Netherlands) (n 33).
44. *NZ Position Paper* 12 (n 35).
45. Dale Stephens, ‘Influence Operations and International Law’ (2020) 19(4) *Journal of Information Warfare* 12.
46. Michael N Schmitt, ‘Computer Network Attack and the Use of Force in International Law: Thoughts on a Normative Framework’ (June 1999) 37 *Columbia Journal of Transnational Law*, abstract.
47. Ibid.
48. Australian Signals Directorate, *ASD Cyber Threat Report 2022–23* (Report, 14 November 2023) 30 <https://www.cyber.gov.au/sites/default/files/2023-11/asd-cyber-threat-report-2023.pdf> .
49. See example: Ongoing UN efforts to clarify views in 2010, 2013, 2015 by the Groups of Governmental Experts as reflected in *Report of the Group of Governmental Experts on*

Advancing Responsible State Behaviour in Cyberspace in the Context of International Security, UN Doc A/76/135 (14 July 2021) 18 ('GGE Final Report 2021'); See further, official compendium of 15 states voluntary submissions as reflected in *GGE Compendium 2021* (n 33).

50. Michael N Schmitt (ed), *Tallinn Manual 2.0 on the International Law Applicable to Cyber Warfare* (Cambridge University Press, 2nd ed, 2017) ('Tallinn Manual 2.0').
51. See generally, *Tallinn Manual 2.0,* (n 50) (rule 19).
52. Tallinn Manual 2.0 (n 50) (rule 71, commentary 6).
53. Tallinn Manual 2.0 (n 50) (rule 71, commentary 4) & (rule 92, commentary 6).
54. Tallinn Manual 2.0 (n 51) (rule 92, commentary 10).
55. Tallinn Manual 2.0 (n 50) (rule 92, commentary 11).
56. Tallinn Manual 2.0 (n 50) (rule 92, commentary 12).
57. Ian Traynor, 'Russia Accused of Unleashing Cyberwar to Disable Estonia' *The Guardian* (Brussels, 17 May 2007) (date accessed 27 March 2024). <https://www.theguardian.com/world/2007/may/17/topstories3.russia> .
58. McLaughlin (n 5) 834.
59. Stephens (n 45) 16; See generally, Authoritarian regimes have successfully implored internet technology to conduct a range of information operations as referred to by Russ Castronovo, 'Information Warfare and Slow Media: Loyalism and the Lesson of Revolutionary Failure' (01 December 2017) 89(4) *American Literature* 821–849.
60. Stephens (n 45) 11; *ICCPR* (n 29) art 17.
61. ICCPR art 17 (n 29).
62. *Criminal Code Act 1995* (Cth) s 92.2 ('*Criminal Code'*).
63. See generally, *Criminal Code* Category B 15.2.
64. Drawing on powers contained within the *Criminal Code Act 1995* (Cth*)*, the I*ntelligence Agencies Act 2001*(Cth), the *Australian Federal Police Act 1979* (Cth), the *Australian Security Intelligence Organisation Act 1979* (Cth) and the *Telecommunications Act 1995* (Cth).
65. *Telecommunications Act 1995* (Cth).
66. Explanatory Memorandum, Telecommunications and Other Legislation Amendment (Assistance and Access) Bill 2018 (Cth) 21.
67. *The Assistance and Access Act 2018* (Cth) Sch 1. See generally; Explanatory Memorandum, Telecommunications and Other Legislation Amendment (Assistance and Access) Bill 2018 (Cth) 3 [8].
68. Angus Grigg, 'Australia claims world first in cyber war' *Australian Financial Review* (Canberra, 27 March 2019) (date accessed 30 March 2024) <https://www.afr.com/technology/australia-claims-world-first-in-cyber-war-20190326-p517q6>.
69. Ibid.
70. Ibid.
71. Tallinn Manual 2.0 (rule 6, commentary 28) (n 50).
72. *GGE Compendium 2021* (n 33).
73. *GGE Compendium 2021* 8 (submission made by Brazil) (n 33).
74. *GGE Compendium 2021* 56 (submission made by the Netherlands) (n 33).
75. *GGE Compendium 2021* 68 (submission made by Norway) (n 33).
76. *GGE Compendium 2021* 33 (submission made by Germany) (n 33).
77. *GGE Compendium 2021* 48 (submission made by Japan) (n 33).
78. *GGE Compendium 2021* 71 (submission made by Norway) (n 33).
79. *GGE Compendium 2021* 59 (submission made by The Netherlands) (n 33).
80. Ministère des Armées, *International Law Applied to Operations in Cyberspace* (Position Paper, September 2019) 12–18 ('French Position Paper'); Government of the Netherlands, Ministry of Foreign Affairs, *Letter to the parliament on the international legal order in cyberspace* (public letter, 5 July 2019) Appendix: International law in cyberspace, p. 5 https://www.government.nl/ministries/ministry-of-foreignaffairs/documents/parliamentary-documents/2019/09/26/letter-to-the-parliament-on-theinternational-legal-order-in-cyberspace.

81. Ireland Department of Foreign Affairs, *Position Paper on the Application of International Law in Cyberspace* (Position Paper, July 2023) 16–19 ('Irish Position Paper').
82. GGE Compendium 2021 (submission made by Singapore) (n 33) 83.
83. GGE Compendium 2021 (submission made by Norway) (n 33) 69.
84. GGE Compendium 2021 (submission made by The Netherlands) (n 33) 57–58.
85. Irish Position Paper (n 81) 18; GGE Compendium 2021 (n 33).
86. French Position Paper (n 33) 13.
87. GGE Compendium 2021 (submission made by Germany (n 33) 36–7.
88. Tallinn Manual 2.0 (n 50) (rule 100, commentary 5); International Committee of the Red Cross (ICRC Commentary, 1987), para 2008–2009.
89. Roy Schöndorf, 'Israel's Perspective on Key Legal and Practical Issues Concerning the Application of International Law to Cyber Operations' (2021) 97(1) *International Law Studies* 395, 399. ('Israel Position Paper').
90. International Committee of the Red Cross, *International Humanitarian Law and Cyber Operations during Armed Conflicts* (Position paper, November 2019) 8.
91. Tallinn Manual 2.0 (n 50) (rule 132).
92. Tallinn Manual 2.0 (n 50) (rule 100, commentary 7); International Committee of the Red Cross (ICRC Commentary, 1987), para 2008–2009.
93. See generally, David W. Shattuck, Stephanie R. Sandor-Leahy et al., 'Magnetic Resonance Image Tissue Classification Using a Partial Volume Model' (May, 2001) 13(5) *Neuroimage* 856–876.
94. See, example, GGE Compendium 2021, the submissions of Australia 6, Brazil 17, Estonia 23–26, Germany 31, The Netherlands 78, Sweden 59, Switzerland 93, United Kingdom 118 (n 33); Israel Position Paper (n 89); Finnish Government, Ministry for Foreign Affairs, *International Law and Cyberspace: Finland's National Positions* (Position Paper, 15 October 2020) 7.

Dale Stephens is a Professor of the University of Adelaide Law School and a Captain in the Royal Australian Navy Reserve who spent over 20 years as a permanent officer in the Royal Australian Navy before taking up his appointment at Adelaide Law School. He has occupied numerous staff officer positions throughout his career in the Australian Defence Force (ADF), including Fleet Legal Officer, Command Legal Officer (Naval Training Command), Chief Legal Officer Strategic Operations Command, Director of Operational and International Law, Deputy Director of the Asia–Pacific Centre for Military Law (a joint venture with Melbourne University Law School), Director Navy Legal and Director of the Military Law Centre. He has deployed twice to East Timor (INTERFET & UNTAET) and twice to Iraq (Baghdad) in senior legal officer positions and has provided extensive advice to Government at the strategic level. He is the recipient of the Conspicuous Service Medal and the (US) Bronze Star, the Red Cross Distinguished Service Award as well as ADF and UN commendations for his service. He holds a Masters and Doctorate from Harvard Law School and is the Director of The Adelaide University Research Unit on Military Law and Ethics.

Old Treaties, New Applications: The Creation of Digital Resilience in International Law via State Practice

Joanna Jarose

Abstract The rapid evolution of cyber capabilities has not only enabled huge advancement in human technology but has also challenged the capacity of legal systems to govern such activities. As cyber operations become an increasing cause of diplomatic tension and a fixture of armed conflicts, setting limits on when such activities will be considered lawful is a priority for States. At a domestic level, the creation of new regimes of law may be comparatively fast-tracked by legislatures to keep up with technological change. However, this is more challenging at an international level, as customary law develops only incrementally and new treaty instruments remain rare. One way that international law can adapt is by the capacity for interpretation of existing treaty instruments to evolve over time. This chapter examines emerging State practice which has begun to reinterpret how longstanding international humanitarian law rules apply to cyber operations and demonstrated a growing consensus about when cyber activities may be considered to violate these key limits.

Introduction: The Unchanging Law

The common law is fairly conservative; the doctrine of *stare decisis* ensures that general legal principles evolve incrementally.[1] Drastic paradigm shifts, when they occur, may be largely driven by parliament via legislation—tempered, if need be, by the judiciary.[2] International law is, by nature, even less disposed to any dramatic change. While the parliament of a single State may drive towards a common goal, hopefully based on what they believe is best for that State, the effort to create a new multilateral treaty is often a decades-long tug of war between dozens of competing State interests. Even agreeing on a common position may be a fruitless endeavour, let alone translating that agreement into binding law. The international law equivalent of the common law is customary international law, that nebulous body of principles which are law simply because States treat them as laws—observing, and expressing

J. Jarose (✉)
University of Adelaide Law School, Adelaide, Australia
e-mail: joanna.jarose@adelaide.edu.au

D. Stephens et al. (eds.), *Digital Resilience*,
https://doi.org/10.1007/978-981-97-9746-2_4

that they are bound to observe, their requirements.[3] While a new treaty may take years to agree (if it happens at all), the establishment of a firm customary international law principle may take decades or even centuries.

Therefore, the creation of new binding international law can be a challenging prospect. This is a particular concern when there are areas of rapid development which cause crises in international affairs—for example, the enormous recent growth in the utilisation of outer space (including plans to mine celestial bodies);[4] the development of AI-enabled military technology and weaponry;[5] and the increasing deployment of unfriendly cyber operations (by both private actors and States).[6] Policies, non-binding recommendations and 'norms' can go some way to controlling certain behaviours. However, a State cannot be held to account by other States for its failure to abide by 'soft law' instruments. When an issue which was not anticipated under existing treaty instruments has become a source of international alarm, requiring the imposition of new boundaries to maintain the peace, it may seem that international law is ill-equipped to respond.

One area in which such tension has arisen is the global use of unfriendly cyber operations. This is a truly international problem, unbounded by domestic borders and thus not capable of being controlled by domestic law alone; the global nature of the internet means that individuals acting from any place in the world can have a detrimental impact on systems literally anywhere else—whether that's the building next door or the diametrically opposite point on the globe.[7] A sub-facet of this problem is the rising trend of States deploying cyber operations as part of their warfighting strategy, whether preparatory to or in conjunction with traditional kinetic operations.[8]

International humanitarian law ('IHL'), the body of law governing armed conflict, is an extensive, well-defined, and widely agreed field. The major IHL treaties are the *Geneva Conventions* and their *Additional Protocols*.[9] Adherence is generally high and it has quite powerful enforcement mechanisms in the International Criminal Court and multiple specialist tribunals which have been created in response to large-scale armed conflicts. However, none of the numerous treaties and customary international law comprising IHL specifically cover cyber operations. Despite many consultations in the forum of the United Nations, States have not yet agreed on any binding legal measures to try and regulate the growing use of this technology in warfare.[10] Does this demonstrate a failing of international law, an inability to adapt quickly enough to serve the needs of humanity? This chapter will argue that the answer is 'no'. International law has built-in resilience, enabling *informal* concurrence by States to shape the way provisions in old treaties may be interpreted to apply to new technologies and new applications. This is what appears to be ongoing in the area of cyber applications and IHL: States are building consensus towards reinterpreting the meaning of 'attack' so that it can apply to limit certain cyber operations despite the strict textualist meaning applied under *Additional Protocol I*.

Applicability of IHL Principles to Cyber-Warfare

The problem of how hostile cyber operations are to be constrained, at an international level, is not new. As far back as 2004, the United States Joint Chiefs of Staff designated cyber 'a "domain" of conflict alongside the air, land, sea and space domains'.[11] The catastrophic potential of cyber operations became clear in the early 21st century—in 2007, widespread DOS and DDOS attacks disabled government and private infrastructure in Estonia;[12] DDOS attacks were used to cause extended outages of Georgian websites before and during the 2008 Russian invasion;[13] and the Stuxnet worm was deployed against Iranian nuclear facilities sites in 2010, causing significant damage which eventually spread well beyond the intended targets.[14] The North Atlantic Treaty Organization ('NATO') recognised cyberspace as a new operational domain in 2016.[15]

However, none of this recognition of the potential issue actually assisted in determining how international law could act to constrain cyber operations. The first significant attempt to do so came with the first edition of the *Tallinn Manual on the International Law Applicable to Cyber Warfare*, which was released in 2013;[16] this ambitious project attempted to survey and outline how international law would govern the use of cyber operations in both the *jus ad bellum* and *jus in bello* contexts. It was later followed by a revised, expanded edition in 2017, the *Tallinn Manual 2.0*,[17] which additionally 'consider[ed] the rules of international law governing cyber incidents that states encounter on a day-to-day basis but which fall below the thresholds of the use of force or armed conflict'.[18]

The *Tallinn Manual* and *Tallinn Manual 2.0* generated significant momentum towards determining how international law does or should govern cyber operations, momentum which was carried on into numerous initiatives conducted by the United Nations ('UN') and seeking to clarify State views. Since 2019, many States have released formal positions on unfriendly cyber operations in response to UN requests, adding their voices to the conversation spurred on by the academic efforts in the *Tallinn Manual*. One significant document in this regard is the compendium of State views arising out of the 2019–2021 UN Group of Governmental Experts on Advancing Responsible State Behaviour in Cyberspace in the Context of International Security ('GGE'),[19] which collected the views of 15 States in regard to whether and how cyber operations could be constrained by certain principles of international law. Many other States have released their views as stand-alone position papers, either on their own initiative or in response to the ongoing UN Open-Ended Working Group on Information and Communication Technologies.[20]

These views vary, not only in perspective but in their finality. However, some clear consensus is evident: for example, States overwhelmingly take the position that existing IHL principles also apply to cyber operations conducted as part of armed conflict.[21] The consensus report issued by the GGE, and endorsed by the UN General Assembly, confirmed this position.[22]

What can be said with certainty, therefore, is that (1) cyber operations can and will be used in armed conflict; and (2) when they are, they will be subject to the very expansive existing body of IHL. This will of course include the four *Geneva Conventions* and, for most States, their additional protocols. Although *Additional Protocol I* has not been ratified by all States, its central targeting principles (at minimum) are considered to be customary international law.[23] However, although States have therefore agreed on what law applies to constrain cyber operations, it is more difficult to assess how this operates in practice. IHL is generally concerned with violence, injury and damage that occurs in the physical world. For example, Part IV of *Additional Protocol I* sets out the protections for civilians and civilian objects in armed conflict; it is part of the crucial 'core' of IHL which is also customary law. Article 49(1) of *Additional Protocol I*, in that part, defines 'attacks' as 'acts of violence against the adversary, whether in offence or defence'.[24] It is therefore unclear, at least based on the plain language of the treaty, how a cyber 'attack' could legally qualify as an 'attack' under *Additional Protocol I*. The International Criminal Court considered the IHL definition of attack in some depth in the *Prosecutor v Ntaganda* appeal,[25] but declined to accept that it could extend beyond acts causing or intended to cause physical injury or destruction.[26]

If a cyber operation cannot sensibly be considered an 'attack', then it is not subject to the majority of rules in Part IV which provide specific protections to civilians: for example, art 51(2) mandates that civilians 'shall not be the object of attack'; art 51(4) prohibits '[i]ndiscriminate attacks' (which includes, under art 51(5)(b), an attack expected to be disproportionate); under art 52(1) '[c]ivilian objects shall not be the object of attack or of reprisals'; art 57 requires precautions '[w]ith respect to attacks' to minimise civilian harm, cancellation of 'attacks' expected to cause excessive harm and, under art 57(2)(c), advance warning to civilians of 'attacks' which may affect them.

The mode of action of cyber operations is also a challenge under IHL, even if they could be considered an 'act of violence' and therefore an attack—as in the examples from Estonia and Georgia discussed above, a cyberattack can cause very significant disruption to civilian lives without leading to the death or injury of any civilians, or leaving physical damage. The metric prescribed in *Additional Protocol I* to determine whether an attack is indiscriminate or whether appropriate precautions have been taken is based on the likely 'loss of civilian life, injury to civilians and damage to civilian objects'.[27] For example, expected 'damage to civilian objects ... excessive in relation to the concrete and direct military advantage anticipated' can make an attack indiscriminate under art 51(5)(b); arts 57(2)(a)(iii) and 57(2)(b) require an attack expected to cause such disproportionate 'damage to civilian objects' to be cancelled; precautions must be taken under art 57(2)(a) to reduce or avoid 'damage to civilian objects'. Whether the meaning of 'damage to civilian objects' could extend to non-kinetic actions is of particular importance for the regulation of cyber operations, which are much less likely to result in actual physical harm to individuals compared with kinetic attack.

Michael Schmitt, general editor of the *Tallinn Manual 2.0* reasoned in 2012 that *Additional Protocol I*'s 'concern was not so much with acts which were violent, but rather with those that have harmful consequences (or risk them)'.[28] 'Harm' is a very general concept not limited to physical impact[29] and at this point in Schmitt's analysis, the line of reasoning could cover even cyber-attacks with no visible physical impact: such attacks may have consequences extending to dire harm to both individuals and objects.

However, Schmitt ultimately concludes that under IHL 'damage' must be physical, akin to that inflicted by traditional kinetic weapons, and that a cyber operation is not an 'attack' unless its consequences extend this far (at the very least requiring a targeted computer system or connected infrastructure to be physically repaired to function again).[30] This is reflected as the majority view in the *Tallinn Manual 2.0*: to qualify as an attack for the purposes of IHL, a cyber operation must cause physical damage 'requir[ing] replacement of physical components'.[31]

Approaching the Problem

If the majority perspective in the *Tallinn Manual 2.0* is correct, this is a problem for the scope of IHL protections. Cyber operations are potentially devastating, especially given the ubiquitous modern reliance on computer systems and internet connectivity.[32] Large-scale internet outages or data losses could be devastating for State economies and government functioning alike, while more and more essential functions rely at least in part on computer hardware, automation and online monitoring. However, on the basis of the plain text of our most recent comprehensive IHL instrument, *Additional Protocol I*, IHL would not seem to apply to constrain cyber operations. If true, this would withdraw crucial protections from civilians and civilian objects—which is problematic, given such protection was one of the main motivations for *Additional Protocol I* and for the whole of IHL more generally.[33] As Kubo Mačák has noted, this may mean that 'many targets whose physical equivalents are firmly protected by IHL from enemy combat action would be considered fair game as long as the effects of the attack remain confined to cyberspace'.[34]

So what is the solution to this? Long term, this could perhaps require negotiation of another IHL treaty or protocol to update and clarify the provisions of *Additional Protocol I*. However, in an age of decreasing multilateralism and rising international tensions, this is a dim prospect. Agreement of international 'norms' or 'soft law' instruments is another potential approach—although their non-binding nature means any protections they can offer are uncertain. However, there is a third option: the reinterpretation of existing hard law to accommodate evolving conditions and global progress. This is generally reliant on State practice.

Subsequent State Practice

As has been hinted at above, the interpretation of attack and damage under *Additional Protocol I* is, to some degree, open to interpretation. The prescribed method for interpreting treaties is summarised in arts 31 and 32 of the *Vienna Convention on the*

Law of Treaties ('*VCLT*').[35] Generally, treaty provisions are interpreted based on the ordinary meaning of the words, the broader context of the provision, and the object and purpose of the treaty. This creates an evident tug of war in the case of the definition of 'attack' in *Additional Protocol I*: the ordinary meaning, as discussed above, suggests that cyber operations could not be considered attacks, because 'violence' and 'damage' appear to be physical concepts. However, the object and purpose of the treaty are at odds with that conclusion, because it would leave civilian objects integral to civilian life without any protection. The context, too, leans in favour of a broad interpretation—given that the treaty, as a rule, extends civilian protections in cases of doubt or uncertainty (for example, by the restatement of the Martens clause in art 1, by the fact that the civilian population must not be the target of any 'military operations' per art 48, and by the presumption of civilian status in cases of doubt set out in arts 50(1) and 52(3)). The message is very much that civilians are to be respected and protected as far as possible.

This leaves the true meaning of 'attack' ambiguous; it cannot be conclusively resolved by art 31(1) of the *VCLT*. However, the *VCLT* has further rules to help resolve such ambiguity.

Article 31(3)(b) of the *VCLT* provides that 'any subsequent practice in the application of the treaty which establishes the agreement of the parties regarding its interpretation' is also relevant in determining the meaning of a provision.[36] The International Law Commission has found that this is not merely a supplementary means of interpretation or confirmation, but can expand or narrow the primary meaning derived from art 31(1).[37] As a result, in circumstances where all States parties eventually reach some express or implied agreement between them about how a treaty should be interpreted in various contexts—for example, about what 'attack' means in *Additional Protocol I* as applied to cyber operations—this can have a practical impact on how the treaty operates. The catch is that for State practice to be applicable as a primary method of interpretation it must reflect a 'sufficient common understanding' between the parties, which such parties recognise as and intend to be evidence of the correct interpretation of the treaty:[38] this genuinely requires that *all* parties 'have taken a position regarding the interpretation'.[39] So while it is theoretically possible for States to reach such a position, the likelihood seems practically remote in the interpretation of *Additional Protocol I*, which has 174 States parties as of 2024.[40]

However, under art 32 of the *VCLT*, even subsequent practice which does not demonstrate specific agreement on interpretation among party States may be used to help determine the meaning of what appear to be otherwise ambiguous, obscure, absurd or unreasonable provisions.[41] Therefore, even in the absence of very uniform State practice, a current consensus between *some* States may be enough to move the needle as to what should be considered the correct interpretation of attack under *Additional Protocol I*. Because art 32 also requires an examination of the 'preparatory work' of the treaty, the negotiations leading to *Additional Protocol I* must also be considered in conjunction with the available State practice to reach the most accurate possible conclusion.

The Emergence of Subsequent State Practice

As noted above, a number of States have begun to take a public stance in regard to some of the interpretive difficulties introduced by the cyber operational domain. The most recent UN Governmental Group of Experts, which submitted its final report in 2021,[42] prompted a wide array of submissions from States[43] which added significantly to the number now 'on the record' regarding cyber operations and IHL.

States have been refreshingly frank in their views. Some have set out clear answers and thresholds as to when they consider a cyber operation a violation of sovereignty, a use of force, an armed attack and an attack in the context of armed conflict. Others have admitted that they can't be certain when a cyber operation would violate certain principles (such as when it would be considered an attack), but that there should be more work done to clarify this: these include Estonia,[44] Kenya[45] and Switzerland.[46] Of those States who have given a firm position in regard to when a cyber operation may be subject to IHL, several have specifically noted that a cyber operation may qualify as an attack even where it does not result in any physical effects—and, as follows, that 'damage' therefore does not have to be physical in nature. These include France, Germany, Pakistan, Ireland and Costa Rica.

For example, in 2019 France's Ministère des Armeés provided that

> [c]ontrary to the *Tallinn Manual*, France considers that an attack within the meaning of Article 49 of AP I may occur even if there is no human injury or loss of life, or physical damage to goods. Thus, a cyberoperation constitutes an attack if the targeted equipment or systems can no longer provide the service for which they were implemented, including temporarily or reversibly, where action by the adversary is required in order to restore the infrastructure or the system.[47]

Not only does this not require physical damage, but it also does not require *permanent* damage; temporary interruptions are also deemed to potentially qualify as attacks. So long as the adversary has to take some action to restore functionality as a consequence of the cyber operation, in the opinion of France this can be considered a cyber 'attack'.

One of the more recent national positions released, that of Costa Rica, adopts a similar position that even temporary loss of function can be 'damage' and the operation resulting in them can therefore be an 'attack' under IHL.[48] It provides that

> Costa Rica defines a cyber-attack under IHL as any conduct initiated in or through cyberspace that is designed or can be reasonably expected to cause injury or death to persons or damage or destruction to objects. … Costa Rica understands damage to include the disabling — temporary or permanent, reversible or not — of the targeted computer, system, or network. For the avoidance of doubt, this means that the existence of physical damage to objects or injury or death to persons is not required for an operation to constitute an attack under IHL.[49]

Costa Rica specifically indicates that 'encrypting data through ransomware, despite being temporary and reversible, would be considered an attack under IHL and therefore must not be directed against civilian systems'.[50]

Germany's submission to the UN compendium outlined that it considers a cyber operation an 'attack' when it 'cause[s] harmful effects on communication, information or other electronic systems, on the information that is stored, processed or transmitted on these systems or on physical objects or persons'[51] and further specifies that '[t]he occurrence of physical damage, injury or death to persons or damage or destruction to objects comparable to effects of conventional weapons is not required for an attack in the sense of art 49 para 1 [of] *Additional Protocol I*'.[52] This perspective, like that of France, is a notable expansion of the traditional understanding of 'attack'—not just extending the definition to include instances where the impact is not felt in terms of physical damage, but also including a very wide array of harmful effects to both the systems themselves and to people and objects reliant on them. Under this framing, even some relatively innocuous cyber operations that are limited in impact to 'inconvenience, irritation, stress [or] fear'[53] could arguably be considered an 'attack'.

Ireland adopted a similar position in 2023, indicating that '[t]he concept of an "attack" in IHL ... extends to cyber operations expected to cause loss of functioning to networks or electronic systems'.[54] As also argued in this chapter, Ireland reasons that a more restrictive interpretation of attack would leave civilians and civilian objects unprotected by IHL, which 'would not be consistent with the object and purpose of the *Geneva Conventions* and their *Additional Protocols*'.[55]

Pakistan's 2023 national position paper presents a very clear view that a cyberattack is capable of being considered an 'attack' in IHL.[56] It also sets a relatively low threshold for this application, including as examples of prohibited attack: 'employment of cyber and other digital weapons which undermines the confidentiality, integrity, and the availability of a critical civilian infrastructure';[57] '[a]ny attempt to delete, destroy and manipulate the data essential for the smooth functioning of [such infrastructure]'; and '[e]mployment of cyber and other digital technologies to spread fear and chaos among the civilian population through disinformation'.[58] Italy's late 2021 position paper maintains that an attack must be 'an act of violence', in accordance with *Additional Protocol I*, but specifies an action could be classified as such if it results in 'disruption in the functioning of critical infrastructure'—a clear shift in the understanding of what can be considered 'damage' under IHL.[59]

The US mentions that '[*i*]*n addition* to the potential physical damage that a cyber activity may cause ... parties must assess the potential effects of a cyberattack on civilian objects that are not military objectives'[60]—this view does not specify what the further 'potential effects' to be considered must be, but clearly an attack is conceptualised as having an impact beyond the physical which is relevant to IHL requirements. The US Department of Defense *DOD Dictionary of Military and Associated Terms* also defines 'cyberspace attack' as '[a]ctions taken in cyberspace that create noticeable denial effects (i.e. degradation, disruption, or destruction) in cyberspace or manipulation that leads to denial that appears in a physical domain',[61] again apparently acknowledging that even where the direct impact of an operation is confined to cyberspace this can still constitute an 'attack' if the effects are of sufficient scale.

However, this wave of State practice is not uniform. Israel's 2020 position paper accords with the *Tallinn Manual 2.0* majority position, in stating that '[o]nly when a cyber operation is expected to cause physical damage, will it satisfy this element of an attack under LOAC'.[62] Supporting this understanding is their observation that 'practices such as certain types of electronic warfare, psychological warfare, economic sanctions, seizure of property, and detention have never been considered to be attacks' due to the lack of physical damage caused, and there is 'no other specific rule to the contrary that has evolved in the cyber domain'.[63] Denmark's 2023 position paper expresses a similar view, indicating that 'a cyber operation will constitute an attack if it can be reasonably expected to cause injury, death or physical damage to individuals or objects'.[64]

The Inter-American Juridical Committee of the Organization of American States canvassed numerous State members about cyber operations and international law in 2019. The responses were usefully summarised in November 2020.[65] Although the full-text State views do not appear to be publicly available, the summary indicates that perspectives on the application of IHL varied. Guatemala and Ecuador indicated that a cyber operation leading to loss of functionality (with or without visible damage) can be an attack under IHL,[66] while Chile and Peru took the view that to meet this threshold would specifically require damage akin to a kinetic attack.[67] However, the report does note that Peru's response is 'a bit ambiguous, as it appears to rely on *jus ad bellum* materials to identify the standards for an IHL attack'.[68] Bolivia and Guyana also responded to the inquiry, but were 'more equivocal' on this specific issue.[69]

Although there is clearly no consensus between States parties, the views demonstrate an emerging convergence of perspectives. Applied under art 32 of the *VCLT* to resolve the ambiguity of how cyber operations may be categorised under *Additional Protocol I*, they on balance—so far—support a less restrictive interpretation of 'attack' and 'damage'.[70]

This is a fast-moving area—unusually so in the realm of international law. While this chapter addresses the State positions available at the time of writing, more States are contributing their perspectives each year. Further UN initiatives will continue to prompt more State engagement with this issue, such as the submissions given in response to the ongoing Open-Ended Working Group on Information and Communication Technologies.[71] As States continue to set out their understanding, a firmer or varied conclusion about the appropriate definition of 'attack' and 'damage' applicable to cyber operations may become possible. The Cyber Law Toolkit project, run jointly by six partner institutions, keeps an accessible online register of national positions as they are released which can be consulted for more information about this ongoing dialogue.[72]

The Travaux and an Evolving Meaning

The definition of 'attacks' given in *Additional Protocol I* is brief and, clearly, doesn't translate well to the cyber context. There are obvious reasons for this: in the mid-1970s the military potential of modern cyber operations could hardly have been imagined, and armed conflict was considered in terms of traditional kinetic operations.

As noted above, placing art 32 'on the scale' of interpretation requires looking not only at examples of sporadic State practice but also at the preparatory work of the treaty or travaux préparatoires. This may offer some further explanation as to what the drafters intended to be prohibited by the limitations on 'attacks'.

The drafting of pt IV was largely the responsibility of Committee III of the Diplomatic Conference. Committee III had a very important role—it was assigned to work on, among others, the articles covering '[g]eneral protection against effects of hostilities' and '[m]ethods and means of combat'.[73] These are absolutely core components of IHL, and determining the correct approach required the Committee to 'reconcile military necessity with humanitarian aims'.[74] One important aspect for the Committee was determining when a military operation should be considered an 'attack' and therefore be constrained by the rules about the conduct of attacks. The outcome, as noted above, was that attacks were 'acts of violence against the adversary'.[75] Interestingly, Committee III did not seem entirely satisfied with the finalised definition; the representative for the Netherlands noted that 'the Drafting Committee could possibly find a better wording'.[76] The 1987 commentary on *Additional Protocol I* indicated that the original definition intended by the drafters for 'attack' was 'to set upon with hostile action';[77] this would have perhaps left it more open for non-physical operations to fall within the definition. However, the final text retained the reference to 'violence'. Committee III appeared concerned to ensure 'attacks' were not confused with 'military operations' generally, which they equated with 'movements or manoeuvres of armed forces in action'.[78] This is interesting, because if cyber operations are to be categorised as either 'movements of manoeuvres of armed forces', on the one hand, or an instance of being 'set upon with hostile action', they would seem to more reliably fall within the latter category.

What also becomes clear from an appraisal of the travaux préparatoires is that the Committees involved in the drafting of *Additional Protocol I* did intend to cover the development of any new technologies that could be used in armed conflict.[79] Like the four primary Geneva Conventions before it, *Additional Protocol I* was intended to be an enduring restatement and reshaping of IHL that would apply regardless of later technological advances—this is why, for example, it contains provision for review of new weapons or means and methods of warfare.[80]

Given that the terms 'attack' and 'damage' are quite general terms in a treaty built for longevity, there is a further argument that they may have an intrinsically *evolving* meaning, which can also be confirmed by recourse to State practice.

The International Court of Justice has expressly noted that general terms used in longstanding treaties are expected to evolve in meaning over time: 'the parties must be presumed, as a general rule, to have intended those terms to have an evolving meaning'.[81] Such intention is confirmed via State practice[82]—which, as discussed above, is a process we appear to be witnessing in real time with a reframing of 'attack' and 'damage'. Even 'violence' is subject to modern reinterpretation: it is generally associated with physical conflict—'rough or injurious action or treatment'[83]—but current understandings of the concept may extend it to 'any unjust or unwarranted exertion of force or power'.[84] This could conceivably include acts beyond physical aggression, such as those intended to intimidate or coerce an actor into compliance.

The natural evolution of general treaty terms' meaning can even 'result in a departure from the original intent on the basis of a tacit agreement'.[85] With this consideration added to the interpretive influence of State practice, and the emphasis in the preparatory work on future-oriented protections, it appears that the balance is in favour of giving 'attack' a broad interpretation that could encompass cyber operations.

A Position of Compromise

An expansion of the concepts of 'attack' and 'damage' under *Additional Protocol I* to encompass all situations where there is non-trivial loss of functionality provides significantly greater protection to civilians affected by armed conflict. Modern examples have clearly demonstrated the chaos and significant loss that can result from cyber operations.[86] Requiring that military forces consider more broadly potential collateral damage beyond the physical impact of their actions is now simply mandated by the world's reliance on digital infrastructure.

A more nuanced interpretation of 'attack' and 'damage', via the operation of State practice, can only assist with upholding the object and purpose of *Additional Protocol I*. This would have flow-on effects in expanding the protective mechanisms accorded to civilians and civilian institutions—especially in application to proportionality assessments and the obligation to take precautions in the means and method of attack.[87] This would not prevent military forces from making use of disabling cyber operations, but would firmly (and appropriately) disallow civilian cyber infrastructure to be their target in armed conflict. At the same time, it would require military forces to comprehensively assess the collateral impact to civilian systems when conducting such operations against valid military targets, even where this is achieved without any damage to infrastructure hardware.[88]

Conclusion

On the day Russia launched its invasion of Ukraine, a multi-pronged cyberattack was also launched against Viasat's KA-SAT network, which provided much of the internet services to Ukraine including to its government. The hackers exploited an error in Viasat's VPN setup to infect the network servers with malware and wipe the flash memory from over 45,000 individual modems.[89] This had strategic military advantages for Russia, but—if classified as an attack under *Additional Protocol I*—was also clearly indiscriminate, as the malware targeted and disabled end-user devices in the system regardless of whether they were relied on by civilians or combatants. Many of these end-users were not even located in Ukraine, but rather in other neutral States across the world.[90] Although Russia denied responsibility for the hack,[91] it provides a powerful example of how impactful cyber operations can be in armed conflict—and how important it is to control their potential impact on civilian populations.

At this stage, there are only limited indications of how States interpret *Additional Protocol I*, and IHL more generally, as applicable to cyber 'attacks' and 'damage'. Many more States remain absent from the conversation, while others have provided only preliminary and tentative views. However, the State positions available suggest that States are not reluctant to reconsider and reinterpret IHL principles to fill apparent gaps in protection in their application to the cyber domain. Further, State positions imply that cyber operations which impose dire consequences on civilians will not generally be tolerated as a valid means of waging war, regardless of whether they cause damage in the traditional, kinetic sense. These views are reminiscent of one minority position stated in the *Tallinn Manual 2.0*: 'should an armed conflict involving such cyber operations break out, the international community would generally regard them as an attack'.[92] There is every expectation, based on the emerging State practice, that this will hold true. As more comprehensive State practice enables a firm reinterpretation, it is likely that the crucial protections IHL provides to civilian populations affected by war will be fully transposed to the cyber context in accordance with the overriding object and purpose of this body of law.

Acknowledgements This chapter is adapted, with permission, from the author's earlier article in the Adelaide Law Review: Joanna Jarose, 'Reconsidering the Definition of "Attack" and "Damage" in Cyber Operations during Armed Conflict: Emerging Subsequent State Practice' (2023) 44(2) Adelaide Law Review 317.

Notes

1. See, eg, Ronald A Heiner, 'Imperfect Decisions and the Law: On the Evolution of Legal Precedent and Rules' (1986) 15(2) *The Journal of Legal Studies* 227; Jeremy Waldron, 'Stare Decisis and the Rule of Law: A Layered Approach' (2012) 111(1) *Michigan Law Review* 1; Sneha Solanki, 'What is Stare Decisis in Simple Terms?', *Thomson Reuters* (online, 30 January 2023) <https://legal.thomsonreuters.com/blog/the-doctrine-of-stare-decisis/>.
2. See, eg, the ongoing process of reform and judicial interpretation of the *Migration Act 1958* (Cth).
3. See, eg, International Law Commission, *Draft Conclusions on Identification of Customary International Law, with Commentaries* (United Nations, 2018).
4. Guy Faulconbridge, 'Explainer: Moon Mining—Why Major Powers are Eyeing a Lunar Gold Rush', *Reuters* (online, 12 August 2023) <https://www.reuters.com/technology/space/moon-mining-why-major-powers-are-eyeing-lunar-gold-rush-2023-08-11/>; Gloria Oladipo, 'NASA Aims to Mine Resources on Moon in Next Decade', *The Guardian* (online, 29 June 2023) <https://www.theguardian.com/science/2023/jun/28/nasa-mining-moon-2032>.
5. Eve Massingham and Dale Stephens, 'Autonomous Systems, Private Actors, Outer Space and War: Lessons for Addressing Accountability Concerns in Uncertain Legal Environments' (2022) 23(2) *Melbourne Journal of International Law* 276; David Vergun, 'US Endorses Responsible AI Measures for Global Militaries', *US Department of Defense* (Web Page, 22 November 2023) <https://www.defense.gov/News/News-Stories/Article/Article/3597093/us-endorses-responsible-ai-measures-for-global-militaries/>.

6. Pia Hüsch and Henning Lahmann, 'Societal Risks and Potential Humanitarian Impact of Cyber Operations' (Geneva Academy Working Paper, June 2022); Michael N Schmitt, 'Cyber Symposium – The Evolution of Cyber Jus Ad Bellum Thresholds', *Articles of War* (Blog Post, 28 July 2022) <https://lieber.westpoint.edu/evolution-cyber-jus-ad-bellum-thresholds/>.
7. 'Conflict in the Cyber Age: Why the World Must Act to End the Cyber Arms Race' (FP Analytics Research Brief, 17 August 2021) <https://fpanalytics.foreignpolicy.com/2021/08/17/the-rise-of-state-sponsored-cyber-attacks-and-the-cost-of-inaction/>; Dennis Broeders, 'Private Active Cyber Defense and (International) Cyber Security – Pushing the Line?' (2021) 7(1) *Journal of Cybersecurity* 1, 4–5 <https://academic.oup.com/cybersecurity/article/7/1/tyab010/6199903>.
8. Jackson Colling, 'Recapping "Cyber in War: Lessons from the Russia-Ukraine Conflict"', *Articles of War* (Blog Post, 8 January 2024) <https://lieber.westpoint.edu/recapping-cyber-war-lessons-russia-ukraine-conflict/>; FP Analytics, 'The Evolution of Cyber Operations in Armed Conflict', *Digital Front Lines* (Web Page, 25 May 2023) <https://digitalfrontlines.io/2023/05/25/the-evolution-of-cyber-operations-in-armed-conflict/>.
9. *Geneva Convention for the Amelioration of the Condition of the Wounded and Sick in Armed Forces in the Field*, opened for signature 12 August 1949, 75 UNTS 31 (entered into force 21 October 1950) ('*Geneva Convention I*'); *Geneva Convention for the Amelioration of the Condition of Wounded, Sick and Shipwrecked Members of Armed Forces at Sea*, opened for signature 12 August 1949, 75 UNTS 85 (entered into force 21 October 1950) ('*Geneva Convention II*'); *Geneva Convention Relative to the Treatment of Prisoners of War*, opened for signature 12 August 1949, 75 UNTS 135 (entered into force 21 October 1950) ('*Geneva Convention III*'); *Geneva Convention Relative to the Protection of Civilian Persons in Time of War*, opened for signature 12 August 1949, 75 UNTS 287 (entered into force 21 October 1950) ('*Geneva Convention IV*'); *Protocol Additional to the Geneva Conventions of 12 August 1949, and relating to the Protection of Victims of International Armed Conflicts (Protocol I)*, opened for signature 8 June 1977, 1125 UNTS 3 (entered into force 7 December 1978) ('*Additional Protocol I*'); *Protocol Additional to the Geneva Conventions of 12 August 1949, and Relating to the Protection of Victims of Non-International Armed Conflicts (Protocol II)*, opened for signature 8 June 1977, 1125 UNTS 609 (entered into force 7 December 1978) ('*Additional Protocol II*').
10. See, eg, General Assembly, *Report of the Group of Governmental Experts on Advancing Responsible State Behaviour in Cyberspace in the Context of International Security*, UN Doc A/76/135 (14 July 2021) 8; General Assembly, *Report of the Open-Ended Working Group on Security of and in the Use of Information and Communications Technologies 2021–2025*, UN Doc A/78/265 (1 August 2023) 11.
11. US Cyber Command, 'Our History' <https://www.cybercom.mil/About/History/>. See also Joint Chiefs of Staff, *The National Military Strategy of the United States of America: A Strategy for Today; A Vision for Tomorrow* (2004) 18.
12. See generally Andrzej Kozłowski, 'Comparative Analysis of Cyberattacks on Estonia, Georgia and Kyrgyzstan' (2014) 3 (Spec Ed) *European Scientific Journal* 237.
13. Ibid.
14. See generally: Gary D Brown, 'Why Iran Didn't Admit Stuxnet was an Attack' [2011] (63) *Joint Force Quarterly* 70; Peter Beaumont, 'Stuxnet Worm Heralds New Era of Global Cyberwar', *The Guardian* (online, 1 October 2010) <https://www.theguardian.com/technology/2010/sep/30/stuxnet-worm-new-era-global-cyberwar>.
15. North Atlantic Council, 'Warsaw Summit Communiqué' (Press Release, 9 July 2016) <https://www.nato.int/cps/en/natohq/official_texts_133169.htm>.
16. Michael N Schmitt (ed), *Tallinn Manual on the International Law Applicable to Cyber Warfare* (Cambridge University Press, 2013).
17. Michael N Schmitt (ed), *Tallinn Manual 2.0 on the International Law Applicable to Cyber Warfare* (Cambridge University Press, 2nd ed, 2017) ('*Tallinn Manual 2.0*').
18. NATO Cooperative Cyber Defence Centre of Excellence, 'The Tallinn Manual', *CCDCOE* (Web Page, 2021) <https://ccdcoe.org/research/tallinn-manual/>.

19. *Official Compendium of Voluntary National Contributions on the Subject of How International Law Applies to the Use of Information and Communications Technologies by States Submitted by Participating Governmental Experts in the Group of Governmental Experts on Advancing Responsible State Behaviour in Cyberspace in the Context of International Security Established Pursuant to General Assembly Resolution 73/266*, UN Doc A/76/136 (13 July 2021) ('*GGE Compendium 2021*').
20. Associated State submissions available at 'Open-Ended Working Group on Information and Communication Technologies', *United Nations Office for Disarmament Affairs* (Web Page) <https://meetings.unoda.org/meeting/57871/documents>. See also 'Category: National Position', *Cyber Law Toolkit* (Web Page, 2021) <https://cyberlaw.ccdcoe.org/wiki/Category:National_position>.
21. See, eg: *GGE Compendium 2021*, the submissions of Australia at 6, Brazil at 17, 22, Estonia at 23, 26, Germany at 31, 36, Japan at 49, The Netherlands at 59, Norway at 66, 74, Romania at 77, Switzerland at 93, United Kingdom at 118 and the US at 138; Ministère des Armeés, *International Law Applied to Operations in Cyberspace* (Position Paper, 2019) 12 ('French Position Paper'); Roy Schöndorf, 'Israel's Perspective on Key Legal and Practical Issues Concerning the Application of International Law to Cyber Operations' (2021) 97(1) *International Law Studies* 395, 399; Ministry for Foreign Affairs, *International Law and Cyberspace: Finland's National Positions* (Position Paper, 2020), discussed in Ministry for Foreign Affairs, 'Finland Published its Positions on Public International Law in Cyberspace', *Finnish Government* (Web Page, 15 October 2020) <https://valtioneuvosto.fi/en/-/finland-published-its-positions-on-public-international-law-in-cyberspace>.
22. *Report of the Group of Governmental Experts on Advancing Responsible State Behaviour in Cyberspace in the Context of International Security*, UN Doc A/76/135 (14 July 2021) 18 ('*GGE Final Report 2021*'). See also: Michael Schmitt, 'The Sixth United Nations GGE and International Law in Cyberspace', *Just Security* (online, 10 June 2021) <https://www.justsecurity.org/76864/the-sixth-united-nations-gge-and-internationallaw-in-cyberspace/>; Adina Ponta, 'Responsible State Behavior in Cyberspace: Two New Reports from Parallel UN Processes' (2021) 25(14) *American Society of International Law: Insights* 1; Anna Maria Osula, 'In Search of a Coherent International Approach to Governing Technologies', *Observer Research Foundation: Digital Frontiers* (online, 17 October 2021) <https://www.orfonline.org/expert-speak/international-approach-to-governing-technologies/>.
23. Jean-Marie Henckaerts and Louise Doswald-Beck (eds), *Customary International Humanitarian Law* (Cambridge University Press, 2005) vol 1, 51–2; Israeli Defence Force, *The 2014 Gaza Conflict 7 July–26 August 2014: Factual and Legal Aspects* (Report, 2015) 138; Bundesministerium der Verteidigung, *Law of Armed Conflict Manual* (Joint Service Regulation (ZDv) 15/2, 2013) 22 [136]; Norwegian Defence University College, *Manual of the Law of Armed Conflict* (Joint Service Publication, 2013) 14; Department of the Navy, *The Commander's Handbook on the Law of Naval Operations: NWP 1-14M* (Navy Warfare Library, rev ed, 2022) 5-3–5-4, 8–18 [8.10.1].
24. *Additional Protocol I* (n 9) art 49(1).
25. *Prosecutor v Ntaganda (Judgment)* (International Criminal Court, Appeals Chamber, Case No ICC-01/04-02/06 A A2, 30 March 2021). The context in which 'attack' was contemplated was whether pillage of medical equipment (a protected object) could be considered an attack: at 505–7 [1147]–[1152].
26. Ibid 511–14 [1164]–[1169].
27. Ibid art 57(2).
28. Michael N Schmitt, '"Attack" as a Term of Art in International Law: The Cyber Operations Context' in C Czosseck, R Ottis and K Ziolkowski (eds), 4th *International Conference on Cyber Conflict* (NATO CCD COE, 2012) 283, 290 ('"Attack" as a Term of Art in International Law').
29. *Macquarie Dictionary* (online at 10 May 2022) 'harm' (def 2); *Oxford English Dictionary* (online at 10 May 2022) 'harm' (defs 1a, 1b, 2).
30. Schmitt, '"Attack" as a Term of Art in International Law' (n 28) 291.

31. *Tallinn Manual 2.0* (n 17) 417 [10].
32. See, eg, Australian Communications and Media Authority, *Communications and Media in Australia Series: How We Use the Internet* (Report, December 2022) 1–2; UN Secretary-General's High-Level Panel on Digital Cooperation, *The Age of Digital Interdependence* (Report, 2019) 6.
33. *Additional Protocol I* (n 9) Preamble, arts 1, 51, 54, 57.
34. Kubo Mačák, 'Military Objectives 2.0: The Case for Interpreting Computer Data as Objects Under International Humanitarian Law' (2015) 48(1) *Israel Law Review* 55, 78.
35. *Vienna Convention on the Law of Treaties*, opened for signature 23 May 1969, 1155 UNTS 331 (entered into force 27 January 1980) art 31 ('*VCLT*'). The interpretation provisions of the *VCLT* apply to *Additional Protocol I* as they codify pre-existing customary international law. See, eg: Richard Gardiner, *Treaty Interpretation* (Oxford International Law Library, 2nd ed, 2015) 163, 174, 210; *Application of the Convention on the Prevention and Punishment of the Crime of Genocide (Bosnia and Herzegovina v Serbia and Montenegro) (Judgment of 26 February 2007)* [2007] ICJ Reps 43, 110 [160]; *LaGrand Case (Germany v USA) (Judgment of 27 June 2001)* [2001] ICJ Reps 466, 501 [99].
36. *VCLT* (n 35) art 31(3)(b).
37. International Law Commission, *Second Report on Subsequent Agreements and Subsequent Practice in Relation to the Interpretation of Treaties by Georg Nolte, Special Rapporteur*, UN Doc A/CN.4/671 (26 March 2014) 120–1 [20].
38. Ibid 125 [43], 128 [55]; International Law Commission, 'Subsequent Agreements and Subsequent Practice in Relation to the Interpretation of Treaties' in *Report of the International Law Commission* UN GAOR, 70th sess, Supp No 10, UN Doc A/73/10 (2018) 11, 75–7 ('ILC Draft Conclusions').
39. ILC Draft Conclusions (n 38) 43.
40. 'Protocol Additional to the Geneva Conventions of 12 August 1949, and relating to the Protection of Victims of International Armed Conflicts', *United Nations Treaty Collection* (Web Page) <https://treaties.un.org/pages/showdetails.aspx?objid=08000002800f3586>.
41. *VCLT* (n 35) art 32; ILC Draft Conclusions (n 38) 13–14, Conclusions 2(4), 4(3), 5(1), 6(3), 7(2). See also Irina Buga, *Modification of Treaties by Subsequent Practice* (Oxford University Press, 2018) 75–6.
42. *GGE Final Report 2021* (n 22).
43. *GGE Compendium 2021* (n 21).
44. Ibid 27 (submission of Estonia).
45. Ibid 54 (submission of Kenya).
46. *GGE Compendium 2021* (n 21) 94 (submission of Switzerland).
47. French Position Paper (n 21) 13 (emphasis omitted).
48. Ministry of Foreign Affairs of Costa Rica, *Costa Rica's Position on the Application of International Law in Cyberspace* (Position Paper, 21 July 2023) 13 [49] <https://docs-library.unoda.org/Open-Ended_Working_Group_on_Information_and_Communication_Technologies_-_(2021)/Costa_Rica_-_Position_Paper_-_International_Law_in_Cyberspace.pdf>.
49. Ibid.
50. Ibid.
51. *GGE Compendium 2021* (n 21) 36–7 (submission of Germany).
52. Ibid 37.
53. Cf Harvard University Program on Humanitarian Policy and Conflict Research, *Commentary to the HPCR Manual on International Law Applicable to Air and Missile Warfare* (Cambridge University Press, 2013) 20, 96.
54. Ireland Department of Foreign Affairs, *Position Paper on the Application of International Law in Cyberspace* (Position Paper, July 2023) [31].
55. Ibid.
56. Pakistan Mission to the United Nations, *Pakistan's Position on the Application of International Law in Cyberspace* (Position Paper, 3 March 2023) 3 [14].

57. Pakistan defines such infrastructure very broadly, including 'but is not limited to health, transportation, energy, banking and financial sector, civilian logistical supply chains, undersea fibre optic cables, satellites, and other telecommunication networks': ibid.
58. Ibid.
59. Ministry of Foreign Affairs and International Cooperation, Presidency of Council of Ministers and the Ministry of Defence *Italian Position Paper on 'International Law and Cyberspace'* (Position Paper, Republic of Italy, December 2021) 9–10.
60. *GGE Compendium 2021* (n 21) 138 (submission of the US) (emphasis added).
61. United States Department of Defense, *DOD Dictionary of Military and Associated Terms* (Department of Defense, 2021) 55.
62. Schöndorf (n 21) 400.
63. Ibid.
64. Jeppe Mejer Kjelgaard and Ulf Melgaard, 'Denmark's Position Paper on the Application of International Law in Cyberspace' (2023) *Nordic Journal of International Law* 1571–8107: 1–10, 9–10.
65. Department of International Law of the Secretariat for Legal Affairs, *Improving Transparency: International Law and State Cyber Operations* (Report, Inter-American Juridical Committee, 1 November 2020) Annex B.
66. Ibid 45–6 [32].
67. Ibid 45 [31].
68. Ibid 45 n 76.
69. Ibid 46 [33].
70. Under *VCLT* (n 35) art 31(3)(a).
71. Associated State submissions available at 'Open-Ended Working Group on Information and Communication Technologies', *United Nations Office for Disarmament Affairs* (Web Page) <https://meetings.unoda.org/meeting/57871/documents>.
72. See 'Category: National Position', *Cyber Law Toolkit* (Web Page, 2021) <https://cyberlaw.ccdcoe.org/wiki/Category:National_position>.
73. See 'Committee III Report: CDDH/236/Rev1' in *Official Records of the Diplomatic Conference on the Reaffirmation and Development of International Humanitarian Law Application in Armed Conflicts: Geneva (1974–1977)* (Federal Political Department, 1976) vol XV, 377.
74. *Official Records of the Diplomatic Conference on the Reaffirmation and Development of International Humanitarian Law Application in Armed Conflicts: Geneva (1974–1977)* (Federal Political Department, 1978) vol VII, 286 [36].
75. *Additional Protocol I* (n 9) art 49(1).
76. *Official Records of the Diplomatic Conference on the Reaffirmation and Development of International Humanitarian Law Application in Armed Conflicts: Geneva (1974–1977)* (Federal Political Department, 1978) vol XIV 128 [8], 85 [4] ('*Diplomatic Conference Records Vol XIV*').
77. Yves Sandoz, Christophe Swinarski and Bruno Zimmermann (eds), *Commentary on the Additional Protocols of 8 June 1977 to the Geneva Conventions of 12 August 1949* (International Committee of the Red Cross, 1987) 603 [1879].
78. *Diplomatic Conference Records Vol XIV* (n 76) 44 [4].
79. See, eg: *Diplomatic Conference Records Vol XIV* (n 76) 157 [32], 234 [4]; *Official Records of the Diplomatic Conference on the Reaffirmation and Development of International Humanitarian Law Application in Armed Conflicts: Geneva (1974–1977)* (Federal Political Department, 1978) vol V, 8 [4], 126 [46], 144 [16].
80. *Additional Protocol I* (n 9) a.
81. *Dispute regarding Navigational and Related Rights (Costa Rica v Nicaragua) (Judgment)* [2009] ICJ Rep 213, 243 [66] ('*Costa Rica v Nicaragua*').
82. ILC Draft Conclusions (n 38) 14 (Conclusion 8).
83. *Macquarie Dictionary* (online at 10 May 2022) 'violence' (def 2).
84. Ibid (def 3).
85. *Costa Rica v Nicaragua* (n 81) 242 [64].

86. See, eg, Beaumont (n 14).
87. Under *Additional Protocol I* (n 9) arts 57(2)(a)(ii)–(iii), 57(2)(b).
88. Ibid art 52.
89. Katrina Manson, 'The Russian Hack Everyone is Finally Talking About' (New York, 6 March 2023) *Bloomberg Businessweek* 42, 45. See also Cynthia Brumfield, 'Incident Response Lessons Learned from the Russian Attack on Viasat', *CSO* (online, 16 August 2023) <https://www.csoonline.com/article/649714/incident-response-lessons-learned-from-the-russian-attack-on-viasat.html>.
90. Manson (n 89) 44.
91. Ibid.
92. *Tallinn Manual 2.0* (n 17) 418 [13].

Joanna Jarose is a PhD candidate and sessional lecturer at the University of Adelaide Law School. She holds a BA (Hons), LLB (Hons) and a MA (Res). She has been a Research Associate for the law school's Research Unit on Military Law and Ethics since 2021, and is also an Associate Editor for the Adelaide Law Review. In 2023, she was the recipient of several academic awards including the University Medal, the Angas Parsons Prize and the title of Stow Scholar. She has a broad range of research interests in international humanitarian law and adjacent fields, with her PhD project centred on the law of naval warfare.

Data Protection Regulations as Disinformation Resilience

J. W. F. Small

Abstract The regulation of personal data serves a dual purpose. While intended to protect personal privacy, it also constrains a bad actor's ability to access the core resource required for online disinformation campaigns: personal data. This chapter discusses the origins of online disinformation campaigns, tracing their development through marketing and advertising methods to their reliance on social media with its tendency to facilitate disinformation and its dissemination. Taking the general data protection regulations (GDPR) as a point of departure and referring to real-world examples, the chapter posits that data protection regulations constrain the scope and intensity of disinformation by implanting constraints into the processes of private enterprises. The characteristics of GDPR and similar data protection regulations are considered from the perspective of the checks that they impose on the exploitation of personal data and the chapter maintains that together such checks constitute a key aspect of a state's resilience to disinformation. As such, the chapter concludes that in addition to their personal privacy purpose, data protection regulations also carry strategic implications that ought to be given specific consideration in questions of doctrine and policy.

Introduction

In July of 2023, Royal Assent was granted to the National Security Act,[1] an act of the parliament of the United Kingdom which, among other objectives, aims to strengthen national security by preventing interference in the political system. This was followed in October of the same year with the passage of the Online Safety Act,[2]

BSc (Hons), MSc, MSc, GDip (Law); Major, Legal Advisor, British Army Legal Services (Res).
The content of this Chapter and the views expressed herein are entirely the work of the author and do not constitute or reflect the position of the British Army Legal Services, the British Army, the Ministry of Defence of the United Kingdom or of His Majesty's Government.

J. W. F. Small (✉)
Directorate of Army Legal Services, IDL 426, Ramilies Building, Andover, SP11 8HJ, United Kingdom
e-mail: John.Small102@mod.gov.uk

D. Stephens et al. (eds.), *Digital Resilience*,
https://doi.org/10.1007/978-981-97-9746-2_5

a primary focus of which is to limit the impact of harmful online information. These two laws constitute significant legislative responses to aspects of the threat posed by manipulated or maliciously intended information. More generally, they both serve as an important part of the legal matrix which underpins the resilience upon which open societies such as the UK rely to counter the threat posed by disinformation[3] and they provide an appropriate starting point for discussions on statutory responses to that threat.

While these laws will be given cursory individual mention, this Chapter does not concern itself in the main with such intentional responses to the challenges emanating from the information environment since their impact is the subject of consideration elsewhere.[4] Instead, the focus of this Chapter is on the consequences and contribution (largely unforeseen at the time of introduction and still largely unacknowledged) of data protection regulations. Regulations which while intended primarily to protect personal privacy, also serve the secondary purpose of constraining a bad actor's ability to access and manipulate a core resource required for targeted disinformation campaigns: personal data. In so doing, the Chapter does not provide a detailed technical assessment or overview of data protection regulations or their application, nor does it follow closely their development. Instead, the Chapter aims to underscore for lawyers and policy makers—particularly those in national security—the role of data protection regulations in constituting a safeguard against disinformation.[5] The Chapter will also seek to assess some of the implications of that safeguard, both from the perspective of its effects on constraining the spread of disinformation and then more broadly from the standpoint of strategic considerations.

Personal Data and Disinformation: Origins and Development

The UK's most recent major defence policy papers, the Integrated Review of Security, Defence, Development and Foreign Policy[6] and its 2023 Integrated Review ("IR") Refresh[7] both featured concerns around disinformation and a recognition of its proliferation. In addition, they both contained a notable focus on data governance, infrastructure and standards. Importantly, there was also reference to the monetisation of data with a clear understanding of the association between private commercial motives, macro-economic imperatives and strategic considerations relating to disinformation. A broad understanding of the relationship between these observations is fundamental to understanding the role of data protection regulations in addressing the threat of disinformation.

Marketing, advertising and influencing behaviour

Beginning in the mid 2000s and driven by analytics software, commercial marketing and advertising began a reliance on the collection of personal data and the surveillance of consumer habits, activities and preferences for the purpose of increasing attention to and engagement with products and services. Data on consumers was harvested from devices such as mobile phones, programs like online games and digital services such as television streaming services while cookie-based tracking allowed consumers to be traced from one web site to the next allowing for an understanding of their behaviour and interests. This facilitated the build-up of detailed pictures of individual consumer desires. The aim of this data collection was the delivery, to unwitting consumers in the most effective place and at the most effective time, of the most potent advertising - the intention being to increase the likelihood of purchase of a particular good or service.

The predictive power that this compiled data was able to bring to bear should not be underestimated and with each new data point a consumer could become the target of increasingly effective advertising, curated specifically in response to their behaviours. Before long, an ability to identify intimate personal characteristics, beliefs, thoughts and vulnerabilities had been developed, allowing personalised content to be delivered to maximum effect.[8] This allowed for predictive analytics so sophisticated that, by way of a real-world example, a father would complain to a major department store that his teenaged daughter had been receiving coupons for baby related items only to discover shortly thereafter that his daughter was in fact pregnant, analytic methods confirming his daughter's pregnancy to the department store before she had told him about it.[9]

The inputs for the construction of such invasive messaging were not demographic alone but also psychometric. The advent of social media and its use at scale by the public allowed marketing and technology companies alike the insights necessary to develop methods of both detecting and eliciting emotions in their users. This meant that understanding of complex personality, behavioural and psychological characteristics could be garnered so that in addition to facts about the circumstances of a consumer's life (such as whether a person was pregnant), details about who they were and how they viewed the world could be determined, allowing for an increasing capability to influence their emotions.[10]

While the ability of a business to effect purchase decisions by means of such targeted personalised advertising itself raises ethical questions, it is the ability to profile and target individuals for political purposes with information curated on the basis of insights from the same data that presents a particular challenge to democratic freedom.[11] What if the complex data sets provided by this "surveillance capitalism"[12] could be used to influence political opinions and decision making with a consistency similar to the influence on purchasing decisions for which the data sets were initially collated? It is this potential alignment of outcomes between marketing, advertising and political messaging which allows for an easy transition between the use of data to effect purchasing decisions to its use to influence politics. To quote Dawson, "The objective of surveillance capitalism-enabled advertising and information warfare is the same: to influence an individual's behaviour change in support of someone else's goals".[13]

Among the key players in the transition from the use of data harnessing in marketing and advertising to its use in politics and ultimately in disinformation were social-media companies which, as a result of their increasing societal penetration, had access to complex data points on users. These companies came to play a pivotal role in the collection and analysis of the personal data on which online disinformation may be based, harvesting the raw material which could give bad actors unique insight into individual behaviour and relaying disinformation based on those insights. The Cambridge Analytica scandal and the predictive modelling that underpinned it provide an acute example of the issue.

Cambridge Analytica

By combining voting lists with data on charity donations, airline loyalty memberships and bank account ownership with user data from Facebook, political consulting firm Cambridge Analytica was shown to have amassed thousands of data points on hundreds of millions of users, using them to build profiles of 100 million US voters who were allegedly targeted for political messaging.[14] The numbers of data points referred to here are not trivial. For example, one study showed that based on 68 Facebook 'likes' analytic models can predict a person's skin colour, sexual orientation, political party affiliation, drug and alcohol use, and whether a person had grown up in an intact or divorced household.[15] More strikingly, a study by *Youyou et al*[16] demonstrated that such predictive modelling when input with 150 Facebook likes can assess a person's character with more accuracy than a parent, with 300 likes personality judgments could be made with more precision than by the subject's partner and with even more likes the model was consistently more accurate in certain categories than a person reporting on their own personality; predictive models based on am algamated data can know us better than we know ourselves.

From marketing and advertising to disinformation

What might happen when detailed personal data and the ability to use it for targeted influence is accessed by bad actors intent on influencing a society to their own ends?[17] Empowered with accrued insights into how individuals think and react, they could produce disinformation intended to promote or suppress particular narratives or to spread confusion, even seeking to manipulate emotions with a view to changing behaviour and encouraging real-world responses. The potential for such deployment of data presents a particular challenge to democracies because as a consequence of their reliance on truth and trust as fundamental currencies of their politics,[18] people's ability to form opinions and make decisions on the basis of the way that things *actually are* is prerequisite to their proper functioning.[19]

Moreover, while the history of disinformation as a tool of statecraft is well known,[20] disinformation in the age of online communication presents a unique challenge because it spreads more quickly[21] and more widely[22] than does truth.[23] This, the contagious spread of emotive content online,[24] threatens the integrity of an informed populous in new ways, beckoning its replacement with one that is disinformed and therefore ill-equipped for its role in a free society.

There is another especially insidious feature of the way that disinformation spreads online. The ability to predict opinions, habits and circumstances by analysing[25] data on the activities that a user engages in is monetised on social media platforms by way of the generation of person-specific content. For example, a Facebook or TikTok feed does not display updates in the chronological order that other users produce them but instead the algorithm processes user's actions, garnering increased advertising revenue by delivering that content which elicits the emotions most likely to keep the user engaged[26] (a more recent phenomenon has been algorithmic preference being given to the content produced by a platform's owner[27]). Since social media stimulates humans in a hormonal way, encouraging feelings of trust,[28] information that is honed to keep users engaged may prove particularly persuasive because it will often be designed to align with their beliefs and opinions. The more a user's beliefs and opinions are reinforced,[29] the more positive their emotional experience. Personalised content delivered online therefore facilitates the spread and entrenchment of disinformation by its specific effects on human emotions and by manipulating the target's propensity to believe information that confirms existing beliefs.[30] Where those beliefs and opinions align with the intentions of a bad actor, the feedback loop assists in further strengthening them and may cause a heightened resistance to accepting alternate views. In countries where societal dynamics require an acceptance of diverse perspectives for continued cohesion, the phenomenon of different groups experiencing different digital realities constructed for them on the basis of an analysis of their innermost urges presents the problem of echo chambers[31] and the fragmentation of politics and of society into positions of polarisation.[32]

It is important to note that for modern autocracies online disinformation may cause fewer concerns. In part because their governance tends to require less responsiveness to the desires of the populous and so the information which the public receives is less relevant but also because the internal propagation of disinformation is a deliberate feature of the approach of some autocratic models. In such systems, rather than disinformation being intended to spur particular action, the state facilitates, encourages or produces information chaos, flooding the public domain with erroneous and often conflicting information. The confusion this causes is relied upon to prevent the citizenry from arriving at any objective truth and to therefore resigning themselves to the view that with respect to politics, the truth is unknowable. In these cases, disinformation may serve both to reinforce autocratic leadership and to undermine any democratic inclination—fed as they are with a stream of misinformation, disinformation and nonsense the electorate is consigned to a perpetual state of fragmentation and apathy. In addition, to the extent that such systems might be vulnerable to information which seeks to challenge the intentional information chaos (such as, for example, the widescale dissemination of truth intruded from outside of the system), they have a distinct advantage in defending against the threat as they are able to close access to the penetration of outside information in ways that if attempted by democracies would stymie their essence.[33]

@TEN_GOP

The objectives of modern disinformation may range from influencing and reinforcing opinions (often with the aim of degrading public trust in institutions[34]), to discrediting political leadership, deepening societal divides and influencing voting decisions and perceptions of the range of acceptable policies. Disinformation will often be implanted by online accounts controlled by bad actors with national online media being drawn in as unwitting purveyors, repropagating it,[35] often under the protection of misunderstood democratic principles such as freedom of speech. Ultimately, disinformation ends up being amplified by other users online some of whom may have been targets of the same data-driven insights discussed above and, who themselves go on to become vectors for its further propogation.[36]

A remarkable case in point is that of the Twitter account TEN_GOP. Ostensibly a Twitter account of the Republican Party of the US State of Tennessee, it was well known and respected among certain sectors of the US body politic. A review of its content reveals that along with ad-hoc commentary on hot button political issues, it also produced and propagated a mish-mash of conspiracy theories, racism, nativism, Euroscepticism and pro-Putin disinformation. The account had more followers than the official Twitter account of the Republican Party in the State and became one of the online heavy weights of the US far-right online ecosystem, interacting directly with leading US conservatives and being retweeted by Republicans which held senior positions in the 2016 election campaign and later in the White House. When the account was shut down by Twitter after two years for allegations that it was not authentic, a number of prominent local Republicans that had been following and reposting its material took to the public airways to protest its closure on the basis that it was being falsely tarred as being pro-Russian, an accusation that they were sure was false. In 2018, the US Department of Justice indicted thirteen individuals including Yevgeny Prigozhin and his Internet Research Agency LLC, for interfering in US elections as far back as 2014[37] using methods which included the establishment and day to day control of the TEN_GOP Twitter account. It is now widely accepted that TEN_GOP had in fact been a Russian disinformation operation run from the St Petersburg offices of Yevgeny Prigozhin's 'troll farm'.[38]

Data Protection Regulations as Disinformation Resilience

It has been argued elsewhere that weak data privacy and data security regimes enable disinformation[39] and so some instances of the abuses of personal data referred to above may have been prevented had there been sufficient levels of legal protection and regulatory oversight in place at the time. However, precise guardrails appropriate to the complex data environment which had emerged by the 2000s did not exist for commercial enterprises in the UK, the European Union (EU) or indeed elsewhere in comprehensive fashion until the enactment of the GDPR (as defined below).[40] This meant that where companies would conduct research and model the behaviour of target consumers for commercial purposes, the data sets could be acquired by entities that intended to use them for disinformation operations, often with limited oversight.[41] The lack of limits on the processing of personal data was a boon for the advertising-and-marketing-to-disinformation pipeline and while intended to protect personal privacy, the implementation of more strict data protection regulations has proved a hamper on this pipeline and has reduced the ease with which data might be accessed and manipulated by bad actors. While in some jurisdictions legal protections for personal data remain inadequate, with technology companies and social media platforms not subject to comprehensive industry regulations,[42] the continued development of data protection legislation in the UK and the EU has proven effective as a counter to the nefarious use of personal data.

The General Data Protection Regulations

The foremost data protection regulations in the UK and the EU are the General Data Protection Regulations[43] (or in the UK, the UK GDPR[44] and the Data Protection Act 2014[45]) (collectively "GDPR"), substantially identical legislation which seek to limit the misuse of personal data.[46]

There are seven characteristics of the GDPR that provide core protections against the kinds of personal data use that facilitate disinformation. These characteristics have come to be seen as among the global standards for personal data protection and together represent a cornerstone for contemporary data protection.

Regulatory compliance: A key characteristic of the GDPR is that it constitutes multi-industry regulation which places positive burdens on regulated entities. From the perspective of this Chapter, the imposition of a framework for private companies which is similar in scale and consequence to those which may govern banking or healthcare may be the most important aspect of the GDPR. It is this, the regulatory nature and implications of the legislation with its imposition of positive obligations that lies at the centre of its role in disinformation resilience.

Classification of data[47]: This facilitates the prevention of exploitation of specific 'sensitive' data (such as personal data revealing political opinions or religious or philosophical beliefs) by categorising it as such and subjecting it to heightened protections.

Limits on access to personal data[48]: This characteristic restricts unauthorised access, collection and processing of personal data and minimises the amount of data collected. It also retains a specific focus on the remission of data outside of the jurisdiction. These limits hinder the ability to misuse data and reduce third party touchpoints thereby providing fewer opportunities for loss or theft. The requirements for oversight of data when it is being sent outside of the jurisdiction also serve to improve data protection procedures in those second jurisdictions.

Breach reporting requirements[49]**and a central enforcement mechanism**[50]: The mandatory reporting of breaches to a national data protection regulatory authority and a robust enforcement mechanism create a commercial compliance incentive (since fines that may be imposed by a statutory regulator can range from mildly admonishing to commercially crippling).

Transparency requirements[51]: The requirement that companies disclose data usage and that they limit (or prohibit) targeted advertising, reduces the prospects for covert disinformation campaigns and increases the likelihood of their being discovered.

Private rights against data handlers[52]: This characteristic grants individuals the right to have their data deleted, providing both a mechanism to reduce the potential exposure of personal data and a private right of action against data handlers.

Consent for political messaging[53, 54]: With this characteristic, explicit consent will usually be required for electronic political messaging based on certain sensitive data categories, thereby reducing the prospects of targeted political disinformation.

The above characteristics represent a paradigm which revolutionised the personal data landscape by driving organisational implementation of personal data security such that bad actors faced a structured, obstacle-laden personal data landscape that was subject to ongoing regulatory oversight. This restricted opportunities for illicit data access and use, including for the purposes of political manipulation.

The GDPR represented a sea change in the protection of personal data and there was an enormous push by commercial enterprises in the years approaching its implementation in 2018 which saw tens of thousands of companies carrying out the 'technical and organizational' measures required by the regulations; conducting data mapping exercises and audits, appointing data protection officers, implementing data protection policies and entering into new contractual relationships to govern data sharing and processing. From the perspective of scale, the implementation process represented one of the largest ever regulatory exercises conducted by private companies and it revolutionised the knowledge which the private sector had in respect of the personal data which it was holding. The post-GDPR data landscape is unrecognisable when compared to that which existed before its implementation.

The Brussels Effect

The scale of the EU economy along with its integration with global data markets gives the GDPR significant sway over the global personal data regulatory landscape.[55] As a result, the GDPR influenced a successive line of legislation in other jurisdictions whose personal data protection regimes came to either substantially replicate or to meaningfully resemble the GDPR.[56] This influence has led to increased harmonisation across jurisdictions and to the general raising of global data privacy standards. In addition, many companies find it more cost effective and less burdensome to conduct a global roll out of GDPR compliant processes than to bring their EU operations into GDPR compliance and leave non-EU operations with legacy processes in place.[57]

As a Western outlier, the US has remained resistant to the comprehensive jurisdictional approach to data protection and so still lacks legislative underpinning to the protection of personal data at the federal level. Constitutional protections and judicial processes have at times insulated US persons from some of the illicit use of personal data[58] but the patchwork assortment of federal and state privacy provisions in America have been a longstanding concern for American privacy advocates.[59] Indeed, there has been an increasing acknowledgement that despite the challenges of passing legislation at the federal level, there is a national security imperative to their being implemented.[60] It is also the case though that the state data protection laws that govern the epicentre of the US technology industry in Silicon Valley in California were drafted to significantly replicate the GDPR[61] and so to the extent that Federal legislation is ever contemplated, some of those enterprises which are of greatest interest from the perspective of data protection will already be familiar with GDPR-style protection procedures and are likely to be some way to having implemented them.

Recent disinformation related legislation in the EU and the UK.

The EU Digital Services Act[62] is both a corollary to the GDPR and a more focused response to the disinformation threat which, in addition to suppressing illegal content and mandating advertising transparency, seeks specifically to mitigate disinformation. The law provides for direct regulation of online platforms and moderation of online content, requires that consumers are able to turn off recommendation algorithms which target them based on information such as race and religion and requires the disclosure of how algorithms work to a specialist statutory authority. Other recent legislative enactments in the area of disinformation resilience include the National Security Act[1] in the UK which makes it an offence for unregistered foreign agents to carry out political influence activities and the UK Online Safety Act[2] which regulates the duties of providers of online services and aims to protect users from illegal and harmful content.

Strategic Considerations

While the implications of the GDPR for disinformation resilience have become increasingly apparent since its enactment,[63] among the main drivers for the Regulations was a concern for the personal privacy of EU citizens, a concern which was accelerated by the discovery of the sharing by social media platforms of user data with various intelligence agencies on the basis of a rationale of terrorism prevention.[64]Governments enjoy varying levels of exemption from GDPR compliance but the question of the tension between personal privacy and national security was always a part of the debate on more robust personal data privacy legislation. Thus far however, there is little indication that the increased protection of personal privacy that has accompanied stricter data protection regulations has diminished national security and most criticisms of data protection laws concern the perceived restraint that they place on commercial activity. Indeed, a persuasive argument could be made with respect to data protection legislation that in its implementation security and freedom are aligned. Personal data protection regimes protect an individual's freedom from manipulation, allow them control over private information about the most intimate aspects of their lives and in so doing also serve their security and, by way of increasing disinformation resilience, the security of the state.

Moreover, it is arguable that the disruption that data protection regulations cause to bad actors is, on a cost benefit analysis, of greater security import than the access to data on individual criminals that could be garnered by more liberal access to personal data. This is because in addition to the general regulatory discipline that legislative data protection instruments impose into private enterprises, they also place a "structural safeguard"[65] in the information landscape and so constitute a key aspect of disinformation resilience and an underpinning to a defensive information posture.

Since witnessing the precursory disinformation operations of the invasion of Ukraine by the Russian Federation, the prevailing view in NATO member states has evolved from one in which disinformation operations were considered a strategic annoyance to a more recent recognition that such operations may be a harbinger of kinetic activity.[66] When considered with the categorisation of the information landscape by the Russian military as a separate operational domain,[67] some fundamental conceptual issues arise, issues which were given expression in the two-staged pre-invasion destabilisation of Ukraine. The campaign, which began with the utilisation of both cyber-attacks and disinformation, culminated in the invasion of Crimea in 2014 and later preceded an attempted full-scale invasion in 2022 with a widespread cyber and disinformation campaign that targeted both Ukraine and its Western allies.[68] This is the context in which the relationship between personal data and disinformation; the relationship between data privacy and national security has become clearer. It is in this context that it is useful to consider the implications of data protection regulations such as the GDPR from a strategic perspective.

Data protection regulations as strategic denial

Both the UK's Integrated Review[6] and the 2023 IR Refresh[7] commit to strengthening deterrence by (or through) denial. In the case of the UK, it is proposed that this be done by developing the Nation's approach to resilience. Likewise, in the 2022 US National Defence Strategy, the US commits to calling on its Allies to enhance their "information protection posture",[69] highlighting the role of information in deterrence. Across NATO and its Global Partners, there has been broad agreement on the need to enhance national resilience to disinformation and to seek to deny bad actors operational freedom within the information space. Since information does not constitute a separate domain for NATO however, conceptualising the impact of the information space will require a multi-domain outlook. Where an environment has multi-domain implications, it can be both easy to lose sight of its unique characteristics and difficult to see the comprehensive picture of its influence across domains.

Plainly put, with respect to data protection regulations, their implementation is suited to doctrinal conception as a strategy of denial. GDPR and similar legislation serves to block certain information channels by which an adversary may learn some fact or set of facts (i.e. those facts gathered from personal data) upon which their disinformation operations would rely. This blocking imposes additional difficulties on an adversary in the carrying out of its intended effect. More precisely, data protection regulations and their contingent compliance requirements serve a non-offensive anti-access denial function, constraining or preventing entry to an area of the information operating environment and thereby off-setting the bad actor effect intended by disinformation. Implied in this conceptualisation is the implication that such regulations also serve a deterrence function by their imposition of a regulatory impediment that has technical consequences in the information environment, making illicit information access more costly, less successful and so less likely to be attempted. Considering the far-reaching implications of the manipulation or misuse of personal data, the broader implications of the above conception may be equally far reaching. While the most immediate impact may be in the cyber domain, there is also possible relevance for issues of civil preparedness, intelligence and force planning.

The idea that strategic deterrence might involve aspects of legislative enforcement is not new and it has previously been argued that law enforcement is one among deterrence mechanisms of action. In the cyber domain this may be by way of criminal indictment, trial and conviction (for cyber-crime).[70] In the context of foreign state actors however, such methods are often less effective because of the complexities involved in conducting successful prosecutions for cyber-crime and because the state which is seeking to impose criminal sanctions may have limited jurisdiction over suspects (whose individual sanction may in any event be unlikely to materially impact the capability of the adversary[71]). A strategy which allows for the imposition of deterrent costs on a hostile state actor will therefore be preferred as more effective in the context of state-to-state disinformation deterrence and one such approach should be considered to include data protection regulations which are likely to have a broad effect on bad actor outcomes with little direct cost implications to a state's defence resources.

Conclusion

This Chapter has set out the origins and trajectory of the online disinformation campaign, its beginnings in marketing and adverting and its reliance on personal data. It has also outlined the strategic role that data protection regulations have in building resilience against disinformation campaigns. Continued attempts to access and exploit personal data remain a central aspect of the information threat and in an era of economic and political uncertainty, once personal data is accessed there is fertile soil for the manipulation of individuals with the aim of influencing behaviour to the benefit of bad actors.

As social media continues to drive the diminishment of trust in institutions, as it allows for the relativisation of truth and as it erodes the ability of expertise and facts to influence discourse, the capacity of the State to exercise authority in acting in the best interests of the nation continues to be challenged. In such an environment, the importance of a framework that can temper the worst consequences of disinformation should not be underestimated. Notwithstanding other legislative responses, it is data protection regulations that provide a conceptual architecture particular to the information environment upon which later provisions may rely and that initiates and sustains an anti-disinformation framework into processes and systems across the data landscape.

As artificial intelligence continues to advance at pace,[72] we face the spectre of spontaneously generated disinformation; of individuals being targeted with content generated in real time on the basis of their momentary emotional vulnerabilities with accelerated levels of analysis and accuracy.[73] In such a world untempered by sufficient controls, not only does it become impossible for an individual to discern whether the information being presented to them is false but increasingly difficult to resist the emotional manipulation to which they are being subjected by a system of superior intelligence that may know and understand them better than they know and understand themselves. For an open society this is a doomsday scenario and one of the only tools available to defend against it is the imposition of compliance and monitoring mechanisms into the data environment such as those mandated by personal data protection regulations.[74]

GDPR compliance costs for Fortune Global 500 companies are estimated to have been 7.8 billion USD in the year that the legislation was brought into force[75] and private enterprises continue to expend many hundreds of millions of dollars annually in ongoing compliance. This expenditure serves to strengthen the data environment against hostile intervention by reducing the vulnerability of personal data to exploitation in a way that might not have been possible had such expenditure been deployed by the state. Indeed, it is difficult to envision what such resilience would look like were it not effected by way of the regulation of personal data-heavy private enterprises and industries.

By mandating the embedding of protective requirements within business processes, data protection regulations have had the effect of cascading disinformation fortification into commercial data handling processes and this regulatory friction now serves as an embedded check on disinformation. Data protection regulations therefore represent the implanting of a structure of strategic denial into the data landscape with limited financial burden being put on the defence resources of the state. Bad actor disinformation strategies which rely on personal data have been made more difficult to implement and more easily discoverable. Policymakers would be well served to precede deployment of resources and capabilities in the information sphere with a recognition of the strategic role that data protection regulations play as such a recognition will allow for clarity on posture and resource allocation requirements.

When assessing how to build resilience to disinformation, one key insight that should guide consideration is that legal instruments which seek to govern the use of personal data will inevitably have effects in the information sphere, with those effects carrying domain consequences in cyberspace and beyond. To put it more broadly, in addition to the personal privacy purpose, data protection regulations retain an unintended national security function that deserves to be afforded specific attention and consideration in relevant discussions of strategy and doctrine.

Postscript (February 2025)

In a September 2024 interview, the incoming US Vice President suggested that if the US social media platform 'X' was subjected to regulation by the EU, the US might in response reconsider its support for NATO.[76] While discerning rhetoric from reality in US politics is no mean feat, what does seem clear is that on its face the new US presidential administration is opposed to the application of regulatory controls to social media companies to the extent that those controls might constrain the operations of US companies. The challenge that such an approach might be interpreted as posing to European security is significant. Indeed, in a place where memories of some of the worst effects of bad actor disinformation in the twentieth century remain vivid and where in the past decade an aggressive land war was preceded by widescale online disinformation operations, much stock may be put into the legislative and regulatory imperatives which keep disinformation at bay. It therefore seems possible that the tenure of the current US presidential administration will be marked by discord between an EU seeking to restrain disinformation on social media and defend personal data rights and a US administration focused more on protecting US corporate interests. It may be this brewing dispute between ostensible allies (and not resilience to disinformation from longstanding strategic adversaries) that proves to be the defining near term political confrontation with respect to disinformation resilience in the NATO alliance.

Notes

1. *National Security Act 2023* (UK).
2. *Online Safety Act 2023* (UK).
3. This chapter adopts the UK Government's definition of disinformation as set out by the Counter Disinformation Unit, namely: "false and/or manipulated information that is intended to deceive and mislead people, either for the purposes of causing harm, or for political, personal or financial gain." See UK Government '*Fact Sheet on the Work of the Government's Counter-Disinformation Unit and Rapid Response Unit*' (Web Page, 9 June 2023) < https://www.gov.uk/government/news/fact-sheet-on-the-cdu-and-rru > .
4. See, eg Lisa-Maria Neudert, 'Regulatory Capacity Capture: The United Kingdom's Online Safety Regime' (2023) 12 (4) *Internet Policy Review* 1730. In respect of the *National Security Act 2023* (UK). See also Paul F. Scott 'State Threats, Security, and Democracy: the National Security Act 2023' (2023). *Legal Studies* 1–17.
5. See generally Ketan Modh, '4.2 Role of Data Protection in Countering Disinformation' in *Handbook on Identifying and Countering Disinformation* (Project: Dominoes Digital Competences Information EcoSystem, 2021) 215.
6. HM Government, 'Global Britain in a Competitive Age: The Integrated Review of Security, Defence, Development and Foreign Policy', HM Government Assets Publishing Service < https://assets.publishing.service.gov.uk/media/60644e4bd3bf7f0c91eababd/Global_Britain_in_a_Competitive_Age-_the_Integrated_Review_of_Security__Defence__Development_and_Foreign_Policy.pdf > .
7. HM Government, 'Integrated Review Refresh 2023', HM Government Assets Publishing Service < https://assets.publishing.service.gov.uk/media/641d72f45155a2000c6ad5d5/11857435_NS_IR_Refresh_2023_Supply_AllPages_Revision_7_WEB_PDF.pdf > .

8. See Eric Rosenbach and Katherine Manstead, 'Can Democracy Survive in the Information Age' *Aspen Strategy Group Series—Technology and National Security* (Harvard Kennedy School, 2018).
9. Kashmir Hill, How Target Figured Out A Teen Girl Was Pregnant Before Her Father Did' *Forbes (Tech)* (Article, 16 February 2012) < https://www.forbes.com/sites/kashmirhill/2012/02/16/how-target-figured-out-a-teen-girl-was-pregnant-before-her-father-did/ > .
10. Damian Clifford, '*Citizen-Consumers in a Personalised Galaxy, Emotion Influence Decision Making, a True path to the Dark Side?*' in Lilian Edwards, Burkhard Schafer and Edina Harbinja (eds) *Future Law Emerging Technology, Regulation and Ethics* (Edinburgh University Press, 2020) 79.
11. Discussed in Joris van Hoboken and Ronan Ó Fathaigh, 'Regulating Disinformation in Europe: Implications for Speech and Privacy' (2021). *6 UC Irvine Journal of International, Transnational, and Comparative Law*, 9.
12. See Shoshana Zuboff, 'A digital declaration: Big data as surveillance capitalism' *FAZ.NET*. (Article, 14 September 2014) < https://opencuny.org/pnmarchive/files/2019/01/Zuboff-Digital-Declaration.pdf > .
13. Jessica Dawson, 'Microtargeting as Information Warfare' (2021). 6 (1) *The Cyber Defense Review*, 63–80, 69.
14. Discussed in Michael Wade,'Psychographics: the Behavioural Analysis that Helped Cambridge Analytica Know Voters Minds' *International Institute for Management Development* (Article, 21 March 2018) < https://imd.widen.net/view/pdf/dmoxqgcgmb/tc018-18.pdf > See also Christopher Wylie, *Mindf*ck: Cambridge Analytica and the Plot to Break America* (New York: Random House, 2019). See also Information Commissioner's Office, 'ICO Investigation into Use of Personal Information and Political Influence' ICO.ORG (Letter, 20 October 2020) < https://ico.org.uk/media/action-weve-taken/2618383/20201002_ico-o-ed-l-rtl-0181_to-julian-knight-mp.pdf > .
15. Michal Kosinski, David Stillwell and Thore Graepel, 'Private Traits and Attributes are Predictable From Digital Records of Human Behavior' (2013) 110 (15) *Proceedings of the National Academy of Sciences*, 5802.
16. Wu Youyou, Michal Kosinski, and David Stillwell 'Computer-Based Personality Judgments Are More Accurate Than Those Made by Humans (2014). 112 (4) *Psychological and Cognitive Science* 1036.
17. See generally Timothy Clack and Louise Selisny, 'Beijing Bloggers to Whitehall Writers' in Timothy Clack and Robert Johnson (eds) *The World Information War: Western Resilience, Campaigning, and Cognitive Effects* (Routledge, 2021) 265.
18. See Regina Rini, 'Social Media Disinformation and the Security Threat to Democratic Legitimacy' in Joseph McQuade (ed) '*Disinformation and Digital Democracies in the 21st Century*'. (NATO Association of Canada, 2019) 10.
19. See Regina Rini, 'Social Media Disinformation and the Security Threat to Democratic Legitimacy' in Joseph McQuade (ed) '*Disinformation and Digital Democracies in the 21st Century*'. (NATO Association of Canada, 2019) 10.
20. See Calder Walton, 'Spies, Election Meddling, and Disinformation: Past and Present' (2019) 26 (107) *Brown Journal of World Affairs*, 107.
21. Michela Del Vicario et al. 'The Spreading of Misinformation Online' (2015) 113 *Proceedings of the National Academy of Sciences* 554.
22. W Lance Bennett and Steven Livingston, 'The Disinformation Order: Disruptive Communication and the Decline of Democratic Institutions' (2018) 33 (2) *European Journal of Communication* 122.
23. Sandeep Suntwal, Susan A Brown and Mark W Patton, 'How Does Information Spread? A study of True and Fake News' (2020) *Proceedings of the 53rd Hawaii International Conference on System Sciences* 5893.
24. Adam Kramer, Jamie Guillory and Jeffery Hancock, 'Experimental Evidence of Massive-Scale Emotional Contagion through Social Networks' (2014) 111 (24) *Proceedings of the National Academy of Science* 8788–90. See also Nadia Alonso-Lopes, Pavel Sidorenko-Bautista and

Fabio Giscomelli, 'Beyond challenges and viral dance moves: TikTok as a Vehicle for Disinformation and Fact-checking in Spain, Portugal, Brazil, and the USA' (2021) 64 *Anàlisi: Quaderns de Comunicació i. Cultura* 65–84.

25. See generally Wayne Unger, 'Katz and Covid: How a Pandemic Changes the Reasonable Expectation of Privacy' (2020) 12 *Hastings Science and Technology Law Journal* 39.
26. See Vincent Hendricks and Mads Vestergaard, 'The Attention Economy' in *Reality Lost* (Springer Open, 2018). See also Zeynep Tufekei, 'View of Engineering the Public: Big Data, Surveillance and Computational Politics' (2014) *First Monday* 19. See also Agnès Festré and Pierre Garrouste, 'The 'Economics of Attention': A History of Economic Thought Perspective' (2015) 5 (1) *Economia, History, Methodology, Philosophy* 3.
27. See Pietro Gravino, Ruggiero D. Lo Sardo and Emanuele Brugnoli 'Cross-platform impact of social media algorithmic adjustments on public discourse', arxiv.org (Occasional Paper, 29 January 2024) <https://arxiv.org/pdf/2405.00008>).
28. See Ronald Deibert, 'The Road to Digital Unfreedom: Three Painful Truths about Social Media' (2019) 30 (1) *Journal of Democracy* 25.
29. See generally Heather Wolters et al., 'The Psychology of (Dis)information: A Primer on Key Psychological Mechanisms' CNA.Org (Research Memorandum, 27 September 2021) 5 < https://apps.dtic.mil/sti/trecms/pdf/AD1151655.pdf > .
30. See Sachin Modgil et al. 'A Confirmation Bias View on Social Media Induced Polarisation During Covid-19' (2021) 26 (2) *Information Systems Frontiers* 417, 419.
31. Terren Ludovic, and Rosa Borge-Bravo, 'Echo Chambers on Social Media: A Systematic Review of the Literature' (2021) 9 *Review of Communication Research* 99.
32. Pablo Barberá, 'Social Media, Echo Chambers, and Political Polarization' in Nathaniel Persily and Joshua A. Tucker (eds) *Social Media and Democracy: The State of the Field, Prospects for Reform* (Cambridge University Press, 2020) 34.
33. See, eg Serhiy Hovyadinov, 'Research of Various Aspects of State Control Over the Internet in Russia and the Role of Online Intermediaries' (Doctor of Science of Law, Stanford University, 2020).
34. Nicholas O'Shaughnessy, 'From Disinformation to Fake News: Forward not the Past' in Paul Baines, Nicholas O'Shaughnessy and Nancy Snow (eds) *The SAGE Handbook of Propaganda* (SAGE Publications Ltd, 2019) 55.
35. See generally Yochai Benkler, Robert Faris, Hal Roberts, *Network Propaganda: Manipulation, Disinformation and Radicalisation in American Politics* (Oxford University Press, 2018). See also Assenmacher et al 'Demystifying Social Bots: On the Intelligence of Automated Social Media Actors' (2020) 6 (3) *Social Media+ Society.*
36. See Steven Lee Myers, Ken Bensinger and Jim Rutenberg 'Russia Secretly Worms Its Way Into America's Conservative Media' *The New York Times* (Online) 9 July 2024 <https://www.nytimes.com/2024/09/07/business/media/russia-tenet-media-tim-pool.html>
37. *United States of America v Internet Research Agency LLC A/K/A Mediasintez LLC A/K/A Glavset LLC A/K/A Mixinfo LLC A/K/A Azimut LLC A/K/A Novinfo LLC* et al. *(Indictment)* (United States District Court for the District of Columbia), 18 U.S.C 2,371, 1349, 1028A, 16 February 2018. < https://www.justice.gov/media/936606/dl. >
38. See generally Kathleen Jamieson *Cyberwar: How Russian Hackers and Trolls Helped Elect a President: What We Don't, Can't, and Do Know* (Oxford University Press, 2019).
39. Wayne Unger, 'How the Poor Data Privacy Regime Contributed to Misinformation Spread and Democratic Erosion' (2020) 22 *The Columbia Science & Technology Review*, 308.
40. It should be noted that while there is a line of EU jurisprudence in this period which addresses various rights with respect to personal data (perhaps most notably Google Spain SL, Google Inc. v Agencia Española de Protección de Datos, Mario Costeja González Case C-131/12 ('*Google Spain*')) in the main claims were brought under human rights legislation and not under data protection legislation.

41. See generally Finn Myrstad and Ingvar Tjostheim, 'Out of Control: How Consumers are Exploited by the Online Advertising Industry' Forbrukerradet (Report, 14 January 2020) < https://nr.brage.unit.no/nr-xmlui/bitstream/handle/11250/2832214/Forbrukerr%C3%A5det_2020-01-14-out-of-control-final-version.pdf?sequence=1 > . See also Lee Fang, 'The Trump Campaign is Deploying Phone Location-Tracking Technology' *The Intercept* (online) 11 December 2024 https://theintercept.com/2019/12/11/the-donald-trump-campaign-is-deploying-phone-location-tracking-technology/.
42. It should be noted that an EU Code of Practice on Disinformation was agreed with Facebook, Google (then) Twitter and other social media platforms in 2018.
43. *Regulation (EU) 2016/679 of the European Parliament and of the Council of 27 April 2016 on the protection of natural persons with regard to the processing of personal data and on the free movement of such data, and repealing Directive 95/46/EC ('General Data Protection Regulation')* [2016] OJ L119/1.
44. *Regulation 2016/679 of the European Parliament and of the Council of 27 April 2016* (EU).
45. *Data Protection Act 2018* (UK).
46. The jurisdiction of the pre-Brexit and post-Brexit data protection regimes as they apply to the UK differ to a small degree however for the purposes of this Chapter it is sufficient to refer to the contemporary framework collectively as "GDPR".
47. *General Data Protection Regulation* ch 1, art 4 and ch 2, art 9.
48. Ibid, ch 2, art 5.
49. Ibid, ch 4, art 33.
50. Ibid, ch 6, art 51.
51. Ibid, ch 3, art 12–14.
52. Ibid, ch 8, art 79.
53. Ibid, ch 2, art 9.
54. The Privacy of Electronic Communications Regulations 2003 sit alongside the GDPR and provide specific rights and rules in relation to electronic communications.
55. Often referred to as part of the 'Brussels Effect'.
56. See, eg Vibhushinie Bentotahewa, Chaminda Hewage and Jason Williams 'The Normative Power of the GDPR: A Case Study of Data Protection Laws of South Asian Countries' (2022) 3 (3) *SN Computer Science*, 183. See also Christian Binnig and Christopher Comstock 'The California Consumer Privacy Act: The First Step Towards an American GDPR' (2018) 58 *Infrastructure*, 1.
57. Simon Gunst and Ferdi De Ville, 'The Brussels effect: How the GDPR Conquered Silicon Valley' (2021) 26 (3) *European Foreign Affairs Review*, 437.
58. See Laura Donohue, 'Bulk Metadata Collection: Statutory and Constitutional Considerations' (2014) 37 *Harvard Journal of Law and Public Policy*, 757.
59. Wayne Unger, 'Reclaiming Our Right to Privacy by Holding Tech Companies Accountable' (2020) 27 (1) *Richmond Journal of Law and Technology*, 4.
60. See, eg Laura Donohue, 'High Technology, Consumer Privacy, and US National Security' (2015) 4 *American University Business Law Review*, 36. See also Laura DeNardis, *The Internet in Everything* (Yale University Press, 2020).
61. Christian Binnig and Christopher Comstock, 'The California Consumer Privacy Act: The First Step Towards an American GDPR. (2018) 58 (4*) Infrastructure, 1.*
62. *Regulation 2022/2065 of the European Parliament and of the Council of 19 October 2022 on a Single Market For Digital Services and Amending Directive 2000/31/EC* 2022 (EU).
63. Christian Binnig and Christopher Comstock, 'The California Consumer Privacy Act: The First Step Towards an American GDPR. (2018) 58 (4) Infrastructure, 1.
64. See Hallie Coyne, 'The Untold Story of Edward Snowden's Impact on the GDPR' (2019) 4 (2) *The Cyber Defense Review* 65. See also Dara Paleski, 'Hanging in the Balance: An Assessment of European Versus American Data Privacy Laws and Threats to US National Security' (2023) 13 (2) *American University National Security Law Brief*, 4.
65. Ibid 32.

66. See Gustav Gressel, 'Protecting Europe against Hybrid Threats' European Council on Foreign Relations ECFR.EU (Policy Brief, 25 June 2019) < https://ecfr.eu/wp-content/uploads/6_Protecting_Europe_against_hybrid_threats.pdf > .
67. See Michael Connell and Sarah Vogler, 'Russia's Approach to Cyber Warfare', CNA.Org (Occasional Paper, 24 March 2017) 5 < https://www.cna.org/archive/CNA_Files/pdf/dop-2016-u-014231-1rev.pdf > .
68. See Japoco Bosica, 'Russia's Information Aggression Before and During the Full-scale Invasion of Ukraine-Identifying Elements of Change and Continuity Amongst the Kremlin's Disinformation Operations vis-à-vis EU's and NATO's Courses of Action to Counter Them' (Masters, Charles University, 2023). See also Ahan Gadkari, 'Nato Responses to Disinformation' (2023) 01 (30) *Ukraine Analytica* 80.
69. National Defense Strategy of the United States (2022) Unclassified Summary. Department of Defense, 7.
70. See generally Aniket Kesari, Chris Hoofnagle, and Damon McCoy, 'Deterring Cybercrime', *Berkeley Technology Law Journal* 32/3 (2017), 1093–1134. See also Zachary Goldman and Damon McCoy, 'Economic Espionage: Deterring Financially Motivated Cybercrime' (2016) 8 (2016), *Journal of National Security Law and Policy* 595–619.
71. See Erica Borgharda and Shawn Lonergan, 'Deterrence by Denial in Cyberspace' (2023) 46 (3) *Journal of Strategic Studies*, 534. See also Deborah Bunker and Maryam Shahbazi, 'Social Media Trust: Fighting Misinformation in the Time of Crisis' (2024) 77 (August 2024) *International Journal of Information Management*.
72. See Xuli Tang et al., 'The Pace of Artificial Intelligence Innovations: Speed, Talent, and Trial-and-Error' (2020) 14(4) *Journal of Informetrics*, 101,094.
73. Noémi Bontridder and Yves Poullet, *'The Role of Artificial Intelligence in Disinformation'* (2021) 3 (e32) *Data & Policy*, 10. See also Chris Marsden, Trisha Meyer & Ian Brown, 'Platform Values and Democratic Elections: How Can the Law Regulate Digital Disinformation?' (2020) 36 *Computer Law and Security Review*, 15.
74. Cf Katarina Kertysova, 'Artificial Intelligence and Disinformation: How AI Changes the Way Disinformation is Produced, Disseminated, and Can Be Countered' (2018) 29 (1–4) *Security and Human Rights*, 55.
75. Nicole Lindsey, 'Global 500 Faces GDPR Compliance Costs of $7.8 Billion' *CPO Magazine* (online) 2 December 2027 < https://www.cpomagazine.com/data-protection/global-500-faces-gdpr-compliance-costs-of-7-8-billion/ >.
76. Rebecca Rommen, 'JD Vance suggested the US's support for NATO could be pulled if Europe tries to regulate Elon Musk's X as free speech debate rumbles on' Business Insider (online) September 2024 https://www.businessinsider.com/jd-vance-nato-support-eu-regulation-x-musk-free-speech-2024-9.

John Small is a reservist Legal Advisor in the British Army Legal Services where his work focuses on advising the Army chain of command on military and administrative law. A graduate of the Royal Military Academy Sandhurst, he was commissioned as a legal officer in 2017 after serving for four years as a Light Gunner in the Honourable Artillery Company. Formerly a corporate lawyer, he has acted for global financial institutions in the structuring of complex transactions, and his practice included advising on the implementation of regulatory data protection requirements. In addition to his military and legal experience and qualifications, he holds MSc degrees in the Evolution of Language and Cognition from the University of Edinburgh and in Developmental Psychology from University College London. He is also a regular panel judge of the National Technology Awards in the UK and has published contributions in academic conference proceedings and the financial services press.

Australia's Proposed Misinformation and Disinformation Law

Aneta Peretko

Abstract Social media has presided over an explosion of innocent misinformation and weaponised disinformation alike. While other structural changes in society have contributed to the prevalence of false narratives, the largely unregulated landscape of digital platforms has fundamentally altered who can publish content, as well as how quickly and widely it spreads. And while misinformation and disinformation occur online, their often devastating consequences, from incitement of ethnic violence to election interference to preventable COVID-19 deaths, occur in the real world. This chapter considers the evolution of misinformation and disinformation online and how governments are safeguarding their democracies from this threat. It examines the range of responses, from deference to the self-regulatory capacity of digital platforms themselves on the one hand to the imposition of coercive legislative control over social media content on the other. It then turns to Australia's proposed law, a co-regulatory structure in which platforms and governments each play a role in addressing misinformation and disinformation online. It looks at how the proposal balances the need to deal with false content with the need to respect freedom of expression and ultimately it assesses the powers and obligations contained in the proposal, as well as their limits and consequences.

Introduction

Foreign interference and espionage is both the principal security concern in Australia today and at the highest level it has ever been in Australian history.[1] Left unchecked, it can erode public trust in our political institutions, damage national security and

[1] Select Committee on Foreign Interference through Social Media, Parliament of Australia, *Report* (Report, August 2023) [2.1]; [2.55], [5.1].

A. Peretko (✉)
Adelaide, Australia
e-mail: aperetko@alumni.unimelb.edu.au

D. Stephens et al. (eds.), *Digital Resilience*,
https://doi.org/10.1007/978-981-97-9746-2_6

economic prosperity, and ultimately undermine confidence in democracy.[2] And yet, threats to democracy present in a variety of ways, which means that so too do the policy responses.[3] Australia's recently implemented restrictions on foreign donations in elections,[4] foreign influence transparency scheme,[5] criminalisation of foreign interference and espionage,[6] protection of critical infrastructure,[7] and closer regulation of arrangements between Australian States and territories and foreign entities[8] can all be seen as efforts to secure its democracy. Within this flood of activity, however, was one somewhat more overlooked measure; Australia's proposed misinformation and disinformation law, a draft amendment to the *Broadcasting Services Act 1992* (Cth) that would have incorporated digital platform services into that statute's remit, had it not been dropped due to a lack of bipartisan support.[9] The nature of the draft amendment was fundamentally regulatory and therefore less obviously part of the government's response to a wave of attacks on our democracy. However, in the last decade, misinformation and disinformation has come to be considered a major national security concern, especially when it emanates from foreign actors,[10] or targets political processes. Such conduct need not actually change an election or other political outcome; as long as it raises the 'spectre of illegitimacy',[11] it weakens democratic resilience by undermining trust in government, pluralism, inclusion and rule of law.[12]

Misinformation and disinformation are not new concepts, but what is new is the scale, speed and reach they can achieve through social media, especially the way they can transcend international borders and become amplified by algorithms.[13]

---

[2] Select Committee on Foreign Interference through Social Media, Parliament of Australia, *First Interim Report* (Report, December 2021) [4.37].

[3] Scott J. Shackelford et al., 'Defending Democracy: Taking Stock of the Global Fight Against Digital Repression, Disinformation, and Election Insecurity' (2020) 77 *Washington and Lee Law Review* 1747, 1753.

[4] *Electoral Legislation Amendment (Electoral Funding and Disclosure Reform) Act 2018* (Cth).

[5] *Foreign Influence Transparency Scheme Act 2018* (Cth).

[6] *National Security Legislation Amendment (Espionage and Foreign Interference) Act 2018* (Cth).

[7] *Security Legislation Amendment (Critical Infrastructure Protection) Act 2022* (Cth).

[8] *Australia's Foreign Relations (State and Territory Arrangements) Act 2020* (Cth).

[9] Parliament of Australia, *Communications Legislation Amendment (Combatting Misinformation and Disinformation) Bill 2023* exposure draft; Minister for Communications, *Communications Legislation Amendment (Combatting Misinformation and Disinformation) Bill 2024* (Media Release, 24 November 2024).

[10] Emiliana De Blasio and Donatella Selva, 'Who Is Responsible for Disinformation? European Approaches to Social Platforms' Accountability in the Post-Truth Era' (2021) 65(6) *American Behavioral Scientist* 825, 841.

[11] Select Committee on Foreign Interference through Social Media, Parliament of Australia, *Report* (n 1) [2.54].

[12] Melissa-Ellen Dowling, 'Foreign Interference and Digital Democracy: is Digital Era Governance Putting Australia at Risk?' (2022) 57(2) *Australian Journal of Political Science* 113, 117.

[13] UN Human Rights Council, *Disinformation and Freedom of Opinion and Expression: Report of the Special Rapporteur on the Promotion and Protection of the Right to Freedom of Opinion and Expression*, A/HRC/47/25 (13 April 2021) [2]; Andrew Gibbons and Andrea Carson, 'What is

Much of the world has experienced recent increases in the circulation of misinformation and disinformation online, with serious consequences playing out in the real world, from external States interfering with domestic elections, to hate speech and attacks on minority groups, to an 'infodemic' of unsafe information relating to the COVID-19 pandemic that 'rivalled the virus itself'.[14] And like a virus, misinformation and disinformation constantly mutates based on environmental factors, ensuring there is no easy cure.[15] This chapter places the problem of misinformation and disinformation in the context of its operation and interplay with social media and considers the different ways misinformation and disinformation on social media can be addressed. With the dominant approach firmly in the regulatory sphere, it situates Australia's scrapped proposed law along the continuum of options States are exploring in an attempt to combat misinformation and disinformation. Acknowledging the critical factor that makes misinformation and disinformation so difficult to target is that the pillars that define democracy, including rights to free speech and privacy, makes democracy more vulnerable to its tactics and can therefore prevent democracies from implementing resilience measures to combat interference,[16] it assesses Australia's proposed law by examining in detail precisely what it purported to do, with particular attention to the powers it would have granted and the obligations it would have imposed, as well as limits thereto and consequences thereof. While this particular proposal will not proceed, it offers valuable lessons for any government attempting to regulate this controversial space.

The Problem

Historians can cite examples of misinformation and disinformation dating back to the nineteenth century, with an 1835 hoax about observable life on the moon planted by a US newspaper that admitted the story was fake but useful for 'diverting the public mind' from debates about slavery.[17] Likewise has democratic interference been prevalent throughout history, with one study claiming that from 1945 to 2000, the United States and Russia together tried to influence foreign elections 117 times,

---

Misinformation and Disinformation? Understanding Multi-Stakeholders' Perspectives in the Asia Pacific' (2022) 57(3) *Australian Journal of Political Science* 231, 231.

[14] Edward Hurcombe and James Meese, 'Australia's DIGI Code: What Can We Learn From the EU Experience?' (2022) 57(3) *Australian Journal of Political Science* 297, 297; Chris Marsden, Trisha Meyer and Ian Brown, 'Platform Values and Democratic Elections: How Can the Law Regulate Digital Disinformation?' (2020) 36 *Computer Law and Security Review* 1, 2; UN Human Rights Council, *Disinformation and Freedom of Opinion and Expression* (n 13) [2].

[15] Andrea Carson and Scott Wright, 'Fake News and Democracy: Definitions, Impact and Response' (2022) 57(3) *Australian Journal of Political Science* 221, 225.

[16] Dowling (n 12) 114. See generally, Thomas Rid, *Active Measures: The Secret History of Disinformation and Political Warfare* (Profile Books, 2020).

[17] See discussion in, e.g., Gibbons and Carson (n 13) 233.

using both covert and overt means.[18] Russia's interference in Warsaw Pact countries in the 1990s preceded more recent efforts in the 2016 US Presidential election and the UK Brexit vote, during which Russian organs spread misinformation and disinformation using Facebook, Twitter and Instagram in attempts to further its preferred outcome.[19] China has been emulating the same strategies in Taiwan and Australia, as have Iran and North Korea in their own targets, and so too have a range of non-state actors, from terrorist and criminal groups to activists and hacktivists.[20] And while much of the focus has been on foreign actors, domestic misinformation and disinformation campaigns are also rife. Racialised disinformation campaigns suppressed votes from communities of colour in several of the most recent US elections,[21] 'deepfakes' emerged domestically in elections in Belgium, Malaysia and Gabon,[22] and, returning to Australia, the baseless 'Mediscare' and 'death tax' campaigns were run by the Australian Labor Party in 2016 and Coalition in 2019, respectively.[23] While the degradation of democracy is the most obvious chronic harm, examples of more acute harms include preventable deaths from COVID-19 misinformation and disinformation,[24] as well as online discrimination against minorities fed by misinformation and disinformation turning into offline physical harm through ethnic violence in places like Ethiopia and Myanmar.[25]

While the harm may be relatively easily identifiable, the actual cause is not. A universal definition of misinformation and disinformation remains elusive. Disinformation includes outright fabricated or manipulated content, but also content in which truthful information is placed in a misleading context, and content in which sources are impersonated.[26] An emerging delineation between disinformation and misinformation is motivation; while both are essential incidents of false information, the former is spread with an intention to mislead, deceive or otherwise cause harm

---

[18] Dov H. Levin, 'When the Great Power Gets a Vote: The Effects of Great Power Electoral Interventions on Election Results' (2016) 60 *International Studies Quarterly* 189, 189.

[19] Dowling (n 12) 121.

[20] Shackelford et al (n 3) 1750, 1760-1.

[21] UN Human Rights Council, *Disinformation and Freedom of Opinion and Expression* (n 13) [24].

[22] Alexander Puutio and David Alexandru Timis, 'Deepfake Democracy: Here's How Modern Elections Could Be Decided by Fake News', *World Economic Forum* (Web Page, 5 October 2020) <https://www.weforum.org/agenda/2020/10/deepfake-democracy-could-modern-elections-fall-prey-to-fiction/>.

[23] Ravi Baltutis, 'South Australia's Truth in Political Advertising Law: A Model for Australia?' (2021) 42(2) *Adelaide Law Review* 597, 598.

[24] Katie Shepherd, 'A Man Thought Aquarium Cleaner with the Same Name as the Anti-Viral Drug Chloroquine Would Prevent Coronavirus. It Killed Him', *Washington Post* (online, 24 March 2020) <https://www.washingtonpost.com/nation/2020/03/24/coronavirus-chloroquine-poisoning-death/>.

[25] UN Human Rights Council, *Disinformation and Freedom of Opinion and Expression* (n 13) [25]; Andrew Dowse and Sascha Dov Bachmann, 'Information Warfare: Methods to Counter Disinformation' (2022) 38(4) *Defense and Security Analysis* 453, 454.

[26] Dowse and Bachmann (n 25) 455.

while the latter is not.[27] Of course, the underlying motivations and goals of such content can range from political to economic, reputational, or even entertainment.[28] Further complicating our understanding of misinformation and disinformation is that terms such as hoaxes, fake news, alternative facts and post-truth are often used interchangeably with misinformation and disinformation.[29] How these differ from poor-quality journalism, satire, spin or public relations is an unresolved question,[30] and reflects the impossibility of a clear and simple division between fact and fiction, and between benign and malicious intent. Facts can be delegitimised, while fiction can be exploited by actors with noble objectives just as much as those with wicked objectives. Opinions, beliefs, parody and satire defy the binary of truth or lies. Disinformation spread with the intention of causing harm can become misinformation when it is shared by innocent agents who spread it without such intent.[31]

Structural changes in society have facilitated the growth of misinformation and disinformation. The current environment is one of political polarisation and increasing social conflict,[32] and foreign actors have enjoyed operating at a distance from a target jurisdiction while still being able to sow false content to wreak havoc.[33] Domestically, the antidote of professional journalism has been threatened by the 24/7 news cycle, the emotionalisation of the news, the profitability of advertising from clickbait content, competition from online platforms, and low media literacy.[34] Bots, fringe news sites, and selective exposure exacerbate the issue.[35] States have also exerted pressure on their legacy media and many States do not themselves support public information regimes, nor do they facilitate access by members of the public to government business. More broadly, economic downturns, social inequality and political disenfranchisement have not just fanned the grievances of individuals but

---

[27] See generally, James Fetzer, 'Disinformation: The Use of False Information' (2004) 14 *Minds and Machines* 231. See also, Carson and Wright (n 15) 222; Gibbons and Carson (n 13) 234. The literature refers to a third category of malinformation, being truthful content spread with harmful intention.

[28] Dowse and Bachmann (n 25) 455.

[29] Gibbons and Carson (n 13) 232.

[30] Kieran McGuinness, Caroline Fisher and Jee Young Lee, 'Australians' Shifting Concerns about Mis- and Disinformation' (2022) 57(3) *Australian Journal of Political Science* 248, 250. See also Edson Tandoc, Zheng Wei Lim and Richard Ling, 'Defining "Fake News": A Typology of Scholarly Definitions' (2018) 6(2) *Digital Journalism* 137.

[31] UN Human Rights Council, *Disinformation and Freedom of Opinion and Expression* (n 13) [9]–[10].

[32] McGuinness, Fisher and Lee (n 30) 250; Florian Saurwein and Charlotte Spencer-Smith, 'Combating Disinformation on Social Media: Multilevel Governance and Distributed Accountability in Europe' (2020) 8(6) *Digital Journalism* 820, 833.

[33] Andrew Ray, 'Disinformation, Deepfakes and Democracies: The Need for Legislative Reform' (2021) 44(3) *UNSW Law Journal* 983, 990; Björnstjern Baade, 'Fake News and International Law' (2019) 29(4) *European Journal of International Law* 1357, 1361–2.

[34] Saurwein and Spencer-Smith (n 32) 821.

[35] McGuinness, Fisher and Lee (n 30) 250.

have also increased their susceptibility to manipulation.[36] Arguably the biggest factor, however, is social media. The number of people who rely on social media as their main source of news is growing, despite users reporting low levels of trust towards news they encounter on it.[37] Despite the hope for a more informed and political participatory society that would emerge from our increased connectivity,[38] the global trend is towards news exposure that is incidental, accessible and shareable, without the need for deep or intentional engagement.[39] The convergence of these trends means individuals are experiencing a disorientated media system in which they are struggling to distinguish fact from fiction, and are prone to alienation and disinterest in political discourse.[40]

To fully appreciate the relevance of social media to disinformation, consider the three components of any disinformation campaign: an organ to create the disinformation, a media source willing to share it without fact-checking it, and accomplices or unknowing agents to spread the story to other sources.[41] In all three stages, digital platforms, and especially social media, have provided unprecedented access. Digital technology such as media manipulation and surveillance have made it cheap and easy to source and distort information,[42] while digital platforms specifically have revolutionised the practice of politics, as movements like the Arab Spring, #BlackLivesMatter and #MeToo demonstrate.[43] Groups of like-minded individuals can shift their political mobilisation online, from participating in discussion to encouraging voting to displaying political affiliation or support for causes, alongside more traditional actions like fundraising and petitioning.[44] So too, however, can authors of disinformation. The partisan environment means a lack of baseline agreements about fact, a mispresenting of opinion as fact and a scorn for institutional sources, with social media platforms by their nature amplifying sensationalist content and multiplying it at unprecedented speed.[45] This, alongside the absence of editorial control, makes social media highly conducive to disinformation and misinformation and explains, at least in part, the correlation between social media exposure of individuals and their vulnerability to falsehoods.[46]

---

[36] UN Human Rights Council, *Disinformation and Freedom of Opinion and Expression* (n 13) [20]–[21].

[37] McGuinness, Fisher and Lee (n 30) 252–3.

[38] See, e.g., Shelley Boulianne, 'Social Media use and Participation: A Meta-Analysis of Current Research' (2015) 18 *Information, Communication and Society* 524.

[39] McGuinness, Fisher and Lee (n 30) 259; Ray (n 33) 989.

[40] McGuinness, Fisher and Lee (n 30) 250–1, citing Yochai Benkler, Robert Faris and Hal Roberts, *Network Propaganda: Manipulation, Disinformation, and Radicalization in American Politics* (Oxford University Press, 2018).

[41] Shackelford et al (n 3) 1759.

[42] UN Human Rights Council, *Disinformation and Freedom of Opinion and Expression* (n 13) [16].

[43] Anika Gauja, 'Digital Democracy: Big Technology and the Regulation of Politics' (2021) 44(3) *UNSW Law Journal* 959, 959–60.

[44] Ibid 960.

[45] Saurwein and Spencer-Smith (n 32) 824.

[46] Dowse and Bachmann (n 25) 453–4.

At its heart, misinformation and disinformation on social media is characterised by overlapping roles and responsibilities. Social media platform users are media audiences who receive information, but unlike traditional news media, platform users also create and distribute content.[47] Platform interactivity allows clicking, liking and sharing, which sends algorithmic signals boosting content visibility. Platforms and their users are directly involved in the production and spread of such content and are therefore targets of regulation, but platforms are not public infrastructure, no matter how much they resemble it, which means that both States and platforms have a role to play in enforcing any regulation. Strategies to address misinformation and disinformation on social media therefore require a multi-dimensional approach that distributes responsibility across these actors.[48] Yet in Australia, despite several high-profile inquiries recently investigating social media, misinformation and disinformation, and interference in political processes,[49] confusion persists as to who is responsible for what.[50] In addition to the legislative responses to foreign interference noted at the beginning of this chapter, relevant vehicles could include the *Online Safety Act 2021*, the *Privacy Act 1988*, the Australian Cyber Security Centre, the Cyber and Infrastructure Security Centre, the National Security Hotline, the Strengthening Democracy Taskforce, the Election Integrity Task force and the eSafety Commissioner, as well as the failed amendment.[51] Despite the severity of the problem, its multifaceted nature and scale mean that any single government response is unlikely to be effectual and needs to be presented as part of a broad strategy to boost democratic resilience.

The Options

So what exactly should be done, by whom and to whom, to address misinformation and disinformation?[52] The characteristics of misinformation and disinformation discussed above, including the range of actors and underlying causes, are a challenge for law and policymakers. Humans and human factors collide with States as well as companies, platform design and algorithms.[53] Definitions, including misinformation

---

[47] Ibid 454.

[48] Saurwein and Spencer-Smith (n 32) 822–4.

[49] See, e.g., Select Committee on Foreign Interference through Social Media, Parliament of Australia, *Report* (n 1); Australian Competition and Consumer Commission, *Digital Platforms Inquiry: Final Report* (Report, 2019); Electoral Matters Committee, Parliament of Victoria, *Inquiry into the Impact of Social Media on Victorian Elections and Victoria's Electoral Administration* (Final Discussion Paper, 3 September 2014).

[50] Select Committee on Foreign Interference through Social Media, Parliament of Australia, *First Interim Report* (n 2) [1.25]–[1.29].

[51] Select Committee on Foreign Interference through Social Media, Parliament of Australia, *Report* (n 1) [4.4]–[4.52].

[52] Marsden, Meyer and Brown (n 14) 3.

[53] Saurwein and Spencer-Smith (n 32) 833.

and disinformation itself, are contested and therefore open to abuse, and for some States, so is the mere existence of the problem, particularly where the State itself relies on the phenomenon. This creates scope for both State and digital platform responses ranging from the very severe, such as States passing legislation that significantly restricts freedom of expression and therefore has the perverse effect of itself undermining democracy,[54] to the very scarce, such as toothless platform policies that do more for corporate public relations than the spread of false content.[55]Furthermore, complementing any direct policy responses is a vast and interconnected web of powers that may also apply, from defamation law for unfounded content, to criminal law for illegal content, to political advertising restrictions, to transparency initiatives and media literacy programs.[56] The underlying issue of media accountability is not just one thing but is in fact any voluntary or involuntary process by which media answers to society.[57]

Some States have focused on disrupting the internet and directly controlling online content, while others have focused on disrupting social media companies and the process by which the platforms themselves manage it.[58] While social media companies are private actors, they provide an increasingly public service, and they do so within the existing parameters of society. Therefore, by default, responsibility for regulating social media is shared between the companies themselves and the governments of the countries in which they operate. Governments set the legal framework in which all entities in their jurisdiction, including platforms, operate. Those relevant to a platform's operation comprise, for example, laws relating to crime, discrimination, elections, expression and others mentioned throughout this chapter. None of those, however, are specific to digital platforms. Thus, if this is the extent of the regulatory environment, then social media companies are largely not subject to any involuntary processes and the model in place can be described as self-regulation. Digital platforms are responsible for their own operation, including content posted by users. Users, in turn, are bound by the terms and conditions of using that platform, as decided by the platform.[59] To apply a more robust model, industry and government can co-operate to create a regulatory environment, for example with the government mandating certain platform processes, with varying levels of external enforcement.[60] Finally, the most coercive option is external regulation consisting of laws imposed

[54] Sarah Sorial, Shireen Morris and Peter Greste, 'Foreign Interference and the Incremental Chilling of Free Speech' (2024) *Federal Law Review* 1 (advance), 2–3.

[55] Gauja (n 43) 977; UN Human Rights Council, *Disinformation and Freedom of Opinion and Expression* (n 13) [3].

[56] Marsden, Meyer and Brown (n 14) 3.

[57] De Blasio and Selva (n 10) 826.

[58] UN Human Rights Council, *Disinformation and Freedom of Opinion and Expression* (n 13) [46], [56].

[59] UN Human Rights Council, *Report of the Special Rapporteur on the Promotion and Protection of the Right to Freedom of Opinion and Expression*, A/HRC/38/35 (6 April 2018) [12]; Gauja (n 43) 976.

[60] De Blasio and Selva (n 10) 837–8. For a more specific breakdown of different regulatory options, see Marsden, Meyer and Brown (n 14).

specifically on digital platforms, and where the government rather than the company is the chief strategist. Each of these three possibilities is considered in turn.

Unsurprisingly, self-regulation is often the preference of digital platforms themselves, many of whom display resistance to being regulated. One example is Facebook's 2021 blocking of Australians from accessing any news content on its platform, done in response to legislation to enable news organisations to bargain with Facebook for payment in exchange for news content.[61] This is not to say, however, that self-regulation is entirely impotent. Social media companies already implement a range of security features and strategies for countering misinformation and disinformation. Responding to violations of its policies, between 2017 and 2022, Meta disabled over 200 covert influence operations, while in the first quarter of 2023 alone, YouTube terminated over 900 and 18,000 channels linked, respectively, to Russian and Chinese influence operations.[62] The COVID-19 'infodemic' also had a profound effect on self-regulation, with platforms proactively removing false content relating to health or at least labelling it as potentially misleading, enlisting third-party fact checkers, suspending accounts and deprioritising certain content.[63] Nevertheless, platforms are still private companies fundamentally motivated by commercial interests.[64] The prevalence of 'share' and 'retweet' buttons and highly secretive algorithms rewarding sensationalist content speaks to such interests and demonstrates how they may be at odds with the broader national interests of limiting misinformation and disinformation.[65] Furthermore, platform executives in California, or unpaid contractors in developing countries who are charged with 'content moderation', are unlikely to be attuned to the specific needs, laws and standards of all the States in which these platforms operate.[66] Nor are removal decisions subject to any sort of due process or transparency associated with democratic government,[67] despite the implications they may have on a range of human rights.[68] For these reasons, self-regulation is increasingly seen as an inappropriate outsourcing of public functions, including protection of freedom of expression and national security, onto unaccountable private actors.[69]

On the other end of the spectrum is an uptick in States passing laws that directly prohibit false content. Most States already require platforms to restrict content that is manifestly illegal, such as child abuse or incitement to violence, but States are

[61] Diana Bossio et al, 'Australia's News Media Bargaining Code and the Global Turn Towards Platform Regulation' (2022) 14 *Policy and Internet* 136, 136.

[62] Select Committee on Foreign Interference through Social Media, Parliament of Australia, *Report* (n 1) [6.9]-[6.16].

[63] Dowse and Bachmann (n 25) 459; Carson and Wright (n 15) 225; Anastasia Kozyreva et al, 'Resolving Content Moderation Dilemmas between Free Speech and Harmful Misinformation' (2023) 120 *Proceedings of the National Academy of Sciences* 1, 1–2.

[64] Gauja (n 43) 977.

[65] Saurwein and Spencer-Smith (n 32) 824.

[66] Marsden, Meyer and Brown (n 14) 17.

[67] UN Human Rights Council, *Report of the Special Rapporteur* (n 59) [40]; Gauja (n 43) 978.

[68] UN Human Rights Council, *Report of the Special Rapporteur* (n 59) [5].

[69] Ibid [1]; Marsden, Meyer and Brown, 'Platform Values and Democratic Elections: How Can the Law Regulate Digital Disinformation?' (2020) 36 (n 14) 2.

increasingly turning to criminalise misinformation and disinformation itself. Such laws have been proposed or passed in numerous States, including Belarus, Brazil, China, Malaysia, Singapore and Taiwan.[70] The difficulty of confirming whether any one piece of content is in fact 'false' all but ensures that these attempts will be either impossible to enforce, or if enforced, will suppress legitimate forms of expression.[71] Others, including France, Germany, Kenya, Pakistan, Singapore and Russia have opted for laws that enable the government to compel platforms to remove content, with various penalties for non-compliance.[72] This typically involves governments issuing notices to platforms to take down content, but again, vague or expansive definitions of disinformation and misinformation mean such laws have been used to target political dissidents and critics such as journalists.[73] In addition to the way such laws can limit important freedoms, a key criticism is a question of speed—the legislative processes of most countries cannot keep up with continuous advances in digital technologies, and the sheer volume of false content is likely to overwhelm governments seeking to moderate each individual instance thereof, especially where enforcement involves the judiciary.[74] For these reasons, reliance on statute can be seen as overly heavy-handed, as well as inherently inefficient.

The middle ground is co-regulation, which seeks to democratise certain aspects of platform governance through industry codes or standards, with scope for a dedicated body to deal with complaints and enforcement.[75] Companies work individually or collectively, and with industry groups, to develop their own standards for regulating users. Depending on the level of co-regulation, compliance might then be subject to no more than self-reporting, to a regular audit by a self-appointed regulator, to a formally appointed regulator, to approval by the legislature or to the creation of a statutory regulator with full enforcement powers.[76] Of course, involving platforms is a double-edged sword. If platforms are involved in drafting a code, they can help craft standards that limit curtailment of efficiency and profitability. Such a code is more likely to be complied with, but also more likely to be more lenient.[77] Nevertheless, this model seeks to balance the two main critiques of self-regulation and external law enforcement. Instead of relying solely on public pressure to ensure companies police standards and implement policies to counteract misinformation and disinformation, a level of third-party pressure is applied in a fast and flexible

---

[70] Saurwein and Spencer-Smith (n 32) 827; 'A Guide to Anti-Misinformation Actions Around the World', *Poynter* (Web page, 18 March 2024) <https://www.poynter.org/ifcn/anti-misinformation-actions/>.

[71] UN Human Rights Council, *Report of the Special Rapporteur* (n 59) [13].

[72] UN Human Rights Council, *Disinformation and Freedom of Opinion and Expression* (n 13) [57]–[58].

[73] Taking the Singapore law as an example, see, e.g., Gibbons and Carson (n 13) 235.

[74] Gauja (n 43) 978.

[75] Ibid 979.

[76] Marsden, Meyer and Brown (n 14) 11–14.

[77] JingYi Tay, 'No News Is Good News, but "Fake News" Is Bad News: A Comparative Analysis of Singapore's and Australia's Measures to Combat Misinformation on Social Media' (2021) 33(1) *Singapore Academy of Law Journal* 600, 618.

manner, without invoking the coercive power of legislation. Platforms themselves have a seat at the table of any third-party grouping, lessening the risk of governments using regulation to suppress freedom of expression.[78] This model is the preferred approach in the European Union, and as this chapter will now discuss, also underpins the proposed Australian misinformation and disinformation law.

The Response

Prior to examining in detail the proposed law, it is important to briefly set out the events preceding its announcement. In 2017, the Australian Competition and Consumer Commission (ACCC), the statutory competition regulator, was directed to consider the impact of social media and other online services on competition in the media. The ACCC's 2019 report made several recommendations, among them the creation of a voluntary Code of Conduct to deal with disinformation on digital platforms, to be drafted by the industry and enforced by an independent regulator.[79] The government agreed in part and asked Digital Industry Group Inc (DIGI), a digital platform industry association, to develop a code, citing the European Union's 2018 *Code of Practice on Disinformation* as an example for DIGI.[80] DIGI released the *Australian Code of Practice on Disinformation and Misinformation* in February 2021. Like the EU Code, the DIGI Code is a set of voluntary commitments to which its signatories (Adobe, Apple, Google, Meta, Microsoft, Redbubble, TikTok and Twitch, and for a time, Twitter/X[81]) can opt-in, among them actions on empowering users to identify misinformation and disinformation, reducing propagation thereof and increasing the transparency of both political advertising and measures taken to combat misinformation and disinformation.[82] Only two commitments are mandatory; those relating to providing safeguards against harms arising from misinformation and disinformation, and publishing reports.[83] Contrary to the ACCC's recommendation, DIGI administers its code rather than an independent regulator, and adherence is

---

[78] Gauja (n 43) 976–7.

[79] Australian Competition and Consumer Commission (n 49) 34.

[80] Australian Government, 'Government Response and Implementation Roadmap for the Digital Platforms Inquiry' (Government Response, 12 December 2019) <https://treasury.gov.au/publication/p2019-41708>. See also Hurcombe and Meese (n 14) 298.

[81] On 27 November 2023, DIGI found that X had committed a serious breach of the Code due to its removal of a function that allowed users to report tweets as misinformation during the Voice to Parliament referendum, and as a result, removed X from the Code. See, Digital Industry Group Inc., 'Complaint By Reset Australia Against X (F.K.A. Twitter) Upheld By Australian Code Of Practice On Disinformation And Misinformation Independent Complaints Sub-Committee' (Media Statement, 27 November 2023) <https://digi.org.au/complaint-by-reset-australia-against-x-f-k-a-twitter-upheld-by-australian-code-of-practice-on-disinformation-and-misinformation-independent-complaints-sub-committee/>.

[82] Digital Industry Group Inc., *Australian Code of Practice on Disinformation and Misinformation* (at 22 December 2022) 13–15.

[83] Ibid 8.

reviewed by a DIGI sub-committee comprising representatives of the signatories[84]; the Australian Communication and Media Authority (ACMA), the statutory communications regulator, was asked to oversee the DIGI Code but given no enforcement powers. For both the EU and DIGI Codes, therefore, the incentive to opt-in is the prospect of evading harsher regulation, and the repercussions for failure to opt-in or meet commitments are mostly reputational.[85] Under this regime, which remains in place given the amendment has been withdrawn, there is no external independent regulation.

Weaknesses in both codes would eventually trigger a desire for their strengthening.[86] In June 2021, ACMA reported on the adequacy of digital platforms' disinformation and news quality measures, concluding that the DIGI Code was an improvement over its EU counterpart and a good first step, but nevertheless required strengthening.[87] It proposed that ACMA be given powers to gather information from platforms and register and enforce an industry code if the voluntary code fails.[88] The government considered these recommendations and in 2023, announced the amendment and released the exposure draft, which would have inserted a new schedule, headed 'Digital platform services', into the *Broadcasting Services Act 1992* (Cth). Broadly, the draft gave ACMA new powers to (1) gather information from or require platforms to keep certain records; (2) request the industry develop a code of practice; and (3) create and enforce an industry standard. These powers were to apply to digital platform services, which were digital service that provides content aggregation, connective media, media sharing, or were otherwise specified by the Minister, but did not include internet, SMS or MMS service providers.[89] Digital services in turn were ones that deliver or allow users to access content by ways of an internet carriage service provided to the public and accessible in Australia, but did not include a broadcasting or datacasting service.[90] This meant instant messaging services, social media, news aggregators and search engines were all captured, whereas email services and media sharing services with no interactive feature were excluded, as were digital platforms specified by the relevant Minister.[91] Private messages were also excluded.[92] The new scheme, therefore, would have covered virtually all social media platforms, but not all activities therein.

Several aspects of these powers warrant further consideration. Turning first to the record-keeping. ACMA would have had the power to create digital platform

---

[84] Ibid 18.

[85] Hurcombe and Meese (n 14) 299.

[86] While this chapter focuses on the DIGI Code, for a comparison of the two and further details about the EU Code, see, e.g., ibid 298–9.

[87] Australian Communications and Media Authority, *Report to Government on the Adequacy of Digital Platforms' Disinformation and News Quality Measures*, 2021, 2–3.

[88] Ibid 5.

[89] Parliament of Australia (n 9) sch 1, cl 4.

[90] Ibid sch 1, cl 3.

[91] Ibid sch 1, cl 2.

[92] Ibid sch 1, cl 14(3), 18(4), 19(4), 34.

rules, enabling it to require digital platforms to keep records about the prevalence of misinformation and disinformation on their platform, efforts to combat it and effectiveness thereof,[93] as well as to compile reports for ACMA based on those records on an 'as and when required' basis, or periodically.[94] Contravening a rule was grounds for a warning, a remedial direction and/or a civil penalty.[95] Digital platforms that made false or misleading records, including by omission, committed an offence and faced up to 100 penalty units or 12 months' imprisonment.[96] Furthermore, ACMA could have compelled information, including documents or evidence, from digital platforms about the prevalence of misinformation and disinformation on their platform, efforts to combat it and effectiveness thereof.[97] Significantly, this power would have also applied to compelling 'other persons', where the information in question is relevant to the exercise of the ACMA's powers relating to digital platforms,[98] the only instance in which the amendment would have applied to individuals, rather than just digital platforms. Notably, for the purposes of the information-gathering powers, the amendment would have retrospectively applied the definitions of misinformation and disinformation,[99] discussed further below. There was no carve out for refusing to provide information that might tend to self-incriminate, but any such information produced would not have been admissible against the platform or person in criminal proceedings.[100] Again, persons who knowingly provided false or misleading information to ACMA, or knowingly omitted matters without which the information is misleading, committed an offence punishable by up to 100 penalty units or 12 months' imprisonment.[101] Finally, ACMA could have published information on its website about misinformation and disinformation, including its prevalence, efforts to combat it and effectiveness thereof, both industry-wide and on individual platforms.[102]

Turning next to the codes and standards. The proposed law would have created a graduated scheme that supported self-regulation in the first instance but empowered ACMA to request the industry make new code of practice containing measures to combat misinformation and disinformation if existing voluntary efforts proved inadequate, with that code becoming mandatory and registered with ACMA for enforcement and ACMA able to issue compliance warnings and remedial directions, as well as attracting civil penalty.[103] These codes could have covered a wide array of matters, from the use of technology like artificial intelligence to address misinformation and

---

[93] Ibid sch 1, cl 14(1).

[94] Ibid sch 1, cl 14(8).

[95] Ibid sch 1, cl 15–16.

[96] Ibid sch 1, cl 17(1).

[97] Ibid sch 1, cl 18.

[98] Ibid sch 1, cl 19.

[99] Ibid sch 2, cl 32(2).

[100] Ibid sch 1, cl 21, except for prosecutions relating to giving false or misleading information.

[101] Ibid sch 1, cl 22(1) sets a maximum penalty for this offence as imprisonment for 12 months.

[102] Ibid sch 1, cl 25, with further practicalities, such as consultation and protection of private information, contained in cl 26–27.

[103] Ibid sch 1, cl 32, 37–38, 43–44.

disinformation, to fact-checking, to user detection and reporting, to complaints procedures.[104] As a last resort in the graduated scheme, ACMA could have created and enforced 'misinformation standards' by legislative instrument, a stronger form of regulation, if the industry did not create the requested code, if the code was deficient, or if there were exceptional or urgent circumstances.[105] Before registering a code or determining a standard, ACMA must have considered any burden on freedom of political communication, and in doing so, may have considered any circumstances it considers relevant,[106] a safeguard that, while welcome, raises questions about what ACMA may have considered relevant. Finally, regarding non-compliance, again it attracted a civil penalty and here, digital platforms that contravened an ACMA standard would have faced a maximum penalty of the greater of 25,000 penalty units or 5% of the corporation's annual turnover during the 12 months before the contravention.[107] The penalty, therefore, was not insignificant and would have likely provided strong incentive for platforms to comply.

The definition of misinformation and disinformation was critical to understanding the scope and implications of this scheme. The proposed law adopted the same intention-based delineation between misinformation and disinformation, the former being online content that is 'false, misleading or deceptive, that is shared or created without an intent to deceive but can cause and contribute to serious harm', while the latter being misinformation that is '*intentionally* disseminated with the intent to deceive or cause serious harm' (emphasis added).[108] However, excluded from that was content which was entertainment, parody or satire, professional news, produced by or for an accredited educational institute, or authorised by an Australian government.[109] These exceptions demand careful consideration. Only the first is based on the nature of the content itself, rather than its source. It could be considered both too narrow, for example by failing to exclude other forms of artistic expression, and too broad, for example by excluding entertainment as a blanket category and therefore allowing blatant disinformation as long as it is presented in the form of 'infotainment'. The exclusion for professional news content swung the other way as being potentially too generous, with ample examples of such outlets disseminating misinformation or disinformation—one example being the spread of COVID-19 conspiracy theories by cable news channel Sky News Australia.[110] Furthermore, though the definition of 'digital service' excluded 'broadcasting service', digital platforms frequently host news content from broadcasting services, for example, news reels or highlights. This seems to have shifted responsibility in the proposed law to the digital platform rather than the broadcaster to consider whether the content is misinformation or disinformation for the purposes of their record-keeping and information-sharing obligations,

[104] Ibid sch 1, cl 33.

[105] Ibid sch 1, cl 46–50.

[106] Ibid sch 1, cl 37, 45.

[107] Ibid sch 2, cl 17, relating to the civil penalty in cl 53 or 54.

[108] Ibid sch 1, cl 7(1)–(2).

[109] Ibid sch 1, cl 2.

[110] Hurcombe and Meese (n 14) 304.

when they may not have been the best placed to do so. The exception for government-authorised content raised the same failure to reckon with the fact that elected officials are often prominent disseminators' misinformation and disinformation,[111] creating an unequal playing field between the government and its critics.

Both definitions of misinformation and disinformation also rested on the concept of 'harm'. This was defined as (a) hatred against a group in Australian society on the basis of ethnicity, nationality, race, gender, sexual orientation, age, religion or physical or mental disability; (b) disruption of Australian public order or society; (c) harm to the integrity of Australian democratic processes or government institutions; (d) harm to the health of Australians; (e) harm to the Australian environment; and (f) economic or financial harm to Australians or the Australian economy.[112] The proposed law did not define 'serious' harm, but did set out factors relevant to the determination of whether content is likely to cause or contribute to serious harm, being the subject matter of the content, the circumstances, potential reach, speed and impact of its dissemination, the author, the purpose, attribution to a source and authority thereof, other related false content, and 'any other relevant matter'.[113] This broadly aligned with the harms flowing from misinformation and disinformation identified by scholars.[114] Recalling that for the purposes of the draft, misinformation was false content reasonably likely to cause or contribute to serious harm, the breadth of these definitions of harm worked with the broad definition of misinformation and disinformation to capture more content than necessary or desirable. For example, lawful protest that is met with opposition, including from governments, could be considered a disruption of public order, as could campaigns for social change. Similarly, while some medical advice, particularly that seen during the peak of the COVID-19 pandemic, is clearly harmful to the health of Australians, in many other instances, medical (and environmental) matters are spaces of significant scientific debate and disagreement. Given the content had to only be reasonably likely to cause such harm rather than directly causative or even highly likely, these wide definitions meant that platforms may have erred on the side of caution and identified legitimate forms of expression and misinformation and disinformation.

A recurring theme in this chapter is the risk that restrictions relating to misinformation and disinformation may bring about the very harms they seek to minimise by repressing free speech and distorting the media landscape to the detriment of democratic resilience.[115] A general protection in the proposed law confirmed that the rules, codes and standards therein would have no effect to the extent that their operation would have infringed on any constitutional doctrine of implied freedom of political communication.[116] Further, the proposed law focused on obligations on digital

[111] Ibid.

[112] Parliament of Australia (n 9) sch 1, cl 2.

[113] Ibid sch 1, cl 7(3).

[114] See, e.g., Gibbons and Carson (n 13) 242–3, discussing electoral harm, physical harm, emotional harm, economic harm and 'other intangible harm'.

[115] Sorial, Morris an Greste (n 54) 21.

[116] Parliament of Australia (n 9) sch 1, cl 60.

platforms to deploy processes that responded to misinformation and disinformation, rather than focusing on individual pieces of content—indeed, it did not give ACMA the power to remove, or request removal of, content. Therefore, its direct interference on freedom of expression was limited. This did not, however, exclude such interference from occurring indirectly. To avoid the public shame of being labelled an outlet of misinformation or disinformation, platforms may have chosen to take a more interventionist approach to content moderation. Similarly, while ACMA would have only had reserve powers if industry efforts failed, platforms may have chosen to implement their own potentially excessive measures to ensure ACMA did not step in. In this sense, the defining feature of this proposal was the assumption that ACMA and digital platforms could, and in fact must, identify misinformation and disinformation. In reality, however, to even attempt this task requires an enormous investment of resources and expertise, and there is no reason to be satisfied that either ACMA or digital platforms are so equipped. Ultimately, even the vastest army of fact checkers is unlikely to be able to resolve the canyon of content that does not fall neatly into the binary of true/false.

Conclusion

When tackling risks, especially ones as severe as those posed by misinformation and disinformation, coercive statutory measures are often the first instinct, especially following reluctance by social media platforms to be regulated. For the media sector, however, government-led responses enshrined in law can create other risks—from repressing free speech and enacting censorship to creating an inflexible statutory scheme unable to respond to the agility of digital innovation.[117] Overall, the proposed law would have tilted Australia's position on the regulatory continuum further towards the coercive end and therefore represented an escalation in Australia's approach to misinformation and disinformation. However, despite being at the more fulsome end of the spectrum, the proposed law still sat firmly within the co-regulation category of possible responses. In the long term, the *ex ante* nature of the proposed law would have been more likely to be effective than more aggressive *ex post* take-down laws that are effectively limited to moderation of individual pieces of content, given the proposed law required the industry to adopt systemic changes to their processes rather than their content. Furthermore, in contrast to vesting responsibility in an elected official of group thereof, an independent regulator like ACMA would have been less likely to misuse its powers for political ends.[118] Nevertheless, questions remained over the ability of both ACMA and digital platforms to apply the definitions of misinformation and disinformation in a way that would have struck the appropriate balance of preserving freedom of expression and legitimate debate, and preserving individual and collective safety and trust.

[117] Saurwein and Spencer-Smith (n 32) 822.

[118] Tay (n 77) 616–9.

While the proposed law has been withdrawn for now, it is highly likely that some form of proposed regulation of misinformation and disinformation will return to the political agenda in the near future and in considering any response to misinformation and disinformation, it is instructive to note that the decades-long trend of declining trust towards government and democracy in Australia was not just stayed, but in fact experienced a reversal, increasing substantially during the COVID-19 pandemic.[119] This was so despite an onslaught of misinformation and disinformation on the virus.[120] Several factors offer a possible explanation; that the early months of the pandemic were characterised by informational reporting and health messaging in the mainstream media, that the approach of Australian politicians to managing the crisis was largely bipartisan, and that this political unity was reflected in a media coverage that had noticeable less conflict-based political reporting.[121] This trend aptly demonstrates the importance of a multi-dimensional approach to misinformation and disinformation, one that considers all of the diverse actors in the informational landscape. The focus on digital platforms and independent regulators should not take away from the critical role of public awareness campaigns, educational initiatives to increase media literacy and critical analytical skills, and appropriate resourcing for independent and pluralistic journalism and fact-checking organisations.[122] Ideally, given democracies all around the world are struggling with this issue, States would share not just information about security and threats but also best practices to foster resilience in their institutions.[123] This is particularly important because, as this chapter has sought to convey, disinformation is both a cause and a consequence of eroding trust in democracy. Governments disconnected from their people create the conditions in which misinformation and disinformation flourishes, capitalising on narratives of government failure.[124] Responses to misinformation and disinformation will not succeed without also targeting the reasons why individuals have become disenfranchised and alienated, and therefore susceptible to its mischief.[125]

---

[119] Shaun Goldfinch, Ross Taplin and Robin Gauld, 'Trust in Government Increased During the Covid-19 Pandemic in Australia and New Zealand' (2021) 80 *Australian Journal of Public Administration* 3.

[120] McGuinness, Fisher and Lee (n 30) 248.

[121] Ibid 248–9.

[122] FSaurwein and Spencer-Smith (n 32) 834; Marsden, Meyer and Brown (n 14) 16; Dowse and Bachmann (n 25) 459.

[123] Shackelford et al (n 3) 1752.

[124] Dowling (n 12) 119.

[125] UN Human Rights Council, *Disinformation and Freedom of Opinion and Expression* (n 13) [20]–[21].

References

'A Guide to Anti-Misinformation Actions Around the World', *Poynter* (Web page, 18 March 2024) <https://www.poynter.org/ifcn/anti-misinformation-actions/>

Australia's Foreign Relations (State and Territory Arrangements) Act 2020 (Cth)

Australian Communications and Media Authority, *Report to Government on the Adequacy of Digital Platforms' Disinformation and News Quality Measures*, 2021

Australian Competition and Consumer Commission, *Digital Platforms Inquiry: Final Report* (Report, 2019)

Australian Government, 'Government Response and Implementation Roadmap for the Digital Platforms Inquiry' (Government Response, 12 December 2019) <https://treasury.gov.au/publication/p2019-41708>

Baltutis, Ravi, 'South Australia's Truth in Political Advertising Law: A Model for Australia?' (2021) 42(2) *Adelaide Law Review* 597

Baade, Björnstjern, 'Fake News and International Law' (2019) 29(4) *European Journal of International Law* 1357

Bossio, Diana, et al, 'Australia's News Media Bargaining Code and the Global Turn Towards Platform Regulation' (2022) 14 *Policy and Internet* 136

Boulianne, Shelley, 'Social Media use and Participation: A Meta-Analysis of Current Research' (2015) 18 *Information, Communication and Society* 524

Carson, Andrea and Scott Wright, 'Fake News and Democracy: Definitions, Impact and Response' (2022) 57(3) *Australian Journal of Political Science* 221

De Blasio, Emiliana and Donatella Selva, 'Who Is Responsible for Disinformation? European Approaches to Social Platforms' Accountability in the Post-Truth Era' (2021) 65(6) *American Behavioral Scientist* 825

Digital Industry Group Inc., *Australian Code of Practice on Disinformation and Misinformation* (at 22 December 2022)

Digital Industry Group Inc., 'Complaint By Reset Australia Against X (F.K.A. Twitter) Upheld By Australian Code Of Practice On Disinformation And Misinformation Independent Complaints Sub-Committee' (Media Statement, 27 November 2023) <https://digi.org.au/complaint-by-reset-australia-against-x-f-k-a-twitter-upheld-by-australian-code-of-practice-on-disinformation-and-misinformation-independent-complaints-sub-committee/>

Dowling, Melissa-Ellen, 'Foreign Interference and Digital Democracy: is Digital Era Governance Putting Australia at Risk?' (2022) 57(2) *Australian Journal of Political Science* 113

Dowse, Andrew and Sascha Dov Bachmann, 'Information Warfare: Methods to Counter Disinformation' (2022) 38(4) *Defense and Security Analysis* 453

Electoral Legislation Amendment (Electoral Funding and Disclosure Reform) Act 2018 (Cth)

Electoral Matters Committee, Parliament of Victoria, *Inquiry into the Impact of Social Media on Victorian Elections and Victoria's Electoral Administration* (Final Discussion Paper, 3 September 2014)

Fetzer, James, 'Disinformation: The Use of False Information' (2004) 14 *Minds and Machines* 231

Foreign Influence Transparency Scheme Act 2018 (Cth)

Gauja, Anika, 'Digital Democracy: Big Technology and the Regulation of Politics' (2021) 44(3) *UNSW Law Journal* 959

Gibbons, Andrew and Andrea Carson, 'What is Misinformation and Disinformation? Understanding Multi-Stakeholders' Perspectives in the Asia Pacific' (2022) 57(3) *Australian Journal of Political Science* 231

Goldfinch, Shaun, Ross Taplin and Robin Gauld,'Trust in Government Increased During the Covid-19 Pandemic in Australia and New Zealand' (2021) 80 *Australian Journal of Public Administration* 3

Hurcombe, Edward and James Meese, 'Australia's DIGI Code: What Can We Learn From the EU Experience?' (2022) 57(3) *Australian Journal of Political Science* 297

Kozyreva, Anastasia et al, 'Resolving Content Moderation Dilemmas between Free Speech and Harmful Misinformation' (2023) 120 *Proceedings of the National Academy of Sciences* 1

Levin, Dov H., 'When the Great Power Gets a Vote: The Effects of Great Power Electoral Interventions on Election Results' (2016) 60 International Studies Quarterly 189

Marsden, Chris, Trisha Meyer and Ian Brown, 'Platform Values and Democratic Elections: How Can the Law Regulate Digital Disinformation?' (2020) 36 *Computer Law and Security Review* 1

McGuinness, Kieran, Caroline Fisher and Jee Young Lee, 'Australians' Shifting Concerns about Mis- and Disinformation' (2022) 57(3) *Australian Journal of Political Science* 248

Minister for Communications, *Communications Legislation Amendment (Combatting Misinformation and Disinformation) Bill 2024* (Media Release, 24 November 2024)

National Security Legislation Amendment (Espionage and Foreign Interference) Act 2018 (Cth)

Parliament of Australia, *Communications Legislation Amendment (Combatting Misinformation and Disinformation) Bill 2023* exposure draft

Puutio, Alexander and David Alexandru Timis, 'Deepfake Democracy: Here's How Modern Elections Could Be Decided by Fake News', *World Economic Forum* (Web Page, 5 October 2020) <https://www.weforum.org/agenda/2020/10/deepfake-democracy-could-modern-elections-fall-prey-to-fiction/>

Ray, Andrew, 'Disinformation, Deepfakes and Democracies: The Need for Legislative Reform' (2021) 44(3) *UNSW Law Journal* 983

Rid, Thomas, *Active Measures: The Secret History of Disinformation and Political Warfare* (Profile Books, 2020)

Saurwein, Florian and Charlotte Spencer-Smith, 'Combating Disinformation on Social Media: Multilevel Governance and Distributed Accountability in Europe' (2020) 8(6) *Digital Journalism* 820

Select Committee on Foreign Interference through Social Media, Parliament of Australia, *Report* (Report, August 2023)

Select Committee on Foreign Interference through Social Media, Parliament of Australia, *First Interim Report* (Report, December 2021)

Shackelford, Scott J., et al., 'Defending Democracy: Taking Stock of the Global Fight Against Digital Repression, Disinformation, and Election Insecurity' (2020) 77 *Washington and Lee Law Review* 1747

Shepherd, Katie, 'A Man Thought Aquarium Cleaner with the Same Name as the Anti-Viral Drug Chloroquine Would Prevent Coronavirus. It Killed Him', *Washington Post* (online, 24 March 2020) <https://www.washingtonpost.com/nation/2020/03/24/coronavirus-chloroquine-poisoning-death/>

Security Legislation Amendment (Critical Infrastructure Protection) Act 2022 (Cth)

Sorial, Sarah, Shireen Morris and Peter Greste, 'Foreign Interference and the Incremental Chilling of Free Speech' (2024) *Federal Law Review* 1 (advance)

Tandoc, Edson, Zheng Wei Lim and Richard Ling, 'Defining "Fake News": A Typology of Scholarly Definitions' (2018) 6(2) *Digital Journalism* 137

Tay, JingYi, 'No News Is Good News, but "Fake News" Is Bad News: A Comparative Analysis of Singapore's and Australia's Measures to Combat Misinformation on Social Media' (2021) 33(1) *Singapore Academy of Law Journal* 600

UN Human Rights Council, *Disinformation and Freedom of Opinion and Expression: Report of the Special Rapporteur on the Promotion and Protection of the Right to Freedom of Opinion and Expression*, A/HRC/47/25 (13 April 2021)

UN Human Rights Council, *Report of the Special Rapporteur on the Promotion and Protection of the Right to Freedom of Opinion and Expression*, A/HRC/38/35 (6 April 2018)

Aneta Peretko is a practising lawyer and specialises in terrorism, national security and transnational crime. She holds undergraduate degrees with honours in law and international relations from Flinders University and a Master of Laws with honours from the University of Melbourne.

Ensuring Digital Resilience in Australia: From Resilience to Security in Critical Infrastructure Protection

Susanne L. Lloyd-Jones

Abstract Secure digital infrastructures form the backbone of any modern, industrialised society and economy, and have been the drivers of policy and legislative developments in Australia and other countries worldwide. Australia launched several initiatives to bolster its digital security and resilience, including the 2023–2030 Australian Cyber Security Strategy and Action Plan. The concept of resilience plays a crucial role in critical infrastructure protection in Australia. Security and resilience work together in a critical infrastructure setting. This chapter outlines the legal framework that underpins the security of critical infrastructure in Australia by exploring the operative provisions of the *Security of Critical Infrastructure Act 2018* (Cth). The chapter considers the complex interplay between regulation, resilience, and security, noting some of the challenges and opportunities of this crucial relationship.

Introduction

In an era where the world, including Australia, is deeply integrated with the international digital economy, the security and resilience of national digital infrastructures are paramount.[1] Secure digital infrastructures form the backbone of any modern, industrialised society and economy, and have been the drivers of policy and legislative developments in Australia and elsewhere. Australia launched several initiatives to bolster its digital security and resilience, including the 2023–2030 Australian Cyber Security Strategy and Action Plan.[2] The international digital landscape has been impacted by numerous high-profile data breaches and hacks, presenting a grim report card for digital insecurity.[3] From the commercialisation of the Internet in the 1990s, which exposed the world's connected computers to espionage and cyber-attacks, to the multi-layered problem of digital insecurity that governments, organisations and individuals face today, the threats are wide-ranging and complex.[4] These threats can originate from various levels—individual, product, service, or infrastructure—and work together to create digital insecurity. Even in environments where individuals,

S. L. Lloyd-Jones (✉)
UNSW Faculty of Law and Justice, Sydney, Australia
e-mail: s.lloydjones@unsw.edu.au

D. Stephens et al. (eds.), *Digital Resilience*,
https://doi.org/10.1007/978-981-97-9746-2_7

organisations, governments and businesses have implemented robust digital security systems and processes and adopted a 'security culture' or 'security posture', adverse events can still occur. This may be due to an undetected vulnerability, an unanticipated problem, or the activities of a highly sophisticated threat actor operating undetected for a long period.[5]

The concept of resilience plays a crucial role in critical infrastructure protection in Australia.[6] It serves to bring strategy, policy and regulation together. Resilience, often defined as 'the capacity of a system to absorb disturbance and still retain its basic function and structure',[7] provides the underlying principle that drives the need for secure digital infrastructures, services, processes, systems, and products.[8] Security and resilience work together in a critical infrastructure setting. It makes sense then that digital resilience is a security concern, especially in a critical infrastructure context, given the ubiquitous reliance on digital communications information technology to deliver core services and provide key systems, networks and processes to critical infrastructure industries.[9] The interconnected supply chains and systems-of-systems aspects of critical infrastructure make their resilience an ongoing concern for governments worldwide.[10] The recognition of the interconnectedness of many critical sectors in the economy led to the introduction and subsequent reforms of the *Security of Critical Infrastructure Act 2018* (Cth)(SOCI).[11]

This chapter will proceed in four parts. The first part lays down a foundation for understanding the link between security regulation and resilience. The second outlines the legal framework that underpins the security of critical infrastructure in Australia. The third part explores in more detail the provisions of the SOCI, which operates to secure digital resilience in Australia. The fourth part considers the complex interplay between regulation, resilience, and security, noting some of the challenges and opportunities of this crucial relationship.

Role of Regulation at the Nexus of Security and Resilience

Regulation provides normative scaffolding for changing behaviour to address societal concerns, practices, and desirable behaviours.[12] Legislation is arguably an expression of a society's underlying values and norms.[13] Australia's national security legislative framework operates to secure national interests and protect Australian society from existential threats and harms. In democratic countries such as Australia, the security framework of critical infrastructure protection and resilience is cited by government as key to stability and protecting Australia's way of life.[14]

Critical infrastructure is legally defined through definitions found in policy documents and legislation. The concept of 'critical infrastructure' was first used in the United States in the 1980s but found its way into Australian policy documents in the 1990s.[15] In Australia, critical infrastructure is currently defined as

> 'those physical facilities, systems, assets, supply chains, information technologies and communication networks which, if destroyed, degraded, compromised or rendered unavailable for an extended period, would significantly impact the social or economic wellbeing of

> Australia as a nation or its states or territories, or affect Australia's ability to conduct national defence and ensure national security'.[16]

The Australian government also defines critical infrastructure as providing 'services that are essential for everyday life such as energy, food, water, transport, communications, health and banking and finance'.[17] SOCI is a key component of building digital resilience because it provides the legal means through which the government can enforce its policy and regulatory agenda to secure Australian critical infrastructure against attack. Australia, along with other Western democracies in Europe, the United States and the United Kingdom, have been implementing multi-layered mechanisms to protect critical infrastructure.[18] The Act builds digital resilience through the 'whole-of-economy' application of its risk management program and its more intrusive powers to intervene in the event of a major cyber incident. SOCI covers 11 sectors of the economy and 22 asset classes, including communications, data storage or processing and energy. The Minister for Cyber Security has already declared over 200 systems of national significance encompassing assets in the energy, communications, transport, financial markets, food and grocery and data storage or processing sectors.[19]

The SOCI framework is fundamentally about risk management and building a culture of security within organisations. The risk management framework obliges critical infrastructure sectors to implement a risk management program with broad parameters and requirements as set out in legislation.[20] It recognises the sectoral and cross-sectoral, and in some cases, global reach of industry participants, by providing the means of adopting international standards and sector-specific frameworks as part of its suite of risk management tools and techniques.[21] The risk management program rules have been developed with industry through a co-design process within the Trusted Information Sharing Network (TISN), leveraging the positive effects of co-designing with those most affected by the regulation.[22] The hope is that the legislation will engender a compliance and audit culture, supported by powers of government intervention, and enforcement through infringements and offences, and that it will be sufficient to motivate critical infrastructure industries to uplift their cyber security posture.[23]

Significance of SOCI in Safeguarding Essential Systems and Services from Cyber Threats

The SOCI regime is a hybrid risk management framework, containing a range of mechanisms for achieving its objects, ranging from direct regulation through to co-regulation and co-design of the risk management rules. The hybrid nature of the regulation lends itself to fostering resilience because hybrid regulation entails 'forms of (combinations of) regulatory instruments based on a mix of origins.'[24] The protection of critical infrastructure became subject to legislation in Australia as a response to changing political, economic and security conditions and circumstances, including the fact that most critical infrastructure in Australia and elsewhere is either privately owned and operated,[25] or owned in a commercial partnership with the Australian government, such as the national broadband network (NBN) or Telstra.[26] When the SOCI legislation was being debated in Parliament, it was noted that these owner-and-operator relationships created an unacceptable risk to national security, especially the government's capacity to respond to those national security risks.[27] The explanatory memorandum to the *Security of Critical Infrastructure Act 2018* (Cth) explains that,

> Existing gaps in the Government's understanding of the ownership and control of critical infrastructure, and the lack of a mechanism at the federal level to intervene where a significant risk to national security has been identified, limit Government's ability to understand, manage and respond to national security risks. Disruption of critical infrastructure sectors can have a serious impact on Australia's national and economic security, both in terms of immediate costs incurred and long-term sector vulnerability.[28]

SOCI lists critical infrastructure sectors and assets that are covered by the Act but does not specifically define 'critical infrastructure' per se. The sector and asset classes provide the scope of the Act's regulatory objects, that is, the 'what' of the regulation. The 'sector' and 'asset' definitions have in-built mechanisms, which allow the Minister for Cyber Security to declare and add sectors and assets as critical infrastructure protection evolves.[29] Through the sector and asset definitions, SOCI operates to safeguard Australia's essential services and systems from cyber threats. It does this through requiring entities to develop and implement comprehensive risk management programs, which assist responsible entities in identifying, assessing and mitigating risks to their critical infrastructure assets.[30] SOCI also requires mandatory incident reporting, which helps create an aggregated threat picture for government, enabling proactive and reactive responses to cyber threats.[31] For assets with 'systems of national significance' status, the Act imposes enhanced cyber security obligations. The enhanced obligations contain additional security measures aimed at improving the security posture of those entities.[32] Finally, the Act safeguards essential services and systems through provisions that permit government intervention and information seeking in certain prescribed circumstances.[33] These provisions will be activated by the Minister for Cyber Security when there are no alternative regulatory options available to respond to an incident.[34]

Implications of SOCI for Strengthening Digital Resilience—A Review of Operative Provisions

Object of SOCI

The object of SOCI as outlined in section 3 of the Act is to provide a framework for managing risks relating to critical infrastructure through several legislative measures.[35] These measures include improving transparency of the ownership and operational control of critical infrastructure in Australia, facilitating cooperation and coordination between all levels of government and the owners of critical infrastructure as a basis to better understand risks.[36] SOCI requires responsible entities for critical infrastructure assets to identify and manage risks relating to those assets.[37] It imposes enhanced cyber security obligations on 'systems of national significance', a special class of critical infrastructure asset, to improve their preparedness for, and ability to respond to, cyber security incidents.[38] SOCI provides a regime for the commonwealth to respond to serious cyber incidents.[39]

Register of CI Asset

The register of critical infrastructure assets in Part 2 of SOCI strengthens resilience providing visibility of the critical infrastructure landscape for government and responsible entities.[40] Arguably, the register helps identify potential vulnerabilities and interdependencies among assets, which is crucial to understand proactive risk management.[41] The register assists entities with identifying risk, as the register requires responsible entities to provide detailed information about their assets, including operational changes and ownership updates. This information is vital for developing and updating risk management programs tailored to the specific needs and risks of each asset.[42] The register may be useful in the event of a cyber incident or other disruptions, as it will provide government with up-to-date information for authorities to identify affected assets and their responsible entities. The requirement to maintain and update the register ensures that entities are held accountable for their critical infrastructure. It also provides a mechanism for the government to enforce compliance with SOCI's provisions, which can affect the overall security posture. Finally, the register is designed to be dynamic, allowing for updates as new assets are identified or as existing assets undergo changes.[43] This adaptability ensures that the resilience framework remains relevant and effective in the face of evolving threats and technological advancements. The register of CI assets under SOCI plays a crucial role in building and maintaining the digital resilience of Australia's critical infrastructure.[44]

Critical Infrastructure Risk Management Programs

The risk management program provisions in Part 2A of SOCI strengthen digital resilience by requiring responsible entities to identify hazards that could materially impact their critical infrastructure assets.[45] In conjunction with the critical infrastructure risk management program[46] (CRIMP) rules, these provisions help critical infrastructure entities understand potential threats and vulnerabilities early on.[47] Once risks are identified, SOCI mandates the development of strategies to minimise, eliminate, or mitigate these risks.[48] This means that entities are prepared to manage various types of hazards, including cyber, physical, and personnel-related threats. The risk management program must be reviewed annually and updated as new risks emerge or existing risks evolve.[49] This review process operates to ensure that the program remains relevant and effective in the face of changing threat landscapes. The program must be formally adopted by the responsible entity and maintained.[50] This formalisation strengthens the commitment to the resilience-building process. Additionally, the rules allow for the adoption of international standards and sector-specific frameworks, which helps align risk management practices with global best practices and industry-specific and sector-specific requirements.[51] There are regular reporting requirements, including annual reports approved by the governing body of the entity.[52] This ensures transparency and accountability, making it easier for regulatory bodies to monitor compliance and enforce the rules. For systems of national significance, the rules impose additional cyber security obligations, such as incident response planning, cyber security exercises, and vulnerability assessments.[53] These measures are designed to enhance the preparedness and resilience of the most interconnected critical infrastructure assets.[54] By integrating these elements, the risk management program rules under SOCI provide a robust framework for building and maintaining the resilience of Australia's critical infrastructure against a wide range of threats.

Reporting Obligations Relating to Certain Assets That Are Not Covered by a CRIMP

Part 2AA ensures that critical infrastructure assets not covered by a formal risk management program are still monitored and reported on within the SOCI framework. Responsible entities must submit an annual report for assets not covered by a critical infrastructure risk management program. If the entity has a governing body (e.g. board or council), the report must be approved by this body.[55] The annual reporting requirement helps maintain oversight and accountability, ensuring that any significant hazards and the effectiveness of mitigation actions are documented and evaluated. Coverage of these entities supports the overall goal of protecting critical infrastructure by ensuring that all relevant assets are subject to scrutiny and that responsible entities remain accountable for their security measures.[56]

Notification of Cyber Security Incidents

The notification of cyber security incidents in Part 2B of SOCI strengthens resilience by ensuring that cyber security incidents are promptly brought to the attention of relevant authorities.[57] This may result in faster mitigation of the impact of the incident and prevent further damage. Incident reports also contribute to a broader understanding of the threat landscape. By collecting data from a range of incidents, authorities can identify patterns, emerging threats, and vulnerabilities, which helps in developing more effective response strategies. Reporting requirements also foster better communication and collaboration between critical infrastructure entities and government agencies. Critical infrastructure entities and governments have indicated that this coordinated approach is crucial for a unified response to cyber threats and for sharing best practices in resilience-building.[58] The obligation to report incidents holds responsible entities accountable for their cyber security practices. This accountability is designed to improve an entity's security measures and adherence to best practices, and contributing to overall resilience. Incident reporting provides valuable feedback that can be used to refine and improve risk management programs. Learning from past incidents helps entities to better prepare for and respond to future threats. The reporting mechanism allows the regulator to monitor compliance with SOCI's provisions and take necessary actions in case of non-compliance.[59] This oversight helps critical infrastructure entities maintain a high standard of cyber security. Reporting cyber security incidents under SOCI contributes to building and maintaining the digital resilience of Australia's critical infrastructure.

Enhanced Cyber Security Obligations for Systems of National Significance

The enhanced cyber security obligations (ECSO) in Part 2C of SOCI may apply to declared Systems of National Significance (SoNS).[60] The ECSO is designed to bolster resilience through four legislative mechanisms. In the first instance, the Minister may declare a system of national significance if it meets certain criteria.[61] Systems of national significance are those systems that have interdependencies with other critical infrastructure assets, and their ongoing functioning is critical to the social, economic, defence and national security of Australia.[62] The Minister looks at what hazards are out there that could impact a SONs and then evaluates the consequences of that hazard occurring, and what it might do to stability, defence or national security.[63] Once declared a SoNS and Part 2C applies to the relevant asset, the responsible entity is required to develop and maintain comprehensive incident response plans.[64] These plans ensure that entities are prepared to respond to cyber incidents. SoNS must conduct regular cyber security exercises, which enables entities to practise their preparedness and response capabilities.[65] The exercises arguably help identify weaknesses and improve the overall readiness of the organisation to respond to cyber threats. SoNS must perform regular vulnerability assessments to identify and address potential security gaps.[66] SoNS must also provide access to system information to provide 'a near-real-time threat picture'.[67] This proactive approach can help in mitigate risks before they can be exploited by malicious actors. The provisions operate to enhance the overall security posture and facilitates a coordinated response to cyber threats.[68]

Directions by the Minister

Part 3 of the Act concerns the direction powers of the Minister of Home Affairs and Minister for Cyber Security. Under the Act, the Minister may require a reporting entity for, or an operator of, a critical infrastructure asset to do, or refrain from doing, an act or thing, if the Minister is satisfied that there is a risk of an act or omission that would be *prejudicial to security*. [69] Risks that might be considered prejudicial to security include sabotage, espionage and coercion.[70] The Minister is satisfied that such risks exist based on an ASIO adverse security assessment, which has the same meaning as in the ASIO Act 1979.[71] The Minister may give the direction only if criteria are met and certain consultation has been undertaken.[72]

Directions by the Minister under Part 3 of SOCI strengthen digital resilience in several ways. The Minister has the authority to direct critical infrastructure entities to take specific actions or refrain from certain activities if there is a risk that could be prejudicial to security.[73] This targeted intervention helps in addressing immediate threats and vulnerabilities, thereby reducing the risk of cyber incidents. The Minister's directions require consultation with various stakeholders, including state and territory leaders.[74] This fosters better coordination and collaboration between different levels of government and critical infrastructure entities.

Responding to Serious Cyber Security Incidents

The provisions for responding to serious cyber security incidents in Part 3A of SOCI strengthen digital resilience through several key mechanisms. The Minister has the authority to issue directions to critical infrastructure entities during serious cyber incidents.[75] The provision is designed to permit action to be taken to mitigate the impact of the incident. In the context of digital resilience, the Minister's power to intervene is crucial when entities are unable or unwilling to respond adequately.[76] The Minister's directions must be proportionate and necessary to respond to the incident.[77] This ensures that the response is appropriate to the severity of the threat, minimising disruption while effectively addressing the cyber threat. Directions issued must be technically capable, ensuring that the actions required can be realistically implemented by the entities.[78] The Minister can authorise the collection of information necessary to respond to the incident, which assists in understanding the scope and nature of the threat, potentially enabling more targeted and effective mitigation strategies.[79] There are various safeguards in place to prevent misuse of these powers, including requirements for proportionality and technical feasibility. Additionally, there are reporting requirements to ensure transparency and accountability in the use of these powers. The Minister exercises the powers under these provisions personally.[80] These provisions are highly intrusive. However, the provisions are designed to give the Australian Signals Directorate and any other authorised agency the ability to manage a serious cyber incident but contain appropriate safeguards.[81]

Gathering and Using Information

Part 4 of the SOCI grants the Secretary of the Department of Home Affairs significant authority to require critical infrastructure entities to provide information or documents.[82] The Secretary can compel critical infrastructure entities to provide specific information or documents if they believe it is relevant to their duties under the Act.[83] The Secretary can use or disclose this information in certain circumstances.[84] Unauthorised use or disclosure is an offence.[85] Entities cannot refuse to provide information on the grounds of self-incrimination.[86] The information obtained can be kept indefinitely and shared with a wide range of officials and agencies, including law enforcement and intelligence services.[87] A large group of officials, including Ministers, senior bureaucrats, and heads of agencies like ASIO and the Department of Foreign Affairs and Trade, can receive this information. Law enforcement bodies and oversight entities like the Ombudsman and IGIS can also access it. The information can be used to assist authorised persons in performing their functions, duties, and exercising their powers.[88] This section essentially provides the Secretary with broad powers to gather and use information from critical infrastructure entities.[89]

Enforcement

The enforcement provisions under the SOCI strengthen digital resilience by providing a reasonable and proportionate mechanism for ensuring compliance with the Act.[90] SOCI includes a range of penalties for non-compliance, such as civil penalties, enforceable undertakings, and injunctions.[91] These penalties ensure that critical infrastructure entities comply with the required cyber security standards, which contributes to overall resilience. The Act employs a graduated enforcement regime, which allows for a proportionate response to different levels of non-compliance. This flexibility ensures that enforcement actions are appropriate to the severity of the breach, fostering a culture of cooperative compliance and continuous improvement.[92] SOCI grants authorities the power to monitor and investigate compliance with its provisions. This includes monitoring for offences such as non-compliance with directions and unauthorised use or disclosure of protected information.[93] These powers help in identifying and addressing vulnerabilities promptly. The Act allows for the issuance of infringement notices for certain breaches.[94] These notices provide a mechanism for addressing minor non-compliance issues, providing entities with an opportunity to rectify their practices. The enforcement provisions operate within the framework established by the *Regulatory Powers (Standard Provisions) Act 2014* (Cth), which provides clear guidelines for compliance and enforcement by regulatory authorities covered by its remit.[95] The regulator, CISC, works to inform and guide critical infrastructure entities about their obligations and the consequences of non-compliance. The enforcement provisions promote accountability and transparency in the management of critical infrastructure. By holding entities accountable for their security practices, SOCI drives improvements in security measures and adherence to best practices.[96]

Declarations by the Minister

Declarations by the Minister under Part 6 of SOCI strengthen digital resilience by permitting the Minister to privately declare an asset as critical infrastructure if it affects national security.[97] This ensures that sensitive assets receive the necessary protection without public disclosure, reducing the risk of targeted attacks.[98] Declaring an asset as critical infrastructure or a system of national significance imposes additional security obligations on the responsible entities.[99] These enhanced measures are designed to better protect the most critical assets against cyber threats. The declaration process involves assessing the potential risks and interdependencies of critical infrastructure assets. This assessment approach helps government and responsible entities identify and mitigate risks before they can be exploited by malicious actors. The Minister's declarations require consultation with relevant stakeholders, including state and territory leaders. Consultation encourages better coordination and collaboration between different levels of government and critical infrastructure entities, enhancing the overall resilience of critical infrastructure assets.[100] The Minister has the authority to declare new assets or systems as critical infrastructure as the threat landscape evolves. This in-built flexibility makes sure that the regulatory framework remains relevant and effective in addressing emerging threats.

Miscellaneous Provisions

SOCI provides comprehensive coverage of a range of circumstances and contains provisions for ensuring its continued operation and efficacy.[101] It applies to various legal entities, including trusts, partnerships, superannuation funds, and unincorporated foreign companies.[102] This ensures that all types of legal arrangements involved in critical infrastructure are covered, preventing entities from using corporate structures to avoid compliance. The Secretary of the Department of Home Affairs has broad authority to assess critical infrastructure assets for national security risks.[103] This anticipatory assessment helps in identifying and mitigating potential threats before they can impact the infrastructure. The Secretary may delegate their powers to senior executive service (SES) officers, ensuring that there is flexibility and efficiency in the administration of the Act. However, certain powers cannot be delegated, such as responding to serious cyber incidents.[104] SOCI mandates periodic reports to Parliament, which include details on notifications, directions, information gathering, cyber incidents, and Ministerial authorisations.[105] The transparency and accountability mechanism keeps Parliament informed about the administration and implementation of the Act. SOCI requires independent reviews of its operation, including by the Independent National Security Legislation Monitor (INSLM).[106] Regular reviews provide a democratic safeguard, ensuring that the Act is continuously reviewed and assessed against its objects and operation. Under SOCI, the Minister has the authority to make rules by legislative instrument, which provides a flexible mechanism for government to adapt to technological change and evolving threats without amending SOCI.[107] The review and oversight provisions by Parliament and the INSLM provide for independent review of the SOCI regime, which provides opportunities to improve and strengthen the digital resilience of Australia's critical infrastructure.

Challenges of Securing Vital Systems in the Digital Age

The interface between SOCI and critical infrastructure security is central to digital resilience in Australia. The interplay between the two is multifaceted and involves many stakeholders, complex sectoral and cross-sectoral regulatory contexts, and the ever-present and evolving threat landscape. Arguably, SOCI has set the tone for the protection of critical infrastructure in Australia. As discussed throughout this chapter, SOCI established a comprehensive, hybrid regulatory framework that mandates critical infrastructure entities to implement risk management programs, report cyber incidents, and maintain asset registers. As a risk management framework, it seeks to be proactive in helping responsible entities identify and mitigate risks. The regulatory framework created by SOCI has stakeholder collaboration as a core function.[108] It encourages collaboration between government agencies, private sector entities, and regulatory intermediaries such as the Trusted Information Sharing Network.[109] The regulator of critical infrastructure security, the Cyber and Infrastructure Security Centre within the Department of Home Affairs, fulfils its functions by providing guidance, information and support for entities subject to SOCI.[110]

SOCI enables the government to intervene in cases of significant threats or noncompliance by critical infrastructure sectors. The 'command-and-control' provisions of the Act are considered 'last resort' powers and are intended to be used when national security and public safety are at grave risk.[111] Finally, SOCI's framework is designed to adapt to the threat landscape, which continues to be influenced by technological change, concentration in cyber security markets,[112] geopolitical tensions in the region and evolving cyber threats and incidents.

Further reforms of SOCI proposed under the 2023–2030 Cyber Security Strategy and enacted by the *Security of Critical Infrastructure and Other Legislation Amendment (Enhanced Response and Prevention) Act 2024 (Cth)* in November 2024 will extend the operation of SOCI to systems that hold business critical data and will consolidate telecommunications sector security within the SOCI regime.[113]

Conclusion

This chapter has demonstrated how the *Security of Critical Infrastructure Act* 2018 plays a pivotal role in ensuring the digital resilience of Australia's critical infrastructure. By mandating comprehensive risk management programs, incident reporting, and maintaining asset registers, SOCI fosters a 'whole-of-economy' approach to identifying and mitigating risks. The Act's hybrid regulatory framework encourages collaboration between government agencies, private sector entities and regulatory intermediaries, such as the TISN, enhancing the overall security posture of entities regulated under the Act. SOCI's provisions for government intervention in significant threats or non-compliance scenarios underscore its importance in safeguarding national security and public safety. SOCI's adaptability to evolving threats and technological changes ensures its continued relevance in the face of new challenges. As digital resilience becomes increasingly critical, the critical infrastructure security and resilience framework will hopefully provide a robust and flexible foundation for protecting Australia's essential services and systems from cyber threats.

Notes

1. NIS Cooperation Group, *EU Cybersecurity Risk Evaluation and Scenarios for the Telecommunications and Electricity Sectors* (24 July 2024) 1. 37–38; Organisation for Economic Cooperation and Development, *Digital Security and Resilience in Critical infrastructure and Essential Services* (OECD Digital Economy Paper No 281, April 2019) 9–10.
2. See e.g., Department of Home Affairs, 2023–2030 Australian Cyber Security Strategy (Strategy Document, 22 November 2023) and Department of Home Affairs, 2023–2030 Australian Cyber Security Strategy Action Plan (Document, 22 November 2023).
3. Christopher Leslie and David Kreps (eds), *Current Directions in ICT and Society: IFIP TC9 50th Anniversary Anthology*, vol 700 (Springer Nature Switzerland, 2024) <https://link.springer.com/10.1007/978-3-031-50758-8> ('*Current Directions in ICT and Society*'). 136; OECD, fn 1, 9, 25–26; Director-General of Security, *Annual Threat Assessment 2024* (Australian Security and Intelligence Organisation, 28 February 2024) <https://www.asio.gov.au/director-generals-annual-threat-assessment-2024>.
4. Robert Osei-Kyei et al., 'Critical Review of the Threats Affecting the Building of Critical Infrastructure Resilience' (2021) 60 *International Journal of Disaster Risk Reduction* 102316. 8.; Amani Ibrahim et al., 'The Challenges of Leveraging Threat Intelligence to Stop Data Breaches' (2020) 2 *Frontiers in Computer Science* 36 <https://www.frontiersin.org/article/10.3389/fcomp.2020.00036/full>, 4.
5. Ibrahim et al (n 4), 3–4.
6. Anthony Bergin, *Critical foundations: Australia's infrastructure and national resilience* (Australian Strategic Policy Institute Policy Analysis No 73, 28 January 2011) 1–2; see also Department of Home Affairs, 'Critical Infrastructure Resilience Strategy'.
7. Nikolas Rose and Filippa Lentzos, 'Making us resilient: responsible citizens for uncertain times' in Susanna Trnka and Catherine Trundle (eds) *Competing Responsibilities: The Ethics and Politics of Contemporary Life* (Duke University Press, 2017) 27, 35; Gary E. Marchant and Yvonne A. Stevens, 'Resilience: A New Tool in the Risk Governance Toolbox for Emerging Technologies' (2017) 51(1) U.C. Davis Law Review 233, 244.
8. Kate O'Donnell, 'Critical Infrastructure Resilience: Resilience Thinking in Australia's Federal Critical Infrastructure Protection Policy' (2020) 1(3) *Salus* 21–23.

9. NIS Cooperation Group (n 1), 2, 10.
10. Ibid.; See also, Cyber and Infrastructure Security Centre, *Critical Infrastructure Resilience Strategy* (Strategy, February 2023) 5–6.
11. Explanatory Memorandum, Security Legislation Amendment (Critical Infrastructure) Bill 2020.
12. Julia Black, 'Constructing and Contesting Legitimacy and Accountability in Polycentric Regulatory Regimes' (2008) 2 *Regulation and Governance* 137, 139.
13. Robert Baldwin, 'Regulation: After Command and Control' in Hawkins, K. (ed) *The Human Face of Law: Essays in Honour of Donald Harris* (1997) Oxford: Oxford University Press, 7.
14. The Hon. Clare O'Neil, 'Address to National Security College' (*Speech*, 9 April 2024).
15. O'Donnell (n 8), 14.
16. Department of Home Affairs, Critical Resilience Strategy (February 2023, Australian Government), 4.
17. Australian Government, 'Critical Infrastructure' (Web Page, Australian National Security, 22 September 2024) https://www.nationalsecurity.gov.au/protect-your-business/critical-infrastructure/overview. See also: https://www.homeaffairs.gov.au/about-us/our-portfolios/national-security/security-coordination/critical-infrastructure-resilience.
18. See e.g., Christer Pursiainen and Eero Kytömaa, 'From European Critical Infrastructure Protection to the Resilience of European Critical Entities: What Does It Mean?' (2023) 8(sup1) *Sustainable and Resilient Infrastructure* 85 <https://www.tandfonline.com/doi/full/10.1080/23789689.2022.2128562> ('From European Critical Infrastructure Protection to the Resilience of European Critical Entities').
19. The Hon. Tony Bourke, 'Protecting Australia's critical infrastructure' (*Media Release*, 5 November 2024).
20. See Part 2A of the *Security of Critical Infrastructure Act 2018* (Cth) and the Security of Critical Infrastructure (Critical infrastructure risk management program) Rules (LIN 23/006) 2023.
21. For example, section 8, Security of Critical Infrastructure (Critical infrastructure risk management program) Rules (LIN 23/006) 2023.
22. See e.g., Department of Home Affairs, *Protecting Critical Infrastructure and Systems of National Significance* (29 March 2021).
23. Cyber and Infrastructure Security Centre, 'Security of Critical Infrastructure Act 2018: General Guidance for Critical Infrastructure Assets (Guidance Material, February 2023).
24. Michiel Heldeweg, 'Hybrid regulation as a legal design challenge', in A. L. B. Colombi Clacchi, M. A. Heldeweg, B. M. J. van der Meulen, & A. R. Neerhof (Eds.), *Law & Governance - Beyond the Public-Private Law Divide?* (2013) 9(9) *Governance & Recht* 107–139.
25. Mubarak Banisakher, Marwan Omar and Wade Clare, 'Critical Infrastructure - Perspectives on the Role of Government in Cybersecurity' (2019) 7(1) *Journal of Computer Sciences and Applications* 37, 41; Matthew Warren, 'Australia Critical Infrastructure Protection: A Twenty-Year Journey' (2021) 20(4) *Journal of Information Warfare* 45, 46.
26. Warren (n 25), 46.
27. Security of Critical Infrastructure Bill 2017, Explanatory Memorandum, 5.
28. Security of Critical Infrastructure Bill 2017, Explanatory Memorandum, 5.
29. *Security of Critical Infrastructure Act 2018* (Cth) pt 6 div 2 ss51–52.
30. *Security of Critical Infrastructure Act 2018* (Cth) pt 2A.
31. *Security of Critical Infrastructure Act 2018* (Cth) pt 2B and pt 3A.
32. *Security of Critical Infrastructure Act 2018* (Cth) pt 2C. See also Cyber and Infrastructure Security Centre, *The Enhanced Cyber Security Framework* (CISC Fact Sheet, February 2022).
33. *Security of Critical Infrastructure Act 2018* (Cth) pt 3A and pt 4.
34. See for example, *Security of Critical Infrastructure Act 2018* (Cth) pt 3A div 2 ss35AB(d).
35. *Security of Critical Infrastructure Act 2018* (Cth) pt 1 div 1 s3.

36. *Security of Critical Infrastructure Act 2018* (Cth) pt 1 div 1 ss3 (a)–(e).
37. *Security of Critical Infrastructure Act 2018* (Cth) pt 1 div 1 ss3 (c).
38. *Security of Critical Infrastructure Act 2018* (Cth) pt 1 div 1 ss3 (d).
39. *Security of Critical Infrastructure Act 2018* (Cth) pt 1 div 1 ss3 (e).
40. Commonwealth, Hansard, House of Representatives, 10 December 2020, 11262 (The Hon. Peter Dutton, Security Legislation Amendment (Critical Infrastructure) Bill 2020—Second Reading).
41. Cyber and Infrastructure Security Centre, *Register of Critical Infrastructure Assets* Guidance (Guidance Material, September 2022), 2.
42. Cyber and Infrastructure Security Centre, *Register of Critical Infrastructure Assets* Guidance (Guidance Material, September 2022), 2–4.
43. Cyber and Infrastructure Security Centre, *Register of Critical Infrastructure Assets* Guidance (Guidance Material, September 2022), 4.
44. Cyber and Infrastructure Security Centre, *Register of Critical Infrastructure Assets* Guidance (Guidance Material, September 2022), 2.
45. *Security of Critical Infrastructure Act 2018* (Cth) pt 2A.
46. The CIRMP is a written program. Section 30AH set out the details that a risk management program needs to contain, including a rule-making provision. Section 30AH goes on to detail matters that the rules may specify, including ensuring personnel security.
47. See Critical Infrastructure (Critical infrastructure risk management program) Rules (LIN 23/006) 2023.
48. For example, the rules contain the requirements for a critical infrastructure risk management program, including the identification of material risk, processes for managing the risks, which are broken into 'all hazards', 'cyber and information security hazards', 'personnel hazards', 'supply chain hazards', and 'physical security hazards and natural hazards.
49. *Security of Critical Infrastructure Act 2018* (Cth) pt 2A s30AE.
50. *Security of Critical Infrastructure Act 2018* (Cth) pt 2A s30AC.
51. *Security of Critical Infrastructure Act 2018* (Cth) pt 2A and Critical Infrastructure (Critical infrastructure risk management program) Rules (LIN 23/006) 2023.
52. *Security of Critical Infrastructure Act 2018* (Cth) pt 2A s30AG.
53. *Security of Critical Infrastructure Act 2018* (Cth) pt 2C.
54. Commonwealth, Hansard, House of Representatives, 10 December 2020, 11262 (The Hon. Peter Dutton, Security Legislation Amendment (Critical Infrastructure) Bill 2020—Second Reading).
55. *Security of Critical Infrastructure Act 2018* (Cth) ss30AP—30AQ.
56. *Security of Critical Infrastructure Act 2018* (Cth) pt 2AA.
57. Revised Explanatory Memorandum, Security Legislation Amendment (Critical Infrastructure) Bill 2020, para 503-505, 91–92.
58. Revised Explanatory Memorandum, Security Legislation Amendment (Critical Infrastructure) Bill 2020, para 503, 91.
59. Revised Explanatory Memorandum, Security Legislation Amendment (Critical Infrastructure) Bill 2020, para 531, 97.
60. Systems of National Significance are declared by the Minister for Cyber Security under the *Security of Critical Infrastructure Act 2018* (Cth) pt 6A.
61. *Security of Critical Infrastructure Act 2018* (Cth) pt 6A div 2.
62. Explanatory Memorandum, Security Legislation Amendment (Critical Infrastructure) Bill 2020, para 1174, 1177–1190.
63. *Security of Critical Infrastructure Act 2018* (Cth) pt 6A div 2.
64. *Security of Critical Infrastructure Act 2018* (Cth) pt 2C div 2.
65. *Security of Critical Infrastructure Act 2018* (Cth) pt 2C div 3.
66. *Security of Critical Infrastructure Act 2018* (Cth) pt 2C div 4.
67. *Security of Critical Infrastructure Act 2018* (Cth) pt 2C div 5.
68. Cyber and Infrastructure Security Centre, *The Enhanced Cyber Security Obligations Framework* (CISC Factsheet, May 2022); see also Explanatory Memorandum, Security Legislation Amendment (Critical Infrastructure) Bill 2020, para 673–674.

69. Security of Critical Infrastructure Bill 2017, Explanatory Memorandum para 34–41.
70. Security of Critical Infrastructure Bill 2017, Explanatory Memorandum para 22.
71. Security of Critical Infrastructure Bill 2017, Explanatory Memorandum para 36.
72. Security of Critical Infrastructure Bill 2017, Explanatory Memorandum para 34–41.
73. *Security of Critical Infrastructure Act 2018* (Cth) pt 3 div 2 s32.
74. Security of Critical Infrastructure Bill 2017, Explanatory Memorandum para 37.
75. *Security of Critical Infrastructure Act 2018* pt 3 div 2 s 33. *Security of Critical Infrastructure Act 2018* (Cth) pt 3A.
76. Security Legislation Amendment (Critical Infrastructure) Bill 2020, Explanatory Memorandum, para 17–22.
77. See e.g., Security Legislation Amendment (Critical Infrastructure) Bill 2020, Explanatory Memorandum, para 645.
78. See e.g., Security Legislation Amendment (Critical Infrastructure) Bill 2020, Explanatory Memorandum, para 787, 791.
79. *Security of Critical Infrastructure Act 2018* pt 3A div 2 s35AB.
80. *Security of Critical Infrastructure Act 2018* pt 3A div 2 s35AJ.
81. Security Legislation Amendment (Critical Infrastructure) Bill 2020, Explanatory Memorandum, para 904.
82. *Security of Critical Infrastructure Act 2018* (Cth) pt 4 div 2.
83. *Security of Critical Infrastructure Act 2018* (Cth) pt 4 div 2 s 37.
84 *Security of Critical Infrastructure Act 2018* (Cth) pt 4 div 2 sub div A.
85. *Security of Critical Infrastructure Act 2018* (Cth) pt 4 div 2 sub div B.
86. *Security of Critical Infrastructure Act 2018* (Cth) pt 4 div 2 s40.
87. *Security of Critical Infrastructure Act 2018* (Cth) pt 4 div 3.
88. *Security of Critical Infrastructure Act 2018* (Cth) pt 4 div 3.
89. Security of Critical Infrastructure Bill 2017, Explanatory Memorandum para 293–297.
90. *Security of Critical Infrastructure Act 2018* (Cth) pt 5.
91. Security of Critical Infrastructure Bill 2017, Explanatory Memorandum para 86.
92. Security of Critical Infrastructure Bill 2017, Explanatory Memorandum para 338.
93. *Security of Critical Infrastructure Act 2018* (Cth) pt 5.
94. *Security of Critical Infrastructure Act 2018* (Cth) pt 5 div 4.
95. *Security of Critical Infrastructure Act 2018* (Cth) pt 5 div 3.
96. Security of Critical Infrastructure Bill 2017, Explanatory Memorandum para 342.
97. *Security of Critical Infrastructure Act 2018* (Cth) pt 6.
98. Security of Critical Infrastructure Bill 2017, Explanatory Memorandum para 354–367.
99. *Security of Critical Infrastructure Act 2018* (Cth) pt 6 div 2.
100. *Security of Critical Infrastructure Act 2018* (Cth) pt 6 div 2 s51A.
101. *Security of Critical Infrastructure Act 2018* (Cth) pt 7.
102. *Security of Critical Infrastructure Act 2018* (Cth) pt 7 div 2.
103. *Security of Critical Infrastructure Act 2018* (Cth) pt 7 div 3 s57.
104. *Security of Critical Infrastructure Act 2018* (Cth) pt 7 div 3 s59.
105. *Security of Critical Infrastructure Act 2018* (Cth) pt 7 div 4.
106. *Security of Critical Infrastructure Act 2018* (Cth) pt 7 div 4 s60A.
107. *Security of Critical Infrastructure Act 2018* (Cth) pt 7 div 4 s61.
108. Commonwealth, Hansard, House of Representatives, 10 December 2020, 11262 (The Hon. Peter Dutton, Security Legislation Amendment (Critical Infrastructure) Bill 2020—Second Reading).
109. Cyber and Infrastructure Security Centre, *Trusted Information Sharing Network* (Webpage, 6 March 2024).
110. Cyber and Infrastructure Security Centre, *About us—our mission* (Webpage, 6 March 2024).
111. Security of Critical Infrastructure Bill 2020, Revised Explanatory Memorandum, paras 585–586, 589, 601, 617, 626, 628, 632, 671, and 770.
112. See e.g., Dan Geer et al., *Cyberinsecurity: The Cost of Monopoly* (24 September 2003).

113. Department of Home Affairs, 2023–2030 *Australian Cyber Security Strategy: Legislative Reforms* (Consultation Paper, 18 December 2023) 30, 54. The author notes that the *Security of Critical Infrastructure and Other Legislation Amendment (Enhanced Response and Prevention) Act 2024* received Royal Assent on 29 November 2024.

Susanne L. Lloyd-Jones is a Cyber Security CRC Post Doctoral Fellow based in the School of Law, Society and Criminology at the UNSW Faculty of Law and Justice. Her professional background spans academia, government, industry, and private practice. Susanne's research focuses on cyber security law and policy, emerging technology, critical infrastructure regulation, law and technological change, and national security regulation in complex industry sectors, such as telecommunications, broadcasting, news media, digital platforms, and cloud services. Susanne's current work focuses on whether Australia's legal and policy settings are sufficient to support the move to quantum-resilient encryption. Susanne's research seeks to apply ideas from public law, regulatory theory, and political economy to improve understanding of the national security obligations of regulated industries and develop effective legal and policy responses to problems posed by emerging technologies. Susanne has presented her research at domestic and international conferences, including at CyberCon (2022), PlatGov (2023), the University of Adelaide's RUMLAE Digital Resilience Conference (2023) and at the 11th Annual Governance of Emerging Technology and Science Conference at Arizona State University (2024).

People Power—A Resilience Work Force

Samuel White and Socrates Giatrakos

Abstract This chapter takes a unique approach by exploring the role of intelligence services and Internet Referral Units in building resilience. This chapter sheds light on how military and intelligence agencies can play a pivotal role in countering digital threats. Utilising case studies from across the globe—open source, but often overlooked—the authors examine the strategies and tactics employed by these entities to combat disinformation and cyber-attacks, offering readers a glimpse into the world of cybersecurity from a military perspective. As readers delve into this chapter, they will gain a deeper understanding of the unconventional methods used to bolster digital resilience and protect national security interests.

Introduction

The Internet has become an indispensable incident of everyday life, and its utility is undeniable. However, with its constant growth also comes constant misuse.[1] Foreign interference operations (IOs) can leverage the ubiquity of the Internet in order to deliver personally tailored, micro-targeted messages to individuals in their homes.[2] And they are not theoretical. This is the real threat that the digital age has brought: not the death and disruption that for nearly 25 years been hypothesised,[3] but the ability to connect to individuals, insidiously, at any time of the day.[4] This was best recognised by Chief of the Russian General Staff, Valery Gerasimov, who opined as early as 2013 that:

> The very rules of war have changed. The role of non-military means of achieving political and strategic goals has grown, and in many cases, they have exceeded the power of force of weapons in their effectiveness... In North Africa, we witnessed the use of technologies for influencing state structures and the population with the help of information networks.[5]

S. White (✉) · S. Giatrakos
University of Adelaide, Adelaide, Australia
e-mail: Samuel.white@adelaide.edu.au

S. Giatrakos
e-mail: socrates.giatrakos@adelaide.edu.au

D. Stephens et al. (eds.), *Digital Resilience*,
https://doi.org/10.1007/978-981-97-9746-2_8

The changing nature of warfare has led, formally and informally, to practitioners of the Profession of Arms to claim that grey zone operations unfairly exploit the gaps between peace and war, exploiting the vulnerabilities of Western democracy—free speech—in an unacceptable manner.

How are States to respond? One course of action is to follow other States in attempting to foster social resilience.[6] Promoting social resilience to interference operations has been the focus of many States. For example, there has been increased focus in primary and secondary education on identification of IOs (Sweden);[7] the establishment of truth verification bodies (Argentina);[8] and the use of military personnel to report suspected interference operations and to write comments, as directed by their chain of command (United Kingdom, Israel).[9] This chapter looks to the latter example as a potential model—so-called Internet Referral Units (IRUs). It does so to highlight that the ultimate form of resilience comes from people and people power.

Internet Referral Units

Many IRUs operate differently across the globe, so it is difficult to draw clear lines. However, by looking at how they operate in different jurisdictions, some lines can be drawn. Many different jurisdictions have IRUs including (1) The United Kingdom, (2) The European Union, (3) France and (4) Israel.[10] A recent controversy regarding Israel's IRU was heard in the Israeli Supreme Court[11] and brought Israel's IRU's, and IRU'S generally, into the public domain.[12] From the above examples, the authors argues that IRUs can be described as operating based on the following methods: (1) a voluntary track; (2) a statutory track; and (3) a mandatory track. However, in our view, it is the voluntary track which is the true epitome of an IRU.

Voluntary Enforcement Track

In September 2015, a cyber-enforcement unit (Israeli IRU) was created in Israel from the need to "confront crime and terror in the cyberspace",[13] and to "coordinate efforts in dealing with crime and terrorism in cyberspace".[14] The unit's focus is to reduce the harm and dangers that arise from crimes that are perpetrated online.[15] To reduce crime in the cyberspace, the Israeli IRU operates through two enforcement tracks: (1) the voluntary enforcement track and (2) the statutory enforcement track.[16]

Under the voluntary enforcement track the Israeli IRU concentrates its efforts on referring content to "network platform operators".[17] Network platform operators include: (1) online social networks (e.g. Facebook), (2) online search engines (e.g. Google) and (3) providers of hosting services as defined in the work procedures.[18] These online operators, in most cases, establish conditions of use and "community rules".[19] For example, Facebook does not allow users to use their services for a purpose "that is unlawful, misleading, discriminatory or fraudulent".[20] In general, network platform operators have the power to, among other things, restrict access to content that infringes their community rules.[21] To enforce these rules, network platform operators, in most cases, allow any person to report content directly to them.[22] Network platform operators, at their own discretion, then determine whether said content violates their rules and whether it should be taken down.[23] This process is referred to as a "Notice and Take Down" mechanism,[24] and appears to be derived from procedures stipulated in US Copyright laws.[25] The Israeli IRU's function is to report content through this process.

Before reporting any online publication to a network platform operator the Israeli IRU considers whether the content: (1) constitutes an offence under Israeli Law, (2) violates the network platform operator's community rules and other factors such as the circulation of the publication, its severity, the date of publication the viral potential and the likely interpretation by those who receive it, and (3) on balance with freedom of expression and access to information vis-à-vis the constitutional right to privacy, dignity and the reputation of the subject of the publication that it is in the public interest to make the report.[26] These factors are required to be considered pursuant to the Israeli IRU "work procedures",[27] (at the time of the *Adalah* judgement the work procedures have not been published).[28] The voluntary enforcement track may thus be described as follows: upon notice of an online publication that the Israeli IRU believes should not be online (on balance of the above factors) the Israeli IRU reports the content to the network platform operator and requests, at the "complete" discretion of the network platform operator,[29] for the content to be taken down.

Another model is the UK's Counter Terrorism Internet Referral Unit ("CTIRU"), which was established in 2010,[30] and is the first IRU.[31] The CTIRU has a primary focus on referring "terrorist content", which includes content that breaches UK terrorism legislation,[32] rather than mandatory removal. This was confirmed when Mr John Haynes stated that "[a]ll referrals are assessed by CTIRU against UK terrorism legislation (Terrorism Act 2000 and 2006). Those that breach this legislation are referred to industry for removal".[33] However, it has also been noted that the CTIRU "refers content that they assess as contravening UK terrorism legislation or company terms and conditions to Communication Service Providers (CSPs) for removal".[34] Although contradictory statements have been made as to whether the CTIRU focuses on terrorist content and content that breaches Internet companies community rules or just terrorist content, it does appear that the main focus is on terrorist content.[35]

Additionally, while the CTIRU uses the voluntary enforcement mechanism to remove content (as shown above), the CTIRU also has a *sui generis* method of enforcement. Sections 1 and 2 of the *Terrorism Act* 2006 (UK) provide criminal offences for those who, among other things, encourage or disseminate terrorist activity.[36] There is a defence for the offences stipulated in ss 1 and 2 if it can be shown that the relevant person did not "endorse" the publication.[37] However, a constable can require someone, pursuant to s 3 of the *Terrorism Act* 2006 (UK), to take down online content within two working days.[38] If the relevant person does not take the online content down within two working days (without a reasonable excuse), it is taken that the relevant person "endorsed" the online content,[39] removing the defence for the offences. This could lead to criminal liability being imposed on "relevant persons" who do not comply with the constables' request to remove online content. Although this power seems quite broad, it has never been formally used (as of 2018).[40]

A final model is the European model. Established in 2015,[41] the European Union Internet Referral Unit ('EU IRU') is a unit within Europol.[42] Inspired by the work of the CTIRU, the EU passed regulation 2016/794, which came into effect on 1 May 2017, to govern the EU IRU and Europol generally.[43] Europol was designed, among other things, to assist member states of the European Union to refer content to "online service providers" for their "voluntary consideration of the compatibility of the referred Internet content with their own terms and condition".[44] One of the key functions of the EU IRU is to give effect to this requirement.[45] So, how does the EU IRU operate?

The EU IRU gathers relevant content through open-source collection, or through referral by EU Member States or third parties with their own IRUs or open-source scanning capabilities (but third parties must have operational cooperation agreements with Europol).[46] All content is assessed by a human analyst or translator and flagged before being referred.[47]

The EU IRU has a focus on terrorist-related content, in particular content from the Islamic State and Al-Qaeda, though it is capable of assessing terrorist-related content from any organisation on the United Nations Security Council Sanctions List.[48] However, any form of terrorist-related content, prior to being referred, is evaluated against the offences set out in Council Framework Decision 2008/919/JHA82 on combatting terrorism.[49]

While the EU IRU has a focus on terrorist-related content, it is not strictly limited to this type of content. Europol's purpose is to prevent and combat, among other things, crime and terrorism, "as listed in Annex I" of the Europol Regulations.[50] Annex I contains various different crimes, from "terrorism" to "motor vehicle crime", and thus the EU IRU potentially has a wide net of content that it can refer.[51] However, based on its Transparency Report the EU IRU appears to focus its resources on terrorist and illegal smuggling content.[52] After undergoing the above process, the content is then referred for "voluntary assessment … against [the network platform operators] own terms and conditions".[53]

Statutory Enforcement Track

Under the statutory enforcement track, the Israeli IRU applies to a District Court judge for an order instructing provider of access, searches and storage of content on the Internet to remove or restrict access to said content.[54] The orders are made pursuant to "Authorities for the Prevention of Committing Crimes through use of an Internet Site Law, 5777-2017",[55] a validly enacted Israeli law. This approach according to the court is the "classic view" of criminal enforcement whereby a prosecutor applies to a court, and the court interprets the law and makes appropriate orders.[56] However, in the view of the authors, this is not the epitome of an IRU.

Mandatory Track

Equally, in 2015 France started granting its own IRU power, the office became officially known as the *L'Office Central de Lutte contre la Criminalité liée aux Technologies de l'Information et de la Communication* ("OCLCTIC").[57] The French government have taken a strong stance towards terrorist content. Following a decree, the Ministry of the Interior can demand that content be removed within forty-eight hours, and if it is not removed then the French government will block the content.[58] Additionally, records indicate that the OCLCTIC has made demands for online content to be removed within 24 hours.[59] The authors shall refer to this method of enforcement as the "mandatory enforcement track". Due to the immense power, the OCLCTIC has been conferred and the unit has a supervisor called the Commission Nationale de l'Informatique et des Libertés ("CNIL").[60] When the IRU files a request for online content to be removed, the request is also sent to the CNIL.[61] If the CNIL does not believe that the content should be removed, they can require that the request be withdrawn.[62] If the IRU disagrees with a decision made by the CNIL, the IRU can seek a judicial review of the decision.[63] The courts almost always side with the IRU, noting that the first successful judicial review made by CNIL was not until February 2019.[64] This method of enforcement is the mandatory track.

Lastly, the powers of the E-Safety Commissioner must be considered. Following concerns relating to cyber-bullying material affecting Australians online,[65] the federal parliament passed the *Online Safety Act 2021* (Cth) ('OS Act'),[66] which replaced the *Enhancing Online Safety Act 2015* (Cth).[67] Pursuant to Parts 5, 6, 7 and 9 of the OS Act, the E-Safety Commissioner is empowered to issue a "removal notice",[68] and under Part 8 the E-Safety Commissioner may issue a "blocking notice". A removal notice can be issued by the E-Safety Commissioner against, depending on the provision, an "end-user", a "hosting service provider" and a "provider of a service" requiring said persons to take down the relevant content within 24 hours after the notice has been given to them.[69] However, a person must make a complaint to the E-Safety Commissioner and the provider of the service before the E-Safety Commissioner is empowered to issue a removal notice.[70] Conversely, a complaint is not required to be made to the E-Safety Commissioner or the relevant provider before a blocking notice may be issued.[71] Confusingly, a removal notice may also be issued to remove "class 1 material" and "class 2 material", but no complaint needs to be made to the E-Safety Commissioner or the service provider.[72] Failure to comply with a removal notice, blocking notice, link deletion notice, app removal notice and remedial notice is a civil penalty, and the E-Safety Commissioner may apply to the relevant Court seeking enforcement of the civil penalty and other remedies.[73]

The E-Safety Commissioner is also empowered to issue a "blocking request".[74] Unlike removal notices, blocking notices, link deletion notices, app removal notices and remedial notices, a blocking request is "voluntary".[75] Failing to comply with a blocking request is not a civil penalty. Similarly to IRUs from other jurisdictions, it appears that the blocking request is intended to bring the relevant material to the provider for them to consider removing at their discretion. This power is much more akin to the "voluntary track". Of course, failure to comply with a blocking request could mean that the E-Safety Commissioner will issue a blocking notice, which is mandatory.[76] Blocking notices and blocking requests can only be issued in relation to "abhorrent violent conduct".[77] The decisions of the E-Safety Commissioner can be reviewed internally[78] and by the Administrative Review Tribunal.[79]

Compared to other jurisdictions, the power of the E-Safety Commissioner is quite comprehensive. The OCA Act provides a clear statutory basis for the referral and removal of online content. There are also provisions which permit affected parties to seek reviews of decisions made by the E-Safety Commissioner. However, unlike other jurisdictions, the power of the E-Safety Commissioner is quite clearly not voluntary. Even though the E-Safety Commissioner may issue formal warnings[80]and blocking requests,[81] there is always the looming threat that the E-Safety Commissioner will issue a mandatory notice requiring the relevant provider to remove said content. Accordingly, in our view, the E-Safety Commissioner is not an IRU in the true sense.

Resilience of People Power

IRUs are a viable model to promote resilience through people power. They allow States to go from being passive to active in the information space and within the cyberdomain. This is fundamental to basic deterrence theory and forms the key pillar for Swedish counter-information operations.[82] Resilience can be built from improving identification of misinformation and disinformation at schools, through to more open discussions around national security.[83]

IRUs need to balance the longer-term impacts of secrecy on public trust and resilience. Principles-based attribution of responsibility for these activities can blunt their impact. It can position the government as an "honest broker" and minimise the confusion and mistrust engendered by future cyber-attacks and disinformation campaigns. Multilateral attribution statements can mitigate the risk that named states will retaliate with diplomatic or economic punishment, but are not always possible. Australia should accelerate efforts to develop common, public frameworks among like-minded for identifying and attributing malign activities. These can act as external benchmarks which support the legitimacy of attribution statements.

As foreshadowed, in the interwar period, airpower strategists theorised that a decisive airstrike on a target's civilian infrastructure would cause political paralysis and social chaos, leading "stricken civilians" to quickly demand that their government capitulate.[84] These theories were not evidence-based and reflected classist assumptions about the emotional susceptibility of the body politic. Although misguided, they inspired mass bombings of cities and untold human suffering. Today, there is a need to ensure we do not give our adversaries the impression that people are Australia's soft underbelly. Showing that the government trusts the public to engage in nuanced debate about the threat environment and response options is one way to do this. Similarly, establishing and signalling that we have processes for trusted government messaging about interference and coercion can reduce the perceived benefits to adversaries of targeting the social realm. This, in turn, can have a deterrence-by-denial effect, reducing the appeal of these tactics to adversary.

Conclusion

IRUs are openly acknowledged to operate in a variety of jurisdictions including France,[85] the United Kingdom,[86] the European Union[87] and Israel.[88] These jurisdictions operate in different manners. Some, like the United Kingdom and France, have a statutory basis.[89] Others, such as Israel and the European Union, utilise governmental employees to search for content that may be in breach of the terms of service of service providers (like Facebook and Twitter). In Israel the IRU has been labelled an "Iron Dome of Truth".[90] The counter-IO tactic in Israel utilises its diaspora, connecting pro-Israeli citizens and military in a civic-military centre to conduct *hasbara*—"explaining". Individuals are directed through a smartphone application that paired users with different missions, including writing positive reviews of pro-Israeli celebrities or reporting certain material. The IRUs then refer that content to the service provider for their discretion as to whether they remove the content.

The Iron Dome of Truth has been noted for its effectiveness, "organized but crowd-sourced, directed but distributed".[91] The Israeli model has an added benefit for Australian use, as being private referrals to private social media companies, for breaches of private policies, the implied freedom of political communication is not likely triggered. While it is unclear whether the implied freedom applies to executive power (as well as legislative power),[92] Israeli jurisdiction would suggest no issues of similar constitutional provisions are triggered (which is clearly not binding but persuasive).[93] It remains a viable, workable and increasingly attractive solution to build resilience online for a State.

Notes

1. See, e.g.: Kit Burden et al, 'Cyber Crime – A New Breed of Criminal?' (2003) 19(3) *Computer Law & Security Review* 222; Bhavna Bora, 'Exploring and analyzing Internet crimes and their behaviours' (2016) 7 *Perspectives in Science* 540; Matt Eddolls, 'Making cybercrime prevention the highest priority' [2016] 8 (Summer) *Network Security* 5.
2. Foreign interference operations are 'covert, coercive or corrupt activities' against a State for the purpose of advancing the actor's interests—see Attorney-General's Department 2019, *Foreign Influence Transparency Scheme: Factsheet 2* (Factsheet No 2, February 2019) <https://www.ag.gov.au/sites/default/files/2020-03/influence-versus-interference.pdf>.
3. Alvin Toffler, *The Third Wave* (William Morrow, 1980); Edward Waltz, *Information Warfare—Principles and Operations* (Artech House, 1st ed, 1998). There are only two known instances of physical destruction from a cyber-attack – the destruction caused by Stuxnet, and apparent

damage caused to a Germany blast furnace would appear the only two. Several major cyber-attacks, most notably at Saudi Aramco and Sony, have rendered computers inoperable, but that was as a result of hard-to-reverse changes in software, not damaged hardware.

4. The use of information as resource, environment and weapon within the 21st century is an emergent capability 'still seeking both language and concepts to become normative for discussions of warfare. See generally Edward Morgan and Marcus Thompson, 'Information Warfare - An Emergent Australian Defence Force Capability' (Discussion Paper No 3, Centre for Strategic & International Studies, October 2018) 6.
5. Valery Gerasimov, 'The Value of Science in Prediction' Military-Industrial Kurier, 27 February 2013).
6. Giulio Douhet, *The Command of the Air,* trans. Dino Ferrari (New York: Coward-McCann Inc., 1942) 188.
7. Peter Roudik et al., *Initiatives to Counter Fake News in Selected Countries* (Library of Congress, 2019) 104.
8. Ibid 38.
9. Peter Singer & Emerson Brooking, *LikeWar* (Mifflin Harcourt, 2018) 198.
10. See generally Rabea Eghbariah and Amre Metwally, 'Informal Governance: Internet Referral Units and The Rise of State Interpretation of Terms of Service' (2021) 23 *Yale Journal of Law & Technology* 542.
11. HCJ 7846/19 *Adalah – The Legal Center for Arab Minority Rights in Israel v. Israeli State Attorney – Cyber Unit* (April. 12, 2021) ('*Adalah*').
12. See Generally Daphane Keller, 'Lawfare', *When Platforms Do the State's Bidding, Who Is Accountable? Not the Government, Says Israel's Supreme Court* (Web Page 6 August 2022) Lawfare <https://www.lawfareblog.com/when-platforms-do-states-bidding-who-accountable-not-government-says-israels-supreme-court>.
13. *Adalah* (n xi) [3].
14. Eghbarish and Metwally (n x) 580 quoting Ministry of Justice, 'The Office of the State Attorney', *About the Cyber Unit* (Web page, 11 May 2021) <https://www.gov.il/en/Departments/General/cyber-about>.
15. *Adalah* (n xi) [3].
16. Ibid; See also Eghbarish and Metwally (n x) 580 quoting Ministry of Justice, *Cyber Unit 2016 Annual Report 4* (Annual Report No 4, 2017).
17. *Adalah* (n xi) [7].
18. Ibid.
19. Ibid [8] citing Jack M Balkin, 'Free Speech is a Triangle' 118(7) *Columbia Law Review* 2011.
20. *Adalah* (n xi) [8]; See also Facebook, *Terms of Service* (Web page, 26 July 2022) <https://www.facebook.com/terms.php>.
21. *Adalah* (n xi) [8].
22. Ibid, See State Attorney's Office, 'Cyber', *Report Offensive Content* (Web page, 5 December 2018) <https://www.gov.il/he/Departments/General/cyber-report>.
23. *Adalah* (n xi) [10].
24. Ibid [8].
25. US Copyright Office, *Section 512 of Title 17: Resources on Online Service Provider Safe Harbors and Notice-and-Takedown System* (Web page) <https://www.copyright.gov/512/#:~:text=Congress%20created%20the%20notice%2Dand,to%20have%20the%20works%20removed>.
26. *Adalah* (n xi) [11].
27. Ibid [8].
28. Ibid [12].
29. See Brian Chang, 'From Internet Referral Units to International Agreements: Censorship of The Internet by The UK And EU' (2018) 49(49.1) *Columbia Human Rights Law Review* 114, 117: there is immense social pressure on network platform operators to take-down content that has been reported by government agencies, so it is not at their "complete" discretion per se.

30. Counter Terrorism Policing, *'#Justicetogether Week: Counter Terrorism Internet Referral Unit* (Web Page, 28 July 2022) <https://www.counterterrorism.police.uk/justicetogether-counter-terrorism-internet-referral-unit/>.
31. See Eghbarish and Metwally (n x) 570.
32. See: Counter Terrorism Policing, *Together, We're Tackling Online Terrorism* (Web page, 19 December 2018) <https://www.counterterrorism.police.uk/together-were-tackling-online-terrorism/>.
33. Eghbarish and Metwally (n x) 570 citing UK Parliament, *Counter-Terrorism Question for Home Office* (UIN 30893, 14 March 2016) < https://questions-statements.parliament.uk/written-questions/detail/2016-03-14/30893>.
34. United Kingdom, *Parliamentary Debates*, House of Lords, 12 July 2016, vol 772, col 8 (Lord Ahmad); See also: Chang (n xxix) 290; Eghbarish and Metwally (n x) 570.
35. See generally: Home Department, *CONTEST The United Kingdom's Strategy for Countering Terrorism: Annual Report for 2015* (Cm 9310, 2015); Counter Terrorism Policing, *Together, We're Tackling Online Terrorism* (Web page, 19 December 2018) <https://www.counterterrorism.police.uk/together-were-tackling-online-terrorism/>.
36. Chang (n xxix) 126; *Terrorism Act* 2006 (UK) ss 1 and 2.
37. *Terrorism Act* 2006 (UK) ss 1, 2.
38. Ibid s 3(2).
39. Ibid.
40. Chang (n xxix) 127.
41. Europol, 'EU Internet Referral Unit EU IRU', *Monitoring terrorism* online (Web Page, 28 July 2022) <https://www.europol.europa.eu/about-europol/european-counter-terrorism-centre-ectc/eu-internet-referal-unit-eu-iru>.
42. Ibid.
43. Chang (n xxix) 134 citing Regulation (EU) 2016/794 of the European Parliament and of the Council of 11 May 2016 on the European Union Agency for Law Enforcement Cooperation (Europol) and replacing and repealing Council Decisions 2009/371/JHA, 2009/934/JHA, 2009/935/JHA, 2009/936/JHA and 2009/968/JHA, [2016] OJ L 135/53 ('*Europol Regulation*'); See also Eghbarish and Metwally (n x) 574.
44. *Europol Regulation* art 4(m).
45. See generally Eghbarish and Metwally (n x) 574.
46. Chang (n xxix) 135 citing Jan Ellermann, 'Terror won't kill the privacy star – tackling terrorism propaganda online in a data protection compliant manner' (2016) 17(4) *ERA Forum* 555.
47. Vox Pol, *Some Recent Trends In The Use Of The Internet/Ict For Terrorist Purposes – Part II* (Web page, 9 November 2016).
48. Chang (n xxix) 136; see United Nations Security Council, *United Nations Security Council Consolidated List* (Web page) <https://scsanctions.un.org/7b48pen-all.html>.
49. Chang (n xxix) 135 citing *Council Framework Decision 2008/919/JHA of 28 November 2008 amending Framework Decision 2002/475/JHA on combating terrorism* OJ L 330/21.
50. *Europol Regulation* art 3(1).
51. Ibid Annex I.
52. Europol, *EU Internet Referral Unit Transparency Report 2021* (Report) <https://www.europol.europa.eu/cms/sites/default/files/documents/EU_IRU_Transparency_Report_2021.pdf >.
53. Ibid 7.
54. *Adalah* (n xi) [4].
55. Ibid.
56. *Adalah* (n xi) [4]. See also: Australian Federal Prosecution Service, 'Prosecution Process', *Eight Steps in the Prosecution Process* (Web page) <https://victimsandwitnesses.cdpp.gov.au/prosecution-process/prosecution-process/prosecution-process-steps/eight-steps-prosecution-process>; United States Department of The United States Department of Justice, 'Criminal Justice Process', *Navigating the Federal Criminal Justice Process* (Web page, 22 March 2022) <https://www.justice.gov/enrd/criminal-justice-process>.
57. Eghbarish and Metwally (n x) 577-8.

58. Ibid, citing W. Gregory Voss, 'After Google Spain and Charlie Hebdo: The Continuing Evolution of European Union Data Privacy in at Time of Change' (2015) 71(1) *Business Lawyer* 281, 287 citing Decret 2015-253 du 4 mars 2015 relatif an d6referencement des sites provoquant A des actes de terrorisme on en faisant l'apologie et des sites diffusant des images et representations de mineurs A caractere pornographiquet [Decree 2015-253 of March 4, 2015 on the Delisting of Websites Inciting Acts of Terrorism or Justifying Them and Websites Distributing Child Pornography] <https://www.legifrance.gouv.fr/jorf/id/JORFTEXT000030313562>.
59. Eghbarish and Metwally (n x) 577 citing Lumen, *French Government Take Down Demand* (Web page, 22 April 2016) <https://www.lumendatabase.org/notices/12128927#>.
60. Eghbarish and Metwally (n x) 577.
61. Ibid.
62. Ibid.
63. Ibid.
64. Ibid citing CNIL, *Contrôle du blocage administratif des sites : première décision rendue sur saisine de la personnalité qualifiée* (Web page, 5 February 2019) <https://www.cnil.fr/en/node/25163>.
65. Commonwealth, *Parliamentary Debates*, House of Representatives, 24 February 2021, 7 (Paul Fletcher).
66. *Online Safety Act 2021* (Cth) ('OS Act'). See also Australian Home Rights Commission, *Tackling technology facilicated modern slavery at the international level* (Submission, 13 April 2023) 4.
67. *Online Safety (Transitional Provisions and Consequential Amendments) Act 2021* (Cth) sch 1.
68. OS Act pt 5 relates to the removal of "cyber-bullying material targeted at an Australian child"; OS Act pt 6 relates to the removal of an "intimate image"; OS Act pt 7 relates to the removal of "cyber-abuse material targeted at an Australian adult"; OS Act pt 9 relates to the removal of "class 1 material" and "class 2 material".
69. See OS Act ss 65, 66, 70, 77, 78, 79, 88, 89, 90.
70. Ibid.
71. Ibid s 99.
72. Ibid ss 109, 110, 114 and 115.
73. Ibid pt 10.
74. Ibid s 95.
75. eSafetyCommissioner, *Abhorrent Violent Conduct Powers Regulatory Guidance eSC RG 5* (Regulatory Guidance, February 2024) 4
76. Ibid.
77. Ibid s 95 and 99.
78. Ibid s 220A.
79. Ibid s 220.
80. See, e.g., ibid s 68, 72, 76, 81, 84, 92, 112, 117, and 122.
81. Ibid s 95.
82. See Conclusion.
83. Katherine Manstead, 'People Power' (2021) *Occasional Paper – Australian National Security College*
84. L. Freedman, *The Future of War: A History* (Penguin, 2018).
85. Rabea Eghbariah and Amre Metwally, 'Informal Governance: Internet Referral Units and The Rise Of State Interpretation Of Terms Of Service' (2021) 23 *Yale Journal of Law & Technology* 542, 577-8.
86. In the United Kingdom, refusing to take content down when asked to do so by a constable removes a defence that can be used to displace guilt in formal court proceedings - *Terrorism Act 2006* (UK), s. 3.
87. Chang (n xxix) 114, 135

88. Peter Singer and Emerson Brooking, *LikeWar* (Mifflin Harcourt, 2018), 198. For the Israeli Supreme Court case that dealt with its constitutionality, see *Adalah Legal Center for Arab Minority Rights in Israel v. State Attorney's Office—Cyber Department* [2021] HCJ 7486/19 (Supreme Court of Israel).
89. Rabea Eghbariah and Amre Metwally, 'Informal Governance: Internet Referral Units and The Rise Of State Interpretation Of Terms Of Service', (2021) 23 *Yale Journal of Law and Technology* 542, 577-8.
90. Peter Singer & Emerson Brooking, *LikeWar* (Mifflin Harcourt, 2018), 198. The nomenclature of the operation reflects the in-service air-to-air anti-missile defence system employed by the Israeli Defence Force (the so-called 'Iron Dome'), but applied in the online environment.
91. Ibid, 200.
92. Gerard Carney, 'A Comment on How the Implied Freedom of Political Communication Restricts the Non-Statutory Executive Power' (2018) 43(2) *University of Western Australia Law Review* 255, 266.
93. Israel utilises its diaspora, connecting pro-Israeli citizens and military in a civic-military centre to conduct *hasbara*, defined as 'explaining': see Peter Singer and Emerson Brooking, *LikeWar* (Mifflin Harcourt, 2018), 198. For the Israeli Supreme Court case that dealt with its constitutionality, see *Adalah Legal Center for Arab Minority Rights in Israel v. State Attorney's Office—Cyber Department* [2021] HCJ 7486/19 (Supreme Court of Israel).

Samuel White is a Senior Lecturer within the faculty of the Adelaide Law School at the University of Adelaide. He is concurrently a Visiting Fellow at the Australian Defence Force Academy and holds positions as an Adjunct Associate Professor at the University of New England. In 2024, he was made an Associate Fellow of the Royal Historical Society and the first Army Visiting Fellow at the Australian War Memorial. He has also served as both a Royal Australian Infantry Corps and an Australian Army Legal Corps officer in a variety of tactical, operational and strategic level postings. His military experiences focused on his doctoral studies, which addressed the constitutional ambit and limitations of responding to foreign interference (both traditional and modern forms) via military responses.

Socrates Giatrakos is a First Class Bachelor of Laws (Honours) graduate from the University of Adelaide. He is an admitted practitioner to practise law in the Supreme Court of South Australia and is currently practising as a Lawyer at Adelta Legal, advising on a range of matters. He has undertaken research and published on issues relating to public law and domestic military issues. He is an author in the Journal of Information Warfare and assisted as a student editor on the Adelaide Law Review. At the undergraduate level, he undertook research with respect to the Implied Freedom of Political Communication and its potential application to non-statutory executive power. He also worked as a Research Assistant for Dr Samuel White, researching issues regarding Public Law and International Law. He also wrote for Rights Resource Network SA on a range of human rights issues.

Building Social Resilience

Samuel White and Matthew Stubbs

Abstract While not the first option posited by national security practitioners, investing in 'soft' options such as education and self-help options for citizens is a low-cost mechanism to build social cyber resilience. This chapter accordingly explores the threat posed by interference operations and cyber threats, and the viability and models by which States can aim to grow social cyber resilience in order to resist these threats, without having to rely upon international or domestic legal frameworks. Through a case study of Cold War active measures, and consideration of the enhanced threat posed in an era of surveillance capitalism and cyber interconnectedness, this chapter demonstrates how with greater capacity to pinpoint engagement in a target population comes a more urgent need to build self-sufficiency and undertake education of the population to enhance its cyber resilience.

Introduction

Cyber resilience is in part a function of technical responses, but it is also essential to consider the social aspects of cyber resilience. As Cavelty, Eriksen and Scharte have observed, 'the predominant technical understandings of cyber security and cyber resilience can lead to an extreme form of "systems thinking" that might obscure human factors'.[1]

In this chapter, we consider human and social factors that are relevant to cyber resilience, reaching across threats from government-inspired information operations and broader cyber attacks undertaken by more diverse actors for financial and other reasons. We begin with historical examples of information operations targeting populations to understand the importance of social resilience. We then explain how modern

S. White (✉) · M. Stubbs
The University of Adelaide, Adelaide, Australia
e-mail: Samuel.white@adelaide.edu.au

M. Stubbs
e-mail: Matthew.stubbs@adelaide.edu.au

D. Stephens et al. (eds.), *Digital Resilience*,
https://doi.org/10.1007/978-981-97-9746-2_9

cyber interconnectedness and technology dependence, along with surveillance capitalism, enable information operations to pose a dramatically more potent threat now than in the past. Having detailed the threat, we then explore the concept of social resilience and address key means of promoting social resilience that in our view should inform our approach to social cyber resilience today and into the future.

Information Operations Targeting Populations

The social realm has always been a decisive battleground in interstate conflict and competition. Foreign state and non-state actors attempting to interfere with others is not a new phenomenon; nor, too, is the use of information in warfare as a resource, environment and weapon.[2] However, historically, there have been some buffer zones. Ancient attempts to interfere were often restricted by close-knit populations who knew their community and the individuals within. This made covert, clandestine or corrupt activities particularly difficult. Two options were available. The first is best highlighted by the campaign of Hellenic admiral, Themistocles:

> As Themistocles sailed along the coasts, wherever he saw places at which the enemy must necessarily put in for shelter and supplies, he inscribed conspicuous writings on stones, some of which he found to his hand there by chance, and some he himself caused to be set near the inviting anchorages and watering-places. In these writings he solemnly enjoyed upon the Ionians, if it were possible, to come over to the side of the Athenians who were risking all in behalf of their freedom; but if they could not do this, to damage the Barbarian cause in battle, and bring confusion among them.[3]

The second involved peripatetic individuals—such as merchants—who were able to infiltrate and interfere within societies through knowledge of likeminded individuals.[4] Their impacts however were limited to verbal communications and, after the invention of the printing press, pamphlets.[5]

The methods and means of such interference operations remained unchanged until the functional reach of Morse's code, Bell's telephone and Marconi's radio was realised. Their operational use was quick to follow, particularly with respect to radios.[6] Radios were the primary means of interfering within targeted societies, and supporting underground movements, allowing the tyranny of distance to be surmounted. They also did not require the audience to be literate.

The mass manipulation of an enemy population, through both overt and covert means, was the subject of fascination and anxiety in the late 19th century. It was initiated by a landmark study by Gustave Le Bon, a French social psychologist, who published *The Crowd: A Study of the Popular Mind* in 1896.[7] The work encouraged the view that ordinary, rational people could lose their reason when caught in crowds, and influenced the view that populations could be manipulated.[8] Importantly, Le Bon and later scholars noted, individuals could not be forced to believe something without a prior disposition. The power of crowds was therefore limited to those that were easily influenced—or in modern parlance, targetable.[9]

This view in turn dominated the thinking of the Great Powers during the First World War, which involved total, national mobilisation. Modern technologies combined with broadcast media, such as film, were believed to offer a 'hypodermic needle' or 'magic bullet' to the masses which they were unable to resist.[10] The military application—of both an offensive and defensive nature—was clear to state and non-state groups.[11]

Non-state groups seeking to exploit vulnerabilities within states are particularly important to the history of active measures (*aktivnyye meropriyatiya*), a term that emerged from the works of Vladimir Ilyaich Ulyanov (Lenin).[12] Specifically, Lenin wrote:

> The more powerful enemy can be vanquished only by exerting the utmost effort, and by the most thorough, careful, attentive, skilful and obligatory use of any, even the smallest, rift between enemies, any conflict of interests among the bourgeoisie of the various countries and among the various groups or types of bourgeoisie within the various countries, and also by taking advantage of any, even the smallest, opportunity of winning a mass ally, even though this ally is temporary, vacillating, unstable, unreliable and conditional.[13]

One difficulty of active measures was identifying, and contacting, target audiences. Under Soviet doctrine, there were two forms of individuals that active measures should try to target: 'fellow travellers' of the Communist cause and 'useful idiots' who did not realise who was funding their research or endeavours.[14] The identification of these individuals was a task that only well-resourced, bureaucratic organisations could afford.[15] So too were the logistics of contacting these individuals. As Table 1 highlights, contacting fellow travellers and useful idiots required messaging in a general, wide manner. At the height of Soviet active measures (being the 1960s and 1970s), there were six monthly brochures that targeted fellow travellers and useful idiots within West Germany (see Table 1).

The difficulty with these magazines was multifaceted. They were high-cost and low-impact, and flawed by an inherent difficulty in measuring effectiveness, including whether or not the target audience was receptive to the messaging and the dissemination of the information.[17] Targeting individuals either required a generic message (mass broadcasting) or intimate knowledge of a target, gained through timely intelligence gathering, complicated by distance.

There was also difficulty in countering active measures. Although *ex post facto* reporting has claimed that 'the high professional standards of U.S. and allied journalism proved a formidable bulwark against Soviet disinformation efforts, including those to plant false stories and "leak" forged documents in the Western press',[18] this is an inherently difficult claim to justify, or deny. There were many instances of disinformation being actively published by the Western press; indeed *Der Bund* in Table 1 was apparently not uncovered as a Soviet magazine until after the end of the Cold War, despite being read by the West German military.[19]

As this section has demonstrated, information operations targeting populations have a long history. When these operations are conducted using cyber means in an era of surveillance capitalism, however, they become radically more powerful, as the next section demonstrates.

Table 1 Soviet active measures in West Germany[16]

Name	Translation	Audience	Intended effect
Die Wahrheit	The truth	General interest, mini-magazine	Spreading soviet concepts
Der Kampfer	The fighter	West German armed forces	Called into question the usefulness of American intervention in Germany
Der Pareiarbeiter	The party worker	Targeted communist functionaries	To maintain support for communism in Western Europe
Giest und Leben	Spirit and life	General interest, mini-magazine	Cultural news outlet with a focus on suppression of the church and spiritual life
Elternhaus und Schule	Home and school	Parents and students	To try to expose women and children to Soviet concepts
Der Bund	Colloquial nickname of the Bundeswehr	West German military personnel	Called into question the usefulness of American intervention in Germany

The Paradigm Shift of Surveillance Capitalism and Cyber Information Operations

As Samuel White has explained elsewhere,[20] surveillance capitalism (enabled by cyber means) has led to a paradigm shift in the ability to target individuals with customised information (or misinformation, disinformation, or overt cyber attacks). This started with Google's 2004 patent titled 'Generating User Information for Use in Targeted Advertising'.[21] As Shoshana Zuboff has noted, Google realised it could 'infer and deduce the thoughts, feelings, intentions and interests of individuals and groups' from data it could collect on individuals.[22] This shifted identification of individual needs from an art, as experienced in active measures in the Cold War, to a science.

There are three key points that we regard as being essential to the threat that is posed by information operations in an era of surveillance capitalism and cyber capabilities: the ability to micro-target advertisements and other messages; the use of fake accounts (bots) to amplify particular perspectives; and the low costs associated with cyber interference in an era of surveillance capitalism. First, the identification of fellow travellers and useful idiots is manifestly easier now due to surveillance capitalism. Unlike the generalist delivery mode relied upon by the makers of the brochures listed in Table 1, threat actors can now micro-target individuals based on their needs and preferences.[23] The individuals who are micro-targeted might also be selected based on their psychological profiling, due to their perceived susceptibility to disinformation. Second, the rise of bots further enhances the ability of malign actors to achieve their goals. It may no longer be necessary to find and use the fellow travellers and useful idiots of the Cold War. They can simply be created. There are 'a potentially unlimited number of accounts on multiple social media platforms that can be orchestrated by one individual, through one single application, spreading content generated by artificial intelligence pursuing a single and coordinated strategic goal'.[24] This is to be contrasted with the time-intensive work of active measures during the Cold War. Third, the rise of surveillance capitalism and conduct of information operations through cyber means has drastically lowered the costs—financial, political, military and opportunity. The cost of Soviet active measures in the 1970s has been estimated at $4 billion annually;[25] cost estimates of Russian information operations during the 2016 US election total no more than $100,000 over two years on advertisements.[26]

Accordingly, while manipulation of the information environment is as old as war itself, shifts in technology have created a unique opportunity for malign actors. In today's increasingly contested social landscape, technology has vastly expanded the range and effectiveness of tools that states can use to influence and target citizens. The digitisation of social and economic activities has enabled states to interfere and exert control on an unprecedented scale and with immediate effect. The massive collection of personal data by both corporations and governments, coupled with advancements in machine learning, has opened new avenues for precise and tailored interference and coercion.

As machines become more adept at predicting human behaviour and the outcomes of complex social interactions, states gain enhanced capabilities to operate within the social sphere. These technological advancements are not limited to guiding cyber interference and sabotage; they can also be harnessed to more effectively target traditional activities such as the infiltration of political organisations or the blackmail of key decision-makers. Machine learning systems, commonly employed by advertisers and digital platforms, can provide real-time feedback to assess and refine the impact of these operations over time. This reduces the risks and uncertainties associated with social manipulation, making such operations more likely to occur with increasing frequency.

The Importance of Social Resilience

Against this threat, it is important to recall, as strategist Kori Schake reminds us, that societies—not militaries—fight wars.[27] The popular will is key to whether a country chooses to contest an adversary, capitulate, or negotiate peace. The last time that this was discussed in war studies was with the advent of the social bomber, and some applied history can be of assistance in understanding this key terrain. As Italian air power theorist Giulio Douhet noted:

The population can and must be inured to the horrors of war, but there is a limit to all resistance, even human resistance. No population can steel itself enough to endure aerial offensives forever. A heroic people can endure the most frightful offensives as long as there is hope that they may come to an end; but when the aerial war has been lost, there is no hope of ending the conflict until a decision has been reached on the surface, and that would take too long. A people who are bombed today as they were bombed yesterday, who know they will be bombed again tomorrow and see no end to their martyrdom, are bound to call for peace at length.[28]

The social realm is vital terrain during conditions of strategic competition—be it the bomber, or code. Today, Australia faces a complex and increasingly fraught security environment. General Angus Campbell, when discussing what warfare would look like in 2025, remarked:

Political warfare subverts and undermines. It penetrates the mind. It seeks to influence, to subdue, to overpower, to disrupt … It can be covert or overt, a background of white noise or loud and compelling. It's not limited by the constructs or constructions of peace and war. It's constant and scalable, and most important, it adapts.[29]

People are key to this. Authoritarian governments like Russia and China pursue 'political warfare' strategies that view democratic institutions, public opinion and civilian infrastructure as legitimate targets. Technological change has also made Australia unprecedentedly porous to these tactics. Since at least the end of WWII, Australians have enjoyed the luxury of being able to draw clear lines between domestic society and external threats. However, faced with the threat of cyber-enabled interference operations, and by cyber threats more generally, there has never been a more important time to consider promoting social cyber resilience.

Measures to Promote Social Resilience

(1) Education—Boosting Individual Cyber Literacy

One means of boosting social resilience is through education. As the Australian Government's *2023–2030 Australia Cyber Security Strategy* acknowledges:

We must do more to lift cyber awareness across our community. … cyber security needs to become part of our everyday routine. It's important to emphasise that basic actions – like maintaining a secure pass-phrase, keeping our software up to date, or not clicking on suspicious links – can have the most effective outcomes.'[30]

There has been much attention paid to education within a corporate context, but as Joinson et al point out, 'the ability to resist a cyber attack, or quickly recover and learn from a successful attack, is as important for individuals' wellbeing as it is for organisations.'[31] They give the example that:

a cyber-resilient household would engage in good 'hygiene' behaviours (including proper password protection and making regular updates) in order to minimize the likelihood of an attack, take actions (backup regularly and adopt cyber insurance) that would minimize the impact of an attack, but also learn, either from their own mistakes or from knowledgeable others, so as to gradually improve their cyber defence in the longer term.[32]

The sort of basic steps advocated in these two extracts for the purpose of proactively reducing the risk posed by cyber attacks, and learning from those that succeed, can be promoted through public education campaigns. Of course, not everyone will be able to be reached, and not every attack will be able to be prevented. Even incremental increases in cyber literacy can have a significant impact on reducing the overall prevalence of loss from cyber attacks. Education is, therefore, an important means of promoting social cyber resilience.

(2) Governmental Capacity, Credibility and Trust as Promoters of Social Resilience

Social resilience depends in part on the maintenance of trust in governments. This requires not merely competence from governments in the leadership they provide in cyber security, but also that there be a level of trust by the population that government messaging on cyber security is credible. We agree with Cavelty, Eriksen and Scharte that 'the existence, capacity, and accountability of government institutions (local to international) have a strong influence on coping capacity and trust.'[33]

Much national security risk in the digital age is contingent and may never materialise. For example, the decision to exclude certain vendors from 5G infrastructure was not based on a 'smoking gun' but on future risk: that access to the network could enable interference or coercion. Further, the facts about disinformation, cyber-sabotage and other operations in the social realm will be contested: agencies must act now to bolster their credibility. In particular, while Australia has robust procedures for crisis communications, agencies must develop more proactive ways to publicly explain and motivate risk assessments before an incident occurs. If they are to be trusted, communications from government should be consistent and personalised. One positive step in this regard is the increased public presence of Australia's spy chiefs.

To further build trust, the Office of National Intelligence should consider ways in which the intelligence community can publicly share key assessments and associated confidence levels, without compromising sources or methods. One example of this approach is the Office of the US Director of National Intelligence's guidance on the processes involved in making 'attribution' assessments for state cyber attacks.[34] Significantly, when providing advice to Ministers on whether and when to make information public, agencies should not limit their evaluation of the trade-offs involved to operational considerations such as the intelligence gain/loss trade-off. They must also weigh the longer-term impacts of secrecy on public trust and resilience. Australia, in coordination with its international partners, should work to dismantle the façade that adversaries use to disguise their involvement in interference, coercion, and preparatory actions. By adopting a more consistent and transparent approach to assigning responsibility for these hostile activities, the government can weaken their impact. This proactive stance would also establish Australia as a credible and impartial actor, helping to prevent the uncertainty and distrust that might arise from future cyber attacks and misinformation campaigns. Although joint attribution efforts can reduce the likelihood of diplomatic or economic backlash from the accused states, they are not always practical. Therefore, Australia should prioritise the creation of standardised, publicly available frameworks with its allies for detecting and attributing malicious actions. These frameworks can serve as external validation, bolstering the legitimacy of attribution efforts.

Institutional trust at the domestic and international levels is an important piece of the cyber resilience puzzle. It is also related to the last means of promoting cyber resilience that we will address—buttressing social cohesion—as '[t]he key formative psychosocial conditions in the context of cyber resilience are arguably trust and social cohesion'.[35]

(3) Society-Centred Deterrence—Social Cohesion as Cyber Resilience

As noted above, in the inter-war period, airpower strategists theorised that a decisive airstrike on a target's civilian infrastructure would cause political paralysis and social chaos, leading 'stricken civilians' to quickly demand that their government capitulate.[36] These theories were not evidence-based and reflected classist assumptions about the emotional susceptibility of the body politic. Although misguided, they inspired mass bombings of cities and untold human suffering.

Understanding the importance of social cohesion to cyber resilience requires us to think about how the human factor interacts with technical and material resources. As Cavelty, Eriksen and Scharte have pointed out,

> [m]aterial and psychosocial resources may interact to influence institutional resources and social vulnerabilities, for example, when tools, know-how, and social cohesion rally staff to work together under pressure to solve urgent problems with potentially catastrophic social outcomes.[37]

The same impact that can be seen in teams can also be seen in societies—where there is a common sense of purpose in responding to cyber threats, this not only strengthens individual responses to cyber threats themselves but also reduces the effectiveness of interference operations targeted against a population generally. Resilience is, in this way, a function of social actions at the micro and macro levels. Social cohesion also boosts the effectiveness of education campaigns and is related to trust in governmental institutions, so it plays a particularly vital role:

> Social cohesion, particularly characteristics like "sense of community" and "collective problem solving," can act as psychosocial resources that support the development of material resources, mitigative behaviour, and knowledge coproduction.[38]

Today, there is a need to ensure we do not give our adversaries the impression that people are Australia's soft underbelly. Showing that the government trusts the public to engage in nuanced debate about the threat environment and response options is one way to do this. Similarly, establishing and signalling that we have processes for trusted government messaging about interference and coercion can reduce the perceived benefits to adversaries of targeting the social realm. This, in turn, can have a deterrence-by-denial effect, reducing the appeal of these tactics to an adversary.

Conclusion

Social resilience is an essential, but often overlooked, piece of the cyber resilience puzzle. As an example, the Australian Government's *2023–2030 Australia Cyber Security Strategy* proposes six 'cyber shields', which cover a range of technical, security and capability issues.[39] Only one shield is socially focussed—'strong businesses and citizens'—and within that shield, the focus is very much on businesses: five of the seven action areas identified within this shield address businesses, only one is proactively socially oriented, looking to 'help Australian defend themselves from cyber threats' through 'cyber awareness programs' and promoting 'cyber literacy' in vulnerable communities.[40] These are important goals—our point is that they are a very small piece of a strategy that prioritises actions involving businesses, as well as technical, security and capability issues. In this, we agree with Cavelty, Eriksen and Scharte that 'cyber security cannot be reduced to a singular matter of technology: technical systems are embedded into, and derived from, social practices and human choices'[41]

In this chapter, we have demonstrated that information warfare is not new, but now thanks to cyber interconnectedness poses a greater threat than it has at any time in the past. A critical aspect of responding to that threat is social resilience. We have explored three means of enhancing social resilience: education to promote cyber literacy; steps to promote the credibility of, and trust in, government institutions and their responses to cyber threats; and enhancing social cohesion. Our intention here is not to be comprehensive or prescriptive about means of promoting social cyber resilience, but to highlight the importance of social cyber resilience and to advance the conversation about practical ways in which it might be promoted.

Notes

1. Myriam Dunn Cavelty, Christine Eriksen and Benjamin Scharte, 'Making cyber security more resilient: adding social considerations to technological fixes' (2023) 26(7) *Journal of Risk Research* 801, 802.
2. John Keegan, *Intelligence in War* (Hutchinson Press, 2003).
3. Plutarch, *The Lives of Noble Grecians and Romans*, tr John Dryden (Encyclopaedia Britannica, 1952) 98. There was fear such operations might occur in North Queensland, where enemies were interned and the large coastline remained unpatrolled, during World War Two. See National Australian Archives A373/1, Letter of 29 June 1943, Director-General of Security.
4. The Mongols, with an incredibly limited number of troops due to the sparsely populated steppes, relied upon spies to plant rumours of their 'huge numbers, stupidity and ferocity' among enemy populations to lower morale and frighten the enemy before an attack: Paul MA Linebarger, *Psychological Warfare* (Duell, Sloan & Pearce, 2nd ed, 1948) 15. So too did the Mexica (Aztecs) utilise merchants to spread rumours in target populations: see Samuel White and Ray Kerkhove, 'Aztec Laws of War' in Samuel White (ed), *The Laws of Yesterday's Wars* (Brill, 2021) 69, 81. Sun Tzu in *The Art of War* (Penguin, 2008) ch 13 advocated the use of 'dead spies' who would spread rumours until killed. Niccolo Machiavelli in *The Prince* (Penguin, 1951) highlighted the benefits of using a diaspora or colonists to interfere.

5. Thomas Rid, *Active Measures* (Macmillan, 2020) 38. Eventually a method of control was found—the resource of paper. See Peter Kenez, *The Birth of the Propaganda State: Soviet Methods of Mass Mobilization, 1917–1929* (Cambridge University Press, 1986) 44–7.
6. Telegraphs allowed for the quick dissemination of information, providing the British Empire with a means to quickly summon reinforcements in Imperial provinces. One Indian mutineer in 1857 is reported as saying that the telegraph was 'the accursed string that strangles me': Niall Ferguson, *The Square and The Tower* (Penguin, 2008) 160.
7. Gustave Le Bon, *The Crowd: A Study of the Popular Mind* (Macmillan, 1896).
8. I.S. Bloch, *Is War Now Impossible? Being an Abridgement of the War of the Future and in Its Technical Economic and Political Relations* (Grant Richard, 1899).
9. Brittany Kaiser, *Targetable* (HarperCollins, 2020).
10. Nicholas Reeves, 'Battle of the Somme' (1997) 17(1) *Historical Journal of Film* 5; Sandra J Ball-Rokeach, *Media, Audiences and Social Structure* (Beverly Hills, 1986).
11. Brock Millman, 'HMG and the War Against Dissent, 1914–1918' (2005) 40(3) *Journal of Contemporary History* 33.
12. George F Kennan, 'The Inauguration of Organized Political Warfare' (Wilson Centre, Digital Archive, 30 April 1948).
13. Vladimir Lenin, 'Left-Wing Communist, an Infantile Disorder' in Vladimir Lenin, *Collected Works*, tr Ronald Vroon (Progress Publishers, 1972) 62, 70–1. Lenin's approach to active measures was recognised in *Australian Communist Party v Commonwealth* (1951) 83 CLR 1, 143 where Latham CJ held 'one of the most effective forms of fifth-column work is to use any real or pretended dispute—political, industrial or religious—as a means of promoting social confusion and dislocating the economy of a country'.
14. Soviet operatives used the term useful idiot to describe Western targets driven by fame and fortune. The term was coined by Polish agents in the 1860s to describe, in turn, Russian nihilists: see Clint Watts, *Messing with the Enemy* (Harper, 2019) p. 133. A good example in the Cold War era is the funding of the Generals for Peace initiative, in an attempt to use Western generals who opposed nuclear proliferation as a disguised Soviet front: see Rid (n v) p. 81. A more modern example is the creation of social media accounts under the guise of supporting Black Lives Matter, but at a critical moment urging followers to not vote in the 2016 US elections, in an attempt to interfere—the risk of this happening in Australia was noted in Joint Standing Committee on Electoral Matters, *Report on the Conduct of the 2016 Federal Election and Matters Related Thereto* (Report, November 2018).
15. One estimate placed it at $4 billion annually, with over 15,000 personnel—see Kevin McCauley, *Russian Influence Campaigns Against the West: From the Cold War to Putin* (North Charleston, 2016) 51.
16. Friedrich Wilhelm Schlomann, 'DDR-Desinformation', *Das Ostpreustenblatt* (Hamburg, 13 November 1993) 46; Rid (n v) 138.
17. Rid (n v) 38–44.
18. Ross Babbage, *Winning Without Fighting—Volume 1* (CSBA, 2019) 19, quoting Denis Kux, 'Soviet Active Measures and Disinformation: Overview and Assessment' (2013) 15(4) *Parameters* 26.
19. Rid (n v) 92.
20. See Samuel White, *Colouring in the Grey Zone: The Legal Capacity of the Australian Defence Force to Respond Domestically to Interference Operations* (Ph.D. Thesis, University of Adelaide, 2023) 49–55.
21. *US Patent, Amendment No 9 to Form S-1 Registration Statement Under the Securities Act of 1933 for Google Inc*, filed on 18 August 2004.
22. Shoshana Zuboff, *The Age of Surveillance Capitalism: The Fight for a Human Future at the New Frontier of Power* (Hachette, 2019) 81.
23. Also known as narrowcasting, hypertargeting, psychographics and pinpoint propaganda. See Hybrid CoE, *Trends in the Contemporary Information Environment* (Trend Report 4, May 2020) 20; Joint Standing Committee on Electoral Matters, *Report on the Conduct of the 2016 Federal Election and Matters Related Thereto* (Report, November 2018) 176 [7.74].

24. Kim Hartmann and Keir Giles, 'The Next Generation of Cyber-Enabled Information Warfare' (Conference Paper, International Conference on Cyber Conflict: 20/20 Vision—The Next Decade, 2020) 233, 244.
25. Kevin McCauley, *Russian Influence Campaigns Against the West: From the Cold War to Putin* (North Charleston, 2016) 51.
26. Robert Muller, *Unclassified Report of the Select Committee on Intelligence: Russian Active Measures Campaigns and Interference in the 2016 U.S. Election—Volume 2* (Report, 2018) 7.
27. Kori Schacka, 'Civilians win wars, Too' (August 2017, Hoover Institution) <https://www.hoover.org/research/civilians-win-wars-too>.
28. Giulio Douhet, *The Command of the Air*, tr Dino Ferrari (Coward-McCann, 1942) 188.
29. Angus Campbell, 'War in 2025' (Speech, ASPI, 13 June 2019).
30. Australian Government, *2023–2030 Australian Cyber Security Strategy* 19.
31. Adam N Joinson et al., 'Development of a new 'human cyber-resilience scale" (2023) 9(1) *Journal of Cybersecurity* 1, 1.
32. Ibid 2.
33. Cavelty, Eriksen and Scharte (n i) 807.
34. Office of the Director of National Intelligence—Report (14 September 2018) accessed 6 August 2024 from https://dl.icdst.org/pdfs/files3/db004a6f55f96c056a23fc4efc6a23ac.pdf.
35. Ibid.
36. Freedman, *The Future of War: A History* (Penguin, 2018).
37. Cavelty, Eriksen and Scharte (n i) 807.
38. Ibid, 808.
39. Australian Government, *2023–2030 Australian Cyber Security Strategy* 7.
40. Ibid 16–27. The action 'secure our identities and provide better support to victims of identity theft' does include a socially-focused *responsive* action to 'expand support services for victims of identity theft'.
41. Cavelty, Eriksen and Scharte (n i) 802.

Samuel White is a Senior Lecturer of the faculty of the Adelaide Law School at the University of Adelaide. He is concurrently a Visiting Fellow at the Australian Defence Force Academy and holds positions as an Adjunct Associate Professor at the University of New England. In 2024, he was made an Associate Fellow of the Royal Historical Society and the first Army Visiting Fellow at the Australian War Memorial. Samuel has also served as both a Royal Australian Infantry Corps and an Australian Army Legal Corps officer in a variety of tactical, operational and strategic level postings. His military experiences focused his doctoral studies, which addressed the constitutional ambit and limitations of responding to foreign interference (both traditional and modern forms) via military responses.

Matthew Stubbs is a Professor of the faculty of the Adelaide Law School at the University of Adelaide, where he serves as Editor in Chief of the *Adelaide Law Review* and Program Coordinator of Postgraduate Coursework Programs and Military Law Programs. Professor Stubbs is involved with professional bodies in the law and academia, and is a member and former Chair of the Space Law Committee and Human Rights Committee of the Law Society of South Australia and a member of the Law Council of Australia's National Human Rights Committee. Matthew was awarded the Law Society of South Australia President's Medal in 2023.

Truth Tribunals and Arbiters of Truth Using the Judiciary to Build Resilience

Hamish Charles McNamara

Abstract The rise of the internet and the increasing prevalence of fake news presents contemporary challenges to democracy and the jurisdictions which seek to uphold it through developing digital resilience within their domestic legal frameworks. This chapter explores innovative mechanisms across jurisdictions to mitigate the challenges presented by fake news. Part I considers the executive model implemented in Argentina which serves as a potential framework that could be sewed into the existing fabric of Australia's administrative law and judicial decision-making. Part II considers the historic role of the judiciary as determiners of truth in Australia's common law and whether the existing court system is resilient enough to respond to these contemporary threats. Part III evaluates Australia's administrative law as a means of facilitating a supposed 'Truth Tribunal', assessing the opportunities and barriers that may hinder the effectiveness of this model. Ultimately, this chapter will flesh out the utility of the judiciary as arbiters of truth and highlight the real limitations that exist within Australia's current administrative law.

Means for Mitigating Fake News

There is an evident need for Australia to create a mechanism for mitigating fake news and discerning what constitutes 'the truth' when the validity of information is disputed.[1] Due to the global threat posed by fake news, several foreign jurisdictions have implemented mechanisms designed at mitigating the impacts of fake news.[2] These mechanisms installed across various jurisdictions vary substantially, with many driven by government-implemented law reform and election reforms.[3]

The pressing need for governments to build resilience to combat contested information is well publicised across borders as the Final Report conducted by the Select Senate Committee on Foreign Interference through Social Media exposed, governments across the world are recognising the pressing need to build resilience during

H. C. McNamara (✉)
The University of Adelaide, Adelaide, Australia
e-mail: hamish.mcnamara@adelaide.edu.au

D. Stephens et al. (eds.), *Digital Resilience*,
https://doi.org/10.1007/978-981-97-9746-2_10

an age where information has been weaponised.[4] In the European context, the European Union Parliament have declared that itself is a 'target of diverse and aggressive foreign influence campaigns' thereby reflecting the urgency of this threat.[5] Further, the urgency of this threat is likely exacerbated by the lack of awareness around the means in which fake news is implored, which is a view supported by the Australian Securities Intelligence Organisations ('ASIO') most recent Annual Threat Assessment. In public remarks relating to this review, the Director-General stated that Australia "is facing an unprecedented challenge from espionage and foreign interference and I'm not convinced we, as a nation, fully appreciate the damage it inflicts on Australia's security, democracy, sovereignty, economy and social fabric".[6]

These public statements by governments, specifically those by ASIO reflect the necessity to combat the utilisation of social media as a means for dispersing fake news. To counter these threats, Australia will need to adopt its framework in pursuit of a model that will allow the jurisdiction to build digital resilience and more likely than not, Government will turn to approaches taken abroad to offer a framework for doing so.

International Approaches to Fake News

Across jurisdictions, a wide range of legislative and executive action has been undertaken to combat fake news. A comprehensive database compiled by disinformation researchers at global thinktank, the Poynter Institute highlights the comprehensive range of means that have been exercised across jurisdictions to build resilience to misinformation, foreign disinformation campaigns and a lack of media awareness. Table 1 as shown in the appendix represents a broad sample drawn from this database of instances where a specific country has made a legislative response or evoked executive powers to respond to mis and/or disinformation.[7] As the below data indicates, the approaches taken across jurisdictions are expansive and include the creation of new laws to combat fake news, intervention by government task forces, criminal sanctions and more.

Addressing Fake News in Argentina

A distinct approach observed across jurisdictions is the governmental approach taken in Argentina to mitigate fake news which may serve as a framework for Australian reform. Prior to the 2019 national elections, the Argentinean Central Government, out of concern that fake news would disrupt the campaigns, established the 'Comiśon de Verificaćion de Notificia Falsas' or Commission for the Verification of Fake News ('Commission').[8] The Commission was responsible for the "detection, recognition, labelling and prevention of fake news" through digital media broadcasts during national election campaigns, possessing investigative powers to achieve this function.[9] The Commission reports to 'Cámara Nacional Electoral' ('CNE') which is the Executive Department responsible for the administration of elections.[10] The Commission is responsible for the "detection, recognition, labelling and prevention of fake news" through digital media broadcasts during national election campaigns and it possesses investigative powers to achieve this function.[11]

The Commission performs its function by observing media content and relying on complaints being made by persons through its website.[12] The Commission reports its findings to the CNE and can award warnings, fines and disqualify parties from government contracts.[13] In more egregious circumstances where an accused party has failed to remove malicious content or content that may lead to the incitement of violence the CNE, acting on the Commission's recommendation, can suspend a party from accessing a media network or portal for two years.[14]

Fake news is a phenomenon requiring efficient action to limit its detrimental effects. Thus, whilst the CNE undertakes the process of awarding sanctions, the Commission possesses powers to issue public warnings about parties being investigated.[15] The Commission may order an internet provider or social media platform to tag information with a caption stipulating a "notice of doubtful credibility".[16] This power exercisable by the Commission exists in the U.S, China and Malaysia and can be utilised by the electoral authority during the course of elections.[17]

Adopting the Argentinean Approach for Australia

Efforts to mitigate fake news are underway in Australia via a legislative solution in the *Communications Legislation Amendment (Combating Misinformation and Disinformation) Bill (Cth) 2023*.[18] This bill proposes expanding the powers of both the Australian Communications Media Authority ('ACMA') as the independent regulator over the media and digital platform sector as well as the powers exercisable by the Federal Minister of Communications.[19] These amendments will allow ACMA to gather information from digital platform providers, require record-keeping on fake news, create and enforce industry standards, or request industry bodies to develop their own industry practices (i.e. code of conduct).[20] These proposed amendments sparked public outcry, particularly from the conventional 'far right' of the political spectrum who preached the bill infringes the individual liberty of free speech.[21] Whether or not the expansion of ACMA's legislative power succeeds, this book chapter seeks not to delve into the issues surrounding a legislative fix but instead will explore enforcement. This chapter will now turn to consider the idea of 'truth tribunals' as an enforcement mechanism if such reforms were to come into force.

Whether or not the expansion of ACMA's legislative power succeeds, there is little discussion of how such changes would be enforced. This chapter therefore explores an enforcement mechanism if such a 'Ministry of Truth' comes into force.[22]

The Argentinean approach to mitigating fake news may appear extreme; however, when considering other approaches taken across jurisdictions, this approaches adaptability to the Australian legal framework becomes apparent. Despite being the more favourable framework to adopt, the Argentinean approach does possess observable limitations which need not be adopted which will now be explored.

The first evident limitation is that the Commission is only active during the course of the electoral process and its scope is limited to election-related content; therefore, it would be limited in the information that it could investigate and the period it operates.[23] To effectively address Australia's need to mitigate fake news, a proposed tribunal could not possess such limitations and therefore, its object and positioning would need to be housed external to the Australian Electoral Commission. Further, consideration for where such a tribunal would exist would need to be compliant with the Australian Constitutions' limitations on executive power being exercised by the legislature and vice versa. If this were to manifest, the likely concerns would arise from the tribunal being responsible for both the investigation and presiding over claims of fake news being brought before it. To counteract this concern, complaints could be brought by parties external to the tribunal for review as they are in administrative appeals and migration matters as opposed to having the tribunal itself conducting investigations in the inquisitorial fashion that the Argentinean model provides for.

The sanction exercisable under the Argentinean framework may be of utility for an Australian approach to mitigate fake news. The ability to punish parties who have been found to have disseminated fake and deceiving information with the intention of inciting violence can be prohibited from accessing the internet would be effective in limiting fake news entering social discourse.[24] Further, the Commission's use of tagging could be adapted to operate like an injunction.[25] Whilst a claim is being heard before the Truth Tribunal, the alleged fake news would be marked with a warning, prompting Australian viewers to question its validity before relying upon it.

Judicial Fitness as Arbiters of Truth

History of Determining the Truth

The creation of a specialist tribunal whose function is to adjudicate the truth will likely prompt questions about the Court's historic role as arbiters of truth. Australian Courts have inherently reprised the function as the "ultimate fact finder" in Australia's legal system, with the system being responsible for the discharge of decisions exceeding 1.2 million various matters between 2020 and 2021.[26] The practical effect of the Courts discharging their responsibilities on such a high volume of disputes every year's is that their verdicts which are effectively determinations of truth carry significant social and legal effect which has been previously observed on issues arising about rate and gender.

The issue of Identity Relativism has had limited application in Australia's legal system since the High Court decision in *Mabo v Queensland (No.2)*.[27] The High Court in this decision adopted a Tripartite Test to determine an individual's Aboriginality.[28]

Deriving from Brennan J's judgement, the Court determined under the Tripartite test that Aboriginal membership is dependent on an individual's biological descent from an indigenous population, combined with mutual recognition of that individual's membership to the group, and 'by the elders or other persons enjoying traditional authority among those people'.[29]

This test's adoption in the Mabo decision limits the issue of self-identifying without a factual basis to support one's proposition.[30] This factual approach to determining the truth of a person's racial identity was recently reaffirmed in *Love v Commonwealth* where the Court determined that an individual who satisfies the Tripartite Test cannot be deemed an 'alien' per the *Migration Act (1958) (Cth)*.[31]

The High Court's role in the Mabo decision determined what true Aboriginality was within Australia's legal system.[32] The consequences of the Court's role manifests in social discourse and informs growing debate regarding identity, equity and truth in Australia. The influence of the Courts weighing on such a contested aspect of culture war and whether it will contribute to what constitutes an individual's legal identity warrants observation in future years.[33]

Characteristics of the Court System Limiting Outcomes

Courts Are Not Fit for Purpose

Despite the Court having a substantial role in discerning the truth in Australia, there are highly public examples where Courts have not found the truth. When most Australians hear the phrase "Dingo took my baby" they likely recall the prosecution of Lindy Chamberlain, whose charges and subsequent prosecution by Northern Territory Police played out in the public eye.[34] A culmination of poorly collated evidence and the media's actions were detrimental to the initial autopsy of Ms. Chamberlain's child, which should have led the Court to finding native animal involvement.[35]

Overwhelming evidence suggests that for prosecutors in a criminal case or an aggrieved party in a civil claim, proceedings should not commence unless there is a high degree of certainty that their claim is the truth.[36] This is corroborated by the fact that 96% of civil proceedings brought before South Australian Magistrates Court are finalised prior to trial, thus distilling confidence in outcomes.[37] In the frequent circumstances where a guilty plea is made or demands for debt fulfilment are met, an opportunity for truth to be discerned before a judge is not provided and therefore, a factual determination is distinguished in lieu of an omission of the truth.

It is in circumstances where the allegations of a party are contested that the Court often plays a role in discerning the truth from the facts.[38] However, when a court is asked to weigh the likeliness of each parties' allegations, the Judge is not isolating the truth, but determining probability on the appropriate standard.[39] In a civil claim, the Court will make a judgment on whether an allegation was more probable or not of having occurred in the way the claimant has stipulated.[40] As opposed to their civil counterparts, it is likely that criminal proceedings inspire greater confidence that a trial verdict is in fact reflective of a true account of events due to the higher burden of proof the prosecution must meet in asserting their case.[41]

Procedural Inefficiencies

Fake news requires a prompt response to limit its influence. Due to the inherent features of court proceedings, redress is unlikely to be efficient or cost-effective for concerned parties.

Resolving civil disputes before Australian Courts reveals several inefficiencies that are undesirable when discerning the truth. Typically, civil proceedings are drawn-out and expensive, meaning-seeking redress through the Courts is often inaccessible for financially limited parties. Further, *Schulz and Cannon* point out, that the adversarial legal system is driven by lawyers and is therefore prone to exploitation.[42] Lawyers can further exacerbate the drawn-out process via discovery and continuance measures if it is in their clients' interests.[43] These characteristics support the argument that a Court may not be the most appropriate institution for determining the truth, particularly for the swift and confident outcomes needed to address fake news.

Tribunals in Australia's Current Administrative Law Environment

Suitability of Tribunals to Hear Fake News Disputes

Considering the Administrative Appeals Tribunal's abolishment, attention should be given to whether a specialist tribunal is a suitable institution for aggrieved parties to have claims of fake news heard before it, or whether a Court could achieve the same function. Proponents to the introduction of a Truth Tribunal may question why an existing Court can't fulfil the same function, considering the Court's role as an evaluator of what the likely true facts in any dispute are. As this paper is concerned with a reviewing process for decisions made involving fake news, the solution needs to be a body whose jurisdiction is to hear appeals and perform reviews. It is imperative to acknowledge that aggrieved parties of decisions by the Commonwealth do reserve the right to have their dispute heard before the Court. However, in the context of fake news and its implications, it is unclear how effective this review process may be. The following section will evaluate the review processes undertaken by each respective institution and other characteristics possessed by tribunals to evaluate their suitability for adjudicating the truth.

Evaluating Processes of Review

The review processes undertaken by administrative tribunals starkly contrast those of superior courts. David Bennett contrasts the two review mechanisms, illustrating that merits review, an inherent feature of administrative tribunals, possess a broader scope of review compared to judicial review.[44] When a tribunal undertakes merits review it is concerned with all aspects of the original decision. Merits review allows for what is described as the Tribunal 'stand[ing] in the shoes' of the original decision maker, meaning fresh assessments can be made about whether the decision was informed by all the available.[45] As merits review is a factual enquiry, the Tribunal can decide on the facts, potentially reversing the original decision.

Comparatively, a superior court undertaking judicial review is not concerned about the facts surrounding the original decision, but whether the original decision was made within the legal constraints of the minister's power.[46] In *Attorney General (NSW) v Quin* (1990), Brennan J states that the reviews conducted by Superior Courts in administrative decisions "do not go beyond the declaration and enforcing of the law which determines the limits and governs the exercise of the repository's power".[47] The scope of judicial review is limited to determining the exercise of power and whether procedural or jurisdictional errors were at play in the original proceedings that led to that outcome. The outcome of judicial review is limited to setting aside the original decision and compelling parties to fulfill unperformed legal duties. Unlike administrative tribunals, courts undertaking judicial review cannot correct a flawed decision as 'that is a step beyond judicial power' and is achievable only through the merits review process.[48]

In the context of the Truth Tribunal, undertaking a merits review would better exposit issues concerning the facts of original proceedings. The overarching goal of the Tribunal is to decide what is and isn't the truth amongst contested information. If the Truth Tribunal was hindered from reviewing the original facts of the dispute, it would be unable to fulfill its overarching goals. Positioning the Tribunal in the same capacity as the original decision maker will broaden its scope to determine truth. If it were to adopt judicial review, the Tribunal would not be able to determine the factual nature of disputes, setting aside concerns arising from the Separation of Powers Doctrine. Merits review, as a key characteristic of administrative tribunals, therefore constitutes an appropriate institution to house this proposal given the Truth Tribunal's purpose in determining truth from issues of fact.

Jurisdictional Errors

If the Truth Tribunal is to adopt the same structure as an administrative tribunal, consideration should be given to its capacity to handle jurisdictional errors as opposed to a court. In *Kirk v Industrial Relations Court (2010) ('Kirk'),* the majority referred to the distinction drawn in *Craig v South Australia* ('Craig') between what constitutes a jurisdictional error in courts versus tribunals.[49] A jurisdictional error in the context of an administrative tribunal arises when it falls into an error of law, potentially leading the tribunal to rely upon irrelevant information, fail to omit key evidence or identify the wrong issues.[50] According to the majority in *Craig*, these issues of law would not constitute a jurisdictional error if they arose in an inferior court.[51] The key distinction drawn in *Craig* and reflected in *Kirk* is that tribunals "do not have the capacity to authoritatively determine issues of law like a court can".[52] This is because the original jurisdiction of a court is a jurisdiction of law.[53] The reason for this distinction is that an administrative tribunal exercises executive power and, per the Separation of Powers Doctrine, an administrative body cannot exercise judicial power.[54] If it were to consider its own issues of law then it would be exceeding its own authority.[55] In the context of the Truth Tribunal, making a jurisdictional error in a given dispute would invalidate any order made on these proceedings. Housing Truth Tribunals in a court would thus mitigate against the potential hindrance of administrative tribunals using executive power.

The Impact of Judicial Review on the Efficiency of the Truth Tribunal

The efficiency of administrative tribunals' review mechanisms is a necessary characteristic to ensure the Truth Tribunal's ability to quickly deliver decisions that prevent the proliferation of fake news. However, the Tribunal's efficiency may be hindered if the body makes an error of law, and an appeal is brought to a Superior Court for judicial review. If a decision by the Tribunal is subject to judicial review, it is likely that many of the desirable features of the model would be extinguished, as the appeal will require the characteristics of a court. When the appeal is brought before a court, the parties will be subject to the formal and costly nature of court proceedings. As recognised throughout this paper, the mitigation of fake news is reliant on the Truth Tribunal reaching a swift outcome in determining the truthful nature of disputed information brought forward by an aggrieved party.

To preserve the Truth Tribunal's intention to provide an efficient and accessible review mechanism, lawmakers may choose to ouster the court's supervisory function. Privative clauses are legislative tools incorporated into the governing legislation of administrative tribunals that attempt to remove certain acts of executive power, such as administrative decisions, from judicial review.[56] However, the following discussion examines how the HCA has been reluctant in depriving the superior courts of their inherent function of review in both the state and federal context.

Challenges Facing A Truth Tribunal

Previous analysis illustrates that an institution focused on deciding the truth amongst disputed information would operate most effectively as a Tribunal, not a court. Since the abolishment of the AAT, there will likely be discussions about how a future tribunal can avoid the politicisation that engulfed the AAT. This section considers whether adapting specific characteristics from the court system will promote confidence in and ensure the longevity of the Truth Tribunal's operation. These limitations must be situated in the model adopted in the AAT's inception, which is:

> [i]n part the strength of legal culture, in part, the unwillingness to move from the known and well-established rules of evidence and in part, the fact that tribunals are sited in an adjudicative system the final tiers of which traditionally operate in an adversarial fashion.[57]

Detention equally affects the ability of litigants to access legal representation, which is necessary in a quasi-adversarial system. The inhibiting effect of failing to secure legal representation is effectively highlighted in a review of the Australian Law Reform Commission: applicants who gained legal representation succeeded in the AAT 53.5% of the time, compared to a 16.7% success rate if self-represented.[58] Taking into account that legal aid may have been more readily available to applicants with more meritorious claims, such a divide is still indicative of practical barriers to justice, created by implementing a quasi-adversarial merits review system that has its roots in traditional legal fora.[59]

Membership of the Truth Tribunal

The AAT's politicisation, leading to its abolishment, is a challenge that a Truth Tribunal must overcome to achieve longevity. Fake news is inextricably linked to political rhetoric, and as previously discussed is politicised in relation to socio-cultural issues.[60] A potential measure mitigating against the politicisation of the institution constitutes changing the AAT's composition to comprise of Chapter III Judges who possess judicial independence. This will promote public confidence in the non-partisan outcomes made by the Truth Tribunals.

Judicial independence

Unlike administrative tribunals, a key feature of Chapter III Courts is the Doctrine of Judicial Independence, which aims to reduce judicial impropriety among judges and promote public confidence in the decisions made by courts.[61] The Doctrine is considered fundamental to the operation of courts and upholding the rule of law.[62] The United Nations Basic Principles on the Independence of the Judiciary requires that judicial independence be guaranteed, enshrined in a state's constitution, and that there is a positive "duty of all governmental and other institutions to respect and observe the independence of the judiciary".[63] A preference for courts to retain their role as the ultimate fact finder in proceedings is likely to exist due to the protection of independence held by Chapter III Judges.[64]

Judicial independence is entrenched in section 72 of the Australian Constitution.[65] The provision provides judges with the enjoyment of lifelong tenure on the court that they have been appointed to.[66] Providing judges with the guarantee of tenure limits the scope for impropriety, as judges are not seeking an election and are less susceptible to influence concerns arising from bias or other interests. Former Chief Justice Brennan once described tenure as a commitment "to serve and protect not the governors but the governed", inferring that it is a mechanism to ensure that the interests of the court remain with the people.[67] The Doctrine of Judicial Independence limits the politicisation of the institution, promoting confidence that the court's outcomes were reached through an independent interpretation of the law, not by one side of the political spectrum.

Tribunals do not conform to the Doctrine, despite being external to other government agencies that allow for a degree of independence.[68] Characteristics of tribunals that limit its separation from governments include that they are established by statute, funded by government, reside under the Attorney-General's portfolio, and they exercise executive power".[69]

Members of the Tribunal do not enjoy the guarantees of tenure like judges and therefore, they are exposed to potential bias.[70] These concerns had recently manifested which led to the Albanese Labor Government upon securing government announcing that the AAT would be abolished due to the way in which the institution had been politicised. Concerns that the public may perceive a Tribunal as biased arose following the announcement that the AAT was to be abolished after years of alleged stacking of conservative-leaning appointees to the AAT.[71]

The use of Chapter III Judges will allow the Truth Tribunal to hear claims of fake news under the shield of judicial independence that will minimise criticism that its decisions are biased or partisan. The Doctrine will also instil confidence that the decision-makers hearing claims of fake news are free from external interests as guaranteed under section 72 of the AC. However, if a Chapter III Judge was to preside over proceedings in the Truth Tribunal, this may present constitutional challenges.

Challenges arising from Chapter III Judges presiding over proceedings in the Truth Tribunal will likely pertain to the Doctrine of the Separation of Powers. Under the Australian Legal System, there is a distinction separation between the Legislature, the Executive and the Judiciary, who all perform separate functions.[1] The Doctrine stems from the AC, which implies that the powers of the Australian Commonwealth should be distinct to ensure no limb possesses all power, also promoting accountability.[72] The Judiciary is responsible for the accountability of the other two limbs and provides an avenue to hear claims of excessive use of power beyond those outlined in the AC.

[1] Parliamentary Education Office, 'Separation of Powers: Parliament, Executive and the Judiciary", *Commonwealth Parliament of Australia* (Webpage, date accessed 1 May 2023) https://peo.gov.au/understand-our-parliament/how-parliament-works/system-of-government/separation-of-powers/

Despite the Separation of Powers Doctrine calling for clear distinctions between the exercise of each power, there is precedent that may allow Chapter III Judges to prescribe over the Truth Tribunal. An argument for Chapter III Judge presiding over the Tribunal can be drawn upon from their utility in disciplinary proceedings of military personnel. The original disciplinary hearings for charges against active members of the Australian Defence Force ('ADF') are heard outside of the Australian Court System, however, where the use of Judges arises is in the right to appeal.[73] Aggrieved ADF Members possess the right to appeal the original judgment to the Defence Force Discipline Appeal Tribunal (DFDAT).[74] Unlike in the original decision, membership of the DFDAT comprises exclusively of members of the Judiciary.[75] The judges that preside in the DFDAT often have extensive military and judicial experience as reflected through their appointments, generally to superior Australian courts.[76] ADF members like those aggrieved in administrative tribunals can seek a further appeal to the Federal Court or the HCA on grounds of error of law.[77]

The DFDAT precedent that Chapter III Judges can preside over tribunals and contribute judicial independence in their proceedings supports the notion that judges can preside over administrative tribunals without infringing upon the Separation of Powers Doctrine, bolstering advocates for a Truth Tribunal.

Stronger Burden of Proof

When determining the truthfulness of a piece of information, observers will likely comment that it is better to deal in absolutes, and that the onus of proof in determining the truth should be beyond a reasonable doubt. However, as matters before administrative tribunals are civil, it may not be feasible to impose a greater onus than on the balance of probabilities.

In the context of administrative tribunals, the general assumption when conducting merits review is that it is the "civil standard that applies".[78] The issue of whether the standard of proof should remain consistent regardless of the dispute in question arose in the matter of *Bringinshaw v Bringinshaw*. Here, Dixon J. elucidated that the standard of proof in disputes before a tribunal may vary depending on the gravity of the facts needing to be proved.[79] However, Dixon J. stops short of saying that the so-called 'Bringinshaw Standard', implied there is a distinction between the criminal and civil standards posing a standard of its own.[80] However, both Dixon J. and subsequent commentators have emphasised that administrative proceedings dont bare the same emphasis on whether a matter surpasses the standard of proof as it does in the context of judicial proceedings. [81] Subsequent decisions have affirmed that the Briginshaw standard is not applicable in the context of the AAT, and that the AAT is not strictly bound to abide by the standards like a court.[82]

The Truth Tribunal's adoption of a greater standard of proof than a conventional proceeding would promote certainty in its outcomes but would likely be applied inconsistently. Further, observers may view the decisions made by the Tribunal as the truth if it adopts an almost curtain standard, presenting a burden claimants cannot easily meet. However, adopting a standard of proof closer to the standard taken in criminal proceedings would be aspirational, not practical. Fake news may hinder the practicality of the standard of proof as the nature of fake news inherently sews doubt in the truthfulness of information. Reforming the standard would likely lead to very few claims that exceed the standard held in civil proceedings. The applicable logic would likely prevail when considering the truthfulness of disputed information and therefore observing the current standard applicable in civil proceedings will likely still achieve the Tribunals intended function and will not hinder its effectiveness.

Conclusion

This chapter's premise was to determine the viability of a Truth Tribunal within the fabric of Australia's administrative law. The nature of this administrative law is complex and ambiguous following the abolishment of the AAT. In its wake, there is much uncertainty as to what characteristics future Tribunals, including the Truth Tribunal, will need to adopt to achieve longevity. This chapter evaluated the nature of review between courts and tribunals and discerned that only the process of merits review can properly adjudicate claims about fake news and discern the truth. After recognising an administrative tribunal as the appropriate vehicle for hearing fake news claims, consideration was given to how lawmakers could create the institution and what characteristics it would possess. Part III centred on the challenges the Truth Tribunal may face from those who oppose its creation and how lawmakers could circumvent these.

With respect to the viability of a truth-seeking model, it appears that tribunals as an institution may be a viable pathway for building digital resilience if those advocating for its creation can navigate the complexity of the current state of administrative law.

Notes

1. Luke Buckmaster and Tyson Wils, 'Responding to Fake News' (Research Paper, Parliament of Australia, July 2019) <https://www.aph.gov.au/About_Parliament/Parliamentary_departments/Parliamentary_Library/pubs/BriefingBook46p>; Anker Gupta et al., 'Combating Fake News: Stakeholder Interventions and Potential Solutions' *IEEE Access* 10, 78268, 78269; Scott Shackleford, 'The Battle Against Disinformation is Global' (Web Page, The Conversation, 20 March 2020) <https://theconversation.com/the-battle-against-disinformation-is-global-129212>; See generally, Tanya Notley, Michael Dezuanni, '*We Live in an Age of Fake News: But Australian Children are not Learning Enough About Media Literacy*', (Date Published 2020), Western Sydney University, <https://www.westernsydney.edu.au/ics/news/in_the_conversation/we_live_in_an_age_of_fake_news_but_australian_children_are_not_learning_enough_about_media_literacy>.
2. See generally, Daniel Funke, and Daniela Flamini, 'A Guide to anti-misinformation actions around the world' (Online Database, The Poynter Institute, 1 May 2023) <https://www.poynter.org/ifcn/anti-misinformation-actions/> ('Funke and Flamini'); See further, Peter Roudik,

'Initiatives to Counter Fake News in Selected Countries: Argentina, Brazil, Canada, China, Egypt, France, Germany, Israel, Japan, Kenya, Malaysia, Nicaragua, Russia, Sweden, United Kingdom' (2019) 1 *University of Nebraska Global Legal Research Directorate* 1, 2 ('Roudik').
3. Ibid.
4. Senate Select Committee on Foreign Interference through Social Media, Parliament of Australia, *Final Report: Chapter 3: International Issues* (Report, July 2023), 4.
5. Special Committee on Foreign Interference in all democratic processes in the European Union, including disinformation, European Union, *Final Report on Foreign Interference in all Democratic Processes in the European Union, including Disinformation* (Report 2022/2075, 15 May 2023), 93 <https://www.europarl.europa.eu/doceo/document/A-9-2023-0187_EN.html>.
6. Mike Burgess, Director-General of Security, 'Director-General's Annual Threat Assessment' (Press Release, 21 February 2023) <https://www.asio.gov.au/director-generals-annual-threat-assessment-2023>.
7. *Flunke and Flamini* (n ii).
8. Graciela Rodriguez-Ferrand, 'Argentina' in Peter Roudik (ed), 'Initiatives to Counter Fake News in Selected Countries: Argentina, Brazil, Canada, China, Egypt, France, Germany, Israel, Japan, Kenya, Malaysia, Nicaragua, Russia, Sweden, United Kingdom' *University of Nebraska Global Legal Research Directorate* (Digital Commons, 2019) 1, 1, 4 ('Rodriguez-Ferrand').
9. Rodriguez-Ferrand citing Comisión Permanente de Justicia, 'Comision De Verificacion De Notificias Falsas Difundias En Redes Sociales Durante Las Campanas Electorales Nacionales Creacion En El Ambito De La Camara Nacional Electoral' *Diputados Argentina* (Webpage, August 2018) <https://www.diputados.gob.ar/comisiones/permanentes/cjusticia/proyecto.html?exp=5228-D-2018>.
10. Ibid.
11. Rodriguez-Ferrand (n viii) 4–5.
12. Rodriguez-Ferrand (n viii) 5.
13. Rodriguez-Ferrand (n viii) 5.
14. Rodriguez-Ferrand (n viii) 5.
15. Rodriguez-Ferrand (n viii) 5.
16. Rodriguez-Ferrand (n viii) 5.
17. Peter Roudik, 'Comparative Summary' in Peter Roudik (ed), 'Initiatives to Counter Fake News in Selected Countries: Argentina, Brazil, Canada, China, Egypt, France, Germany, Israel, Japan, Kenya, Malaysia, Nicaragua, Russia, Sweden, United Kingdom' *University of Nebraska Global Legal Research Directorate* (Digital Commons, 2019) 1, 1.
18. *Communications Legislation Amendment (Combating Misinformation and Disinformation) Bill (Cth) 2023.*
19. Department of Infrastructure, Transport, Regional Development, Communications and the Arts, 'New ACMA Powers to Combat Misinformation and Disinformation' *Australian Government* (Webpage, accessed 20 March 2023) <https://www.infrastructure.gov.au/have-your-say/new-acma-powers-combat-misinformation-and-disinformation>; See generally, Andrea Carson, 'More Stick, Less Carrot: Australia's New Approach to Tackling Fake News' *Australian Strategic Policy Institute* (Webpage, 17 July 2023) <https://www.aspistrategist.org.au/more-stick-less-carrot-australias-new-approach-to-tackling-fake-news>.
    Ibid.
20. Ibid.
21. Paul Karp, 'Australian Christian Lobby says plans to combat social media misinformation will cancel Christian posts', *The Guardian Australia* (Online article, 5 August 2023) <https://www.theguardian.com/australia-news/2023/aug/05/australian-christian-lobby-social-posts-labor-misinformation-campaign>.
22. Ibid (n xxi).
23. Rodriguez-Ferrand (n viii) 5.
24. Rodriguez-Ferrand (n viii) 5.
25. Rodriguez-Ferrand (n viii) 5.

26. Pamela DH Schulz OAM, Andrew Cannon AM FAAL, 'The Discourse of Deception: Are the Media, the Community or Courts the Arbiters of Truth' (2022) 32(1) *Journal of Judicial Administration* 26, 32. ('Schulz and Cannon') citing Australian Government, Productivity Commission, Report of Government Services: 7 Courts (Final Report, 28 January 2022) <https://www.pc.gov.au/research/ongoing/report-on-government-services/2022/justice/courts>.
27. Schulz and Cannon (n xxvi) 33.
28. Schulz and Cannon (n xxvi) 33.
29. *Mabo v Queensland (No 2)* (1992) 175 CLR 1 70; Schulz and Cannon (n xxvi) 33.
30. Schulz and Cannon (n xxvi) 33.
31. Tess McGuire, 'Aboriginal Australians cannot be deported as 'Aliens' High Court holds' *Human Rights Law Centre* (Webpage, accessed 21 February 2023) <https://www.hrlc.org.au/human-rights-case-summaries/2020/2/21/aboriginal-australians-cannot-be-deported-as-aliens-high-court-holds#:~:text=The%20tripartite%20test%20is%20derived,by%20the%20elders%20or%20other>.
32. Schulz and Cannon (n 4) 33.
33. Schulz and Cannon (n 4) 33.
34. Malcolm Brown, 'Dingo Baby Ruling Ends 32 Years of Torment for Lindy Chamberlain', *The Guardian Australia*, (Webpage, 13 June 2012) <https://www.theguardian.com/world/2012/jun/12/dingo-baby-azaria-lindy-chamberlain>.
35. University of Technology Sydney 'Evidence in the museum: Curating a miscarriage of justice' *UTS OPUS* (Webpage, date accessed 10 February 2023) <https://opus.lib.uts.edu.au/bitstream/10453/98953/1/Evidence%20in%20the%20museum%20%20revised%20after%20referees%2010%2002%2017%20%20author%20details%20removed%20and%20after%20LCC%20changes%20made.docx>.
36. Schulz and Cannon (n xxvi) 41.
37. Schulz and Cannon (n xxvi) 44.
38. Schulz and Cannon (n xxvi) 42–43.
39. Schulz and Cannon (n xxvi) 42–43.
40. Schulz and Cannon (n xxvi) 43–44.
41. Schulz and Cannon (n xxvi) 43.
42. Schulz and Cannon (n xxvi) 43.
43. Schulz and Cannon (n xxvi) 43–44.
44. David Bennett, 'Balancing Judicial Review & Merits Review' (2000) 53 *Administrative Law Review Journal* 3, 4 <http://classic.austlii.edu.au/au/journals/AdminRw/2000/2.html> ('Bennett').
45. Ibid.
46. Bennett (n xliv) 5.
47. *Attorney General (NSW) v Quin* (1990) 170 CLR 1, 36.
48. Duncan Kerr 'The Intersection of Merits and Judicial Review' (2013) 32(1) *University of Queensland Law Journal* 1, 15.
49. *Kirk v Industrial Relations Court of New South Wales* (2010) 239 CLR 531, 66.
50. Ibid 67–68.
51. *Craig v South Australia* (1995) 184 CLR 163, 179–80.
52. Kristen Walker, 'The Jurisdictional Errors since Craig' (26 February 2016) 86 *Australian Institute of Administrative Law Forum* 35, 42 <http://classic.austlii.edu.au/au/journals/AIAdminLawF/2016/27.pdf> ('Walker').
53. Ibid.
54. Walker (n lii) 35.
55. Ibid.
56. Nicholas Gouliaditus, 'Privative Clauses: Epic Fail Critique and Comment' (2010) *Melbourne University Law Review* 34(3) 870, 871 <https://law.unimelb.edu.au/__data/assets/pdf_file/0003/1703523/34_3_7.pdf>.
57. Narelle Bedford and Robin Creyke, 'Inquisitorial Processes in Australian Tribunals' (2006) *Australia Institute of Judicial Administration Incorporated* 1, 66.

58. Australian Law Reform Commission, *Part One: Empirical Information about the Administrative Appeals Tribunal* (Report, 1999) 187, 7.5.
59. Samuel C. Duckett White, 'God-Like Powers: The Character Test and Unfettered Ministerial Discretion', (2020) 41(1) *Adelaide Law Review* 1, 27.
60. Rosa Scardigno, '*The Rhetoric Side of Fake News: A New Weapon for Anti-Politics?*' (31 December 2019) 76(1) *The Journal of New Paradigm Research* 1, 85.
61. Gerard Brennan, 'Judicial Independence' (Speech, A symposium delivered to the Australian Judicial Conference, 2 November 1996) 1.
62. Rebecca Ananian-Welsh and George Williams, 'Judicial Independence from the Executive: A First-Principles Review of the Australian Cases' 40(3) *Monash University Law Review* 593, 594. <https://www.monash.edu/__data/assets/pdf_file/0005/232637/ananianwelshwilliams.pdf>.
63. Ibid citing the Basic Principles on the Independence of the Judiciary, UN DOC A/CONF.122/22/Rev.1 (26 August-6 September 1985) art 1.
64. *Australian Constitution* s 72.
65. Ibid.
66. Ibid.
67. Gerard Brennan, 'Judicial Independence' (Speech, A symposium delivered to the Australian Judicial Conference, 2 November 1996) 1.
68. Administrative Appeals Tribunal, '*Tribunals in Australia: Their Role and Responsibilities*', (2004), *Australian Federal Government* (Webpage, accessed 4 May 2023) <https://www.aat.gov.au/about-the-aat/engagement/speeches-and-papers/the-honourable-justice-garry-downes-am-former-pres/tribunals-in-australia-their-roles-and-responsibilties>.
69. Judith Bannister, Anna Olijnk, et al, '*Government Accountability-Australian Administrative Law*', (Cambridge University Press, 2nd edition, January 2020) 245.
70. Ibid.
71. Jake Evans, ''Politicised' Administrative Appeals Tribunal abolished, after attorney-general declares its reputation ruined' (16 December 2022) *Australian Broadcasting Corporation* (Webpage, date accessed 3 May 2023) <https://www.abc.net.au/news/2022-12-16/administrative-appeals-tribunal-abolished-by-attorney-general/101781300>.
72. See generally, *Australian Constitution* Ch I, II and III; Geoffrey Lindell 'Why is Australia's Constitution Binding? The Reasons in 1900 and Now, and the Effect of Independence' (1986) 16(1) *Federal Law Review* 29.
73. Samuel C. Duckett White, 'A Soldier by Any Other Name: A Reappraisal of the "Citizen in Uniform" Doctrine in Light of Part IIIAAA of the *Defence Act 1903* (Cth)' (2019) 57(2) *Military Law and Law of War Review* 279 1, 68 ('White').
74. Ibid 71.
75. Ibid 71.
76. Ibid 71.
77. Ibid 71.
78. Ian Harvey, 'Applying the Rules of Evidence in Administrative Proceedings' (February 2019) *Precedent Australian Lawyers Alliance* 150 18, 40–43 ('Harvey').
79. *Briginshaw v Briginshaw* (1938) 60 CLR 336 362.
80. Ibid.
81. Harvey (n lxxviii).
82. Harry Stratton 'Perfectly Safe, Five Times out of Six: The Briginshaw Principle and its Paradoxes' (2019) 42(2) *University of New South Wales Law Journal* 427 <https://www.unswlawjournal.unsw.edu.au/wp-content/uploads/2019/06/1-UNSWLJ-422-Stratton-Final.pdf>.

Hamish Charles McNamara is an early career professional working within the dispute resolution branch at the Department of Veterans' Affairs. Nearing towards the completion of his Bachelor of Laws and Bachelor of Commerce (Int. Bus) at the University of Adelaide, Hamish seeks to work at the intersect of international law and trade. The breadth of Hamish's pre-admission

Table 1 Extracts from Poynter institute database relating to misinformation

Country	Action	Focus	Orientation
Argentina	Government task force	Misinformation; election interference	Monitoring; sanctions
Belarus	Law	Misinformation	Sanction
Belgium	Expert group	Misinformation	Awareness
Cambodia	Law	Misinformation	Sanction
Cambodia	Arrests	Media regulation	Sanction
Canada	Media literacy campaign	Media literacy	Awareness
Canada	Government task force	Foreign disinformation campaigns	Monitoring
Chile	Bill	Misinformation	Sanction
Democratic Republic of Congo	Government WhatsApp account	Misinformation	Monitoring
Denmark	Government task force and action plan	Misinformation	Monitoring
France	Law	Election misinformation	Accountability
India	Bill	Misinformation	Sanction
Indonesia	Government task force, arrests	Election misinformation	Sanction
Italy	Online reporting portal	Misinformation	Sanction
Italy	Arrests	Misinformation	Sanction
Italy	Authority report	Misinformation	Awareness
Kazakhstan	Government investigation	Misinformation	Sanction
Kenya	Law	Misinformation	Sanction
Malaysia	Law	Misinformation	Sanction
Mexico	Government task force	Misinformation	Awareness
Myanmar	Law	Misinformation	Sanction
Myanmar	Arrests	Misinformation	Sanction
Netherlands	Media literacy campaign	Foreign disinformation campaigns	Awareness
Nigeria	Media literacy campaign	Misinformation	Awareness
Nigeria	State radio broadcasts	Misinformation	Awareness
Oman	Government task force	Misinformation	Awareness
Pakistan	Government Twitter account	Misinformation	Awareness

(continued)

Table 1 (continued)

Country	Action	Focus	Orientation
The Philippines	Dismissed bill	Misinformation	Accountability
The Philippines	Bill	Misinformation	Sanction
Rwanda	Policy proposals	Misinformation	Sanction
Saudi Arabia	Government threats	Misinformation	Sanction
Singapore	Law	Misinformation	Sanction
South Korea	Government task force	Misinformation	Sanction
South Korea	Proposed law amendments	Misinformation	Sanction
Spain	Committee recommendation	Misinformation	Monitoring
Spain	Joint cybersecurity group	Misinformation	Monitoring
Spain	Government fact-checking	Misinformation	Monitoring
Sri Lanka	Internet shutdowns	Misinformation	Accountability
Sri Lanka	Legal revisions	Misinformation	Sanction
Sweden	Government authority	Foreign disinformation campaigns	Awareness
Sweden	Public handbook	Foreign disinformation campaigns	Awareness
Taiwan	Bill	Misinformation	Sanction
Taiwan	Legal revisions	Misinformation	Sanction
Taiwan	Legal revisions	Misinformation	Sanction
Thailand	Arrests	Misinformation	Sanction
Thailand	Government task force	Misinformation	Sanction
Turkey	Government investigation	Misinformation	Sanction
United Kingdom	Governmental task force	Foreign disinformation campaigns	Monitoring
United Kingdom	Parliamentary report	Misinformation	Awareness
Vietnam	Law	Misinformation	Sanction

experience encompasses working across state and federal government, consulting and academia including the Research Unit on Military Law and Ethics ('RUMLAE'). Working closely with Dr. Colette Langos of RUMLAE, Hamish's research has focussed on the commercial challenges of working with defence, commercial space law, government contracting and most recently sustainable public procurement. Hamish's research interests lie at the intersect of international law, technology, and individual freedoms and how each interacts. Hamish has a particular interest in Indo-Pacific affairs and as a result actively engages in initiatives that strengthen the bilateral relationship including previously living and working in Indonesia as a Delegate on behalf of the Department of Foreign Affairs and Trade. The author wishes to thank Dr. Samuel White for his continuous and unwavering support on this project.

Resilience of the Prerogative

Samuel White

Abstract Determining whether an exercise of constitutional executive power is a manifestation of the royal prerogative or merely a new excuse for executive excess, is notoriously difficult. The royal prerogative remains elusive, notwithstanding a millennium of its exercise. Often its use is viewed as falling on the fringes of government action—honours and awards, the exercise of mercy, or the movement of troops around the country. Other times it has been abridged by statute: either explicitly or implicitly. Yet, its breadth and depth remain potent within modern Australia. This chapter looks to address specifically the oft-referenced and historically well-used prerogative of reading the royal mail as a model for digital resilience. It does so to highlight the residual power that remains in section 61 of the Australian *Constitution* and to provide a useful case study on the fine line between valid prerogative evolution and invalid expansion of executive power unsanctioned by parliament.

Introduction

It is often held that in the absence of legislation, the Commonwealth executive government generally has no power to create new offences.[1] This is particularly important within the ambit of emerging threats, such as those the cyber domain offers. How can governments respond? Oddly, with the oldest tool available—executive power. All States have some level of power within their various constitutions (written or unwritten) to respond to emergencies outside of legislation. Australia—the focus of this case study—is no different.

The Australian Government generally has no power to impose obligations or compel behaviour (including producing documents or information),[2] or to levy taxes.[3] In addition, the Commonwealth executive government is subject to requirements under the general law (including the common law and statute), unless its conduct is authorised by legislation or otherwise lawfully justified.[4] The reference to conduct which infringes the 'law' includes statute law and the common law.[5] This

S. White (✉)
The University of Adelaide, Adelaide, Australia
e-mail: Samuel.white@adelaide.edu.au

D. Stephens et al. (eds.), *Digital Resilience*,
https://doi.org/10.1007/978-981-97-9746-2_11

includes (among other rights) the common law right to bodily integrity protected by the torts of negligence and trespass,[6] the common law right to liberty protected by the tort of false imprisonment and the writ of habeas corpus,[7] and common law rights in relation to private property protected by the tort of trespass and other torts.[8]

This principle finds its antecedents in the eighteenth-century decision in *Entick v Carrington.*[9] John Entick's house was entered and sacked, without warrant, by the King's Chief Messenger, Nathan Carrington, under orders by Lord Halifax, the newly appointed Secretary of State for the Northern Department. The search was conducted under a general warrant in the hope of finding incriminating, seditious pamphlets. None were found, and Entick sued for trespass. The Court held that the general warrants were illegal, and the Secretary of State could not order searches of private property without authority conferred by an Act of Parliament or the common law.[10] *Entick* reflects a watershed moment in the common law, for establishing a firm limit on executive power.[11]

The ratio of *Entick* forms part of Australia's constitutional inheritance and was confirmed in the decision of *A v Hayden.*[12] In that case, Australian Secret Intelligence Service (ASIS) officers, employees and an army representative were directed to participate in a security training exercise, which involved freeing a 'hostage' from a hotel room in Melbourne. The training exercise went awry and it was alleged that the participants had committed criminal offences under Victorian legislation.[13] There was no Commonwealth legislation which authorised the relevant conduct or provided an exemption from the Victorian legislation. The High Court emphasised that the fact that the Commonwealth executive government had authorised the training exercise did not excuse the commission of criminal offences. Chief Justice Gibbs emphasised: 'It is fundamental to our legal system that the executive has no power to authorise a breach of the law and that it is no excuse for an offender to say that he acted under the orders of a superior officer.'[14]

Yet, as Professor Leslie Zines has commented, an exercise of constitutional executive power does not necessarily result in a breach of the law. Declarations of war and peace, the alteration of national boundaries, acts of state, the pardoning of offenders, and various immunities and privileges are capable of lawfully interfering with the legal rights and duties of others.[15] Ultimately, the difficulty in interpretation arises from the fact that executive power is 'described but not defined in section 61'[16] of the *Constitution*, which reads as follows:

> [t]he executive power of the Commonwealth is vested in the Queen and is exercisable by the Governor-General as the Queen's representative, and extends to the execution and maintenance of this *Constitution*, and of the laws of the Commonwealth.

It is a power of the Crown, to be used for the Crown.[17] Executive power is not solely limited to authorising ADF operations: it applies to and through any number of organs of the State. Yet it provides the clearest, historically resilient, legal authority for the Australian Government to respond to digital threats.

The Royal Prerogative

Constitutional executive power can be divided into three ways: statutory, prerogative, and a power that is neither statutory nor a prerogative (nationhood power). It can be both an art and a science to find the exact nature of power being relied upon—be it in war, national emergencies, or peacetime.

Professor George Winterton assisted in this field through advocating a methodology of 'breadth' and 'depth'.[18] This practice was adopted by the (now Chief) Justice Gageler, who explained 'breadth' to relate to 'the subject-matters with respect to which the Executive Government of the Commonwealth is empowered to act having regard to the constraints of the federal system',[19] while depth denotes 'the precise actions which the Executive Government is empowered to undertake in relation to those subject matters'.[20] This is an area where national emergencies raise particular friction points, being outside the enumerated areas of Commonwealth responsibility in s 51 of the *Constitution*. The problem is solved through interpretation. The implied nationhood power has increased the **breadth** of Commonwealth action (being anything with a national flavour) but having no **depth**.[21]

Yet there remains a clear branch of executive power which has significant depth: the royal prerogative. Sir William Blackstone was not the first to describe the Royal prerogative, but he was the first to attempt to do so comprehensively. Blackstone declares:

> By the word prerogative we usually understand that special pre-eminence which the King hath, over and above all other persons, and out of the ordinary course of common law, in right of his regal dignity... it can only be applied to those rights and capacities which the King enjoys alone, in contradiction to others, and not to those which he enjoys in common with any of his subjects.[22]

Such a position reflects the theocratic nature of the Crown, a power that is only exercised by the Monarch and the Monarch alone. AV Dicey rejected this and accused Blackstone of 'applying old and inapplicable terms to new institutions, and especially of ascribing in words to a modern and constitutional King the whole, and perhaps more than the whole, of the powers actually possessed and exercised by William the Conqueror.'[23] Dicey proposed alternatively that:

> The prerogative appears to be historically and as a matter of fact nothing else than the residue of discretionary or arbitrary authority which at any given time is legally left in the hands of the crown. The prerogative is the name of the remaining portion of the Crown's original authority ... Every act which the executive government can lawfully do without the authority of an Act of Parliament is done in virtue of the prerogative.[24]

Such a position reflects a more mundane and human approach to power. Dicey is popular in the United Kingdom,[25] but as Munro has noted it is a rather careless articulation which has proven unfortunately resilient.[26] It fails to acknowledge the concept of the duality of the Crown. In comparison, Blackstone's strict approach is supported in Australian case law and will accordingly be adopted here.[27]

This recognises the impact of the Glorious Revolution in 1688, which provided that the Crown's powers that can only be used in accordance with convention and the principle of responsible government.[28] Importantly, prerogative power is to always be assessed from its existence in 1688, for 'it is 350 years and a civil war too late for the Queen's court to broaden the prerogative'.[29] As the prerogative in the colonies cannot be deeper or wider than the Crown in the British Isles,[30] it is important to note that any prerogative recognised within the Commonwealth—as a matter of law—applies automatically across the other colonies (as all British colonies occurred after 1688).

This is not only because the constitutional executive power is informed by the British common law,[31] but because the Court does not **create** the common law; it **recognises** it. Recognised in one jurisdiction in the Commonwealth, it is recognised everywhere in the Commonwealth.

Resilience of the Prerogative

It may shock individuals just how wide this remaining residual power or the rights and capacities really are. It extends across immunities, capacities and historic rights of priority; to the military and armed forces and their daily operation; to the minerals in the soil. Under the Royal prerogative, the Queen could dismiss all the officers from the Governor-General down; or could appoint any individual as an officer. The prerogative of war allows for operations to be declared unilaterally in order to conquer land, and is 'the only source of authority to kill or capture an enemy in war.'[32] Equally, under the prerogative of peace, any or all part of Australian territory could be sacrificed to another State or non-State group in order to cease hostilities. Likewise, the Royal Prerogative of Mercy could allow for every offender to be pardoned, regardless of their guilt;[33] and every Australian could be appointed a Member of the Order of Australia.

While it is accepted that the prerogative can evolve in a resilient way to meet emerging threats, the exact manner in which this happens is difficult to assess. The author suggests two possible options: a public policy test, and originalism.

Public Policy Test

Professor Winterton in 1983 wrote for the *Law Quarterly Review* a short but critical about article whether the 'questionable' prerogative to open and read mail could extend to telephone communications.[34] He stated that although the objectives of intercepting mail and intercepting telephone communications are the same—to protect state security and to prevent crime—the senders' expectations are different, as telephone communications are not intended to fall into an unintended person's hands.[35] He recognised that distinguishing between creation (which is not permitted) and resilience evolution (which is) 'may be a fine one'.[36] He further noted that due to the speed with which legislation can grant executive power where thought necessary, and the ambiguity regarding judicial review of the prerogative power, courts should be careful when adapting the old prerogatives.[37] This latter warning is of less relevance since jurisprudential developments.[38]

While Winterton's method of adapting the prerogative has been discussed by various academic papers,[39] it does not appear that any court has adopted the *public expectation* test to adapt the prerogative to novel situations. Winterton's public expectation test does help to provide some clarity in relation to the evolution of the prerogative, but it is questionable whether it is an entirely accurate reflection of the law. The requirement that the public must accept the development of the Crown's power seems quite unorthodox for the evolution of law. Therefore, the progression of the prerogative could be grounded elsewhere, and it is appropriate to determine whether the prerogative to open and read mail could evolve to different forms of communication by using different methods. Examining case law pertaining to the evolution of the prerogative may help to provide clarity.

Originalism

In contrast to the public policy test, an alternative arises originalism. The author argues that originalism is the true approach the Courts take with respect to adapting the prerogative. Therefore, in this section, the author outlines various authorities whereby the Courts adapted the prerogative to novel situations. Thereafter, the author applies this test to the prerogative to open and read mail to ascertain whether it can adapt to modern forms of communication.

A case that discussed the issue was *Re a Petition of Right*, a UK matter that was disputed during WW1.[40] The suppliants were the owners of land used for airstrip.[41] The Crown took possession of their land.[42] The issue in this case was whether the suppliants were entitled to compensation for the possession of their land.[43] They submitted on several grounds that they were entitled to compensation, and the Crown submitted on various grounds that they were not entitled to compensation. One of those grounds included whether the prerogative could adapt to the novel situation that was in dispute in this matter. Specifically, determining whether the prerogative could be used to take possession of an aerodrome free from any compensation, even though aerodromes were non-existent prior to the 1900s.[44] Warrington L. J. phrased the question as whether the prerogative is limited to circumstances where the enemy is against the 'soil' of the country.[45]

It was held that the Crown had a prerogative right to take possession of any man's land for the defence of the Commonwealth free from any compensation,[46] and could be used to take possession of an aerodrome, even though aerodromes were non-existent prior to the 1900s.[47] Warrington L. J. stated that the prerogative must vary with the 'advance of military science'.[48] Noting that to limit it to the soil of the country would limit the prerogative practically useless for the *purpose* for which it was entrusted to the King.[49] Further qualifying that the only condition that must be satisfied to exercise the prerogative is that the act must be necessary for the public safety and defence of the realm, and that view must be formed in good faith.[50] Similarly, Lord Cozens-Hardy M. R. also held that the prerogative must change with the advancement of technology.[51] His Lordship noted that the prerogative applied to what is reasonably necessary for preventing and repelling an invasion at the present time.[52]

It is submitted that the Court, in this matter, when ascertaining whether an action of the Crown was within the scope of the prerogative power did so by looking at the purpose for which the prerogative was entrusted to the King. Warrington LJ and Lord Cozens-Hardy M. R. noted that the prerogative was entrusted to the King for the public safety and defence of the realm. While aeroplanes were non-existent during the Glorious Revolution, taking possession of land for public safety and the defence of the realm did occur prior to the end of the Glorious Revolution. Since the aerodrome was taken for the defence of the realm, it was within the scope of the Crown's power.

Similarly, *De Keyser's Royal Hotel* was a case regarding a petition seeking that the Crown provide compensation to the Respondent for taking possession of their hotel.[53] The Crown submitted, inter alia, that the alleged act was done pursuant to the prerogative, and therefore no compensation was due and payable.[54] One issue Lord Sumner dealt with was whether the prerogative could capture the conduct that was in dispute in the matter.[55] Specifically, whether the prerogative applied to the trespass that occurred, or whether it was stricter and only applied to actions within a 'category of urgency'.[56]

To deal with the issue, Lord Sumner stated that 'with the progress of the art of war, the scope both of emergencies and of acts to be justified by emergency extends, and the prerogative adjusts itself to new discoveries'.[57] However, some acts 'are simply committed to the general administration of the Crown' and do not fall within the scope of the prerogative,[58] and the trespass that occurred in this matter fell within this category. It is submitted that Lord Sumner made this determination by ascertaining the purported purpose of the prerogative, and then ascertained whether the Crown's actions fell within that purpose. Lord Sumner held that the prerogative provides the Crown the right to intervene with private life in matters of urgency,[59] so matters of general administration do not fall within that purpose.

Therefore, whether the prerogative can adapt to a novel situation requires ascertaining whether it is being exercised for the *purpose* for which it was entrusted to the Crown. Being a part of the common law,[60] judges can give effect to the purpose through case law. So long as the new conduct falls within the general purpose for which the prerogative was entrusted to the Crown, then the conduct falls within its parameters. If the purpose or objectives of the prerogative can be ascertained, then the parameters of it can be drawn. This method of interpretation is similar to the one described by Professor Goldsworthy in his article 'Originalism in Australia'.[61]

Professor Goldsworthy states that new discoveries can still be captured by the original meaning for which a provision was enacted if it falls within the purpose for which it was created.[62] To better describe this method, he uses the example of a swan. He submits that if there was a law that pertained to swans, and at the time the law was enacted all swans were white feathered, and then a black feathered swan was discovered after the enactment of the law, the black swan would still be caught within the meaning of the provisions.[63] If the apparent purpose for which the provision was enacted was to regulate swans, then irrespective of the colour of the swan, all swans must be captured by its provisions.[64]

A similar view was also shared by the Birkett Committee while discussing adapting the prerogative to open and read mail. While discussing *Re a Petition of Right* in relation to adapting the scope of the prerogative, they stated that

> [t]he prerogative power in question in that case [*Re a Petition of Right*] was the power to take lands without compensation for the purposes of the Defence of the Realm, but if in the question we have to consider, the existence of a prerogative power to intercept all communications was established, the objection that the telephone was a modern invention would not defeat the application of the power.[65]

For the present issue at hand, if there was a prerogative that was entrusted to the Crown to read the general public's communications, and then new forms of communication were discovered, then those new forms of communication would have to be captured by the original prerogative. From mail to telegram to email to text messages, as communication develops, so does the prerogative's scope to regulate those new discoveries. So then, this requires asking, what was the purpose of entrusting the Crown to open and read mail? If this question is answered, then it can be determined whether all forms of communication fall within the scope of the prerogative.

An analysis of history is necessary to determine the purpose for which the prerogative was exercised. The proclamation by Elizabeth I in 1590 appears to have directed the executive to intercept mail for the purpose of centralising the use of the Royal Postage service.[66] Additionally, the ordinance by Cromwell in 1654 appears to have directed the executive to intercept mail for the purpose of thwarting rebels.[67] This would restrict the scope of the exercise of the prerogative to matters pertaining to treason and preventing the use of private communication. However, in Bernard Keenan's thesis, he quotes Samuel Morland, the first master-technician of letter interception in which he said

> a skilful Prince ought to make watch towers of his General Post Office of all his kingdoms and there to place such careful Sentinels as that, by their gaze and diligence, he may have a constant view of all of any moment throughout the universe but more especially of the various tempers of his own subjects, and of the first ferments of all factions, without which it is morally impossible for him long to sit on his throne.[68]

On this view, although intercepting mail can be used to view the 'the first ferments of all factions' it can also be used to 'have a constant view of all of any moment throughout the universe' and to view 'the various tempers of [the Crown's] subjects'. It is not a matter which necessarily specifically pertains to thwarting rebels but may apply more broadly to gazing and retrieving information from the public generally. Therefore, so long as the government is intercepting communication for the purpose of understanding the tempers of the public, then it is supported by the prerogative to open and read mail. This view is supported by the 1657 Post Office Act which established the need for a post office on the basis of finding 'intelligence' in the post.[69] This is broader than specific rebellious matters, but a need for the Post Office to be able to identify general intelligence from the public which could not be found except through the post.

A similar view was also held by the Birkett Committee. Finding that the purpose for creating a Crown monopoly in 1657 over the delivering of mail was done 'with the object of enabling the Crown to inspect the contents of the letters carried'.[70] Rather than being completely restricted to specific matters, the purpose was to allow the Crown to have broad powers to inspect mail for various purposes, not simply to thwart rebels. The purpose of intercepting mail was to ensure that the Crown could have a constant view over all their subjects and gather intelligence that would not be available but in the mail.

In a modern context, this could mean that the old prerogative could be adapted to apply to modern technology. If the government was intercepting text messages for the purpose of gathering intelligence from its subjects, then it would still fall within the ambit of the prerogative to open and read mail. So long as the government is exercising its power for the purpose of gathering intelligence, then the action would be lawful and conferred by the prerogative to open and read mail. Perhaps more appropriately, the prerogative to open and read mail should be referred to as the prerogative to intercept communications.

Conclusion

Applying both originalism and the public policy test, the prerogative to open and read mail can and does expand to include new forms of communication. However, the question remains which test is more appropriate.

For the author of this paper, originalism is the preferred test. It is submitted that originalism is a more accurate reflection of the law and gives effect to the methodology applied by the courts to adapt the prerogative to novel situations. It follows wider common law methodologies of 'always speaking', which allows for the common law to advance with both social needs and scientific advances.[71]

Although the public policy test does provide a useful means of adapting the prerogative, it seems quite odd for the power that 'the King enjoys alone' to be controlled by his subject's temperaments. Rather, it is submitted that the Courts should adapt the prerogative to novel situations by examining the original purpose that the prerogative was entrusted to the Crown, or exercised by the Crown, and determine whether the novel situation falls within that purpose. Within constitutional monarchies, and as a result of the Glorious Revolution, Parliament ultimately decides which powers are to remain within the remit of non-statutory executive power. They can be confirmed, expanded, limited or abridged by legislation. Originalism, rather than a form of ancestor worship,[72] also results in the millennia-old check-and-balance system of the royal prerogative. Responsible government, a pillar upon which Australian democracy stands, ultimately was developed in order to provide an effective check against excessive use of the plenary royal prerogative. Through either coarse or gentle review,[73] a constitutionally enshrined power is wielded responsibly. Applying Winterton's public policy test undermines this process.

Applying an originalism lens, the exercise of the prerogative to open and read mail resulted from a need for the Crown to gather intelligence from the public. It is, therefore, appropriate to adapt that prerogative to new forms of communication, so long as the Crown is only intercepting communication for intelligence-gathering purposes. This position has been mirrored across the Commonwealth where the prerogative is operationalised.

Notes

1. See, e.g., *Davis v Commonwealth* (1988) 166 CLR 79, 112 (Brennan J.); *Williams [No 1]* (n 7) [135] (Gummow and Bell J. J.).
2. *McGuiness v Attorney-General (Vic)* (1940) 83 CLR 73; *Victoria v Commonwealth* (1996) 187 CLR 416, 481.
3. *Williams [No 1]* (n 7) [135] (Gummow and Bell J. J.).
4. See, e.g., *Clough v Leahy* (1904) 2 CLR 139, 155–6 (Griffith C. J.); *Pirrie v McFarlane* (1925) 36 CLR 170; *Shaw Savill and Albion Co v Commonwealth* (1940) 66 CLR 344, 355 (Starke J.); *A v Hayden* (1984) 156 CLR 532, 540 (Gibbs C. J.), 562 (Murphy J.), 582, 588–9, 591 (Brennan J.), 593 (Deane J.); *Re Tracey; Ex parte Ryan* (1989) 166 CLR 518, 575–6 (Brennan and Toohey J. J.); *Re Residential Tenancies Tribunal (NSW) v Henderson; Ex parte Defence Housing Authority* (1997) 190 CLR 410, 427–9 (Brennan C. J.), 442–4 (Dawson, Toohey and Gaudron J. J.), 472–3 (Gummow J.); *Plaintiff M68* (n 15) 91 (Gageler J.).
5. See, eg, *Plaintiff M68* (n 15) [159] (Gageler J.).
6. *Binsaris v Northern Territory* [2020] HCA 22, [25] (Gageler J.).
7. *Plaintiff M68* (n 15) [162] (Gageler J.).
8. *Coco v R* (1994) 179 CLR 427, 435 (Mason C. J., Brennan, Gaudron and McHugh J. J.).
9. (1765) 19 Ste Tr 1029.
10. Ibid.
11. The case was later applied in *A v Hayden* (1984) 156 CLR 532, to extend the principle within the Australian common law jurisdiction.
12. Ibid.
13. Royal Commission on Australia's Security and Intelligence Agencies, *Report on the Sheraton Hotel Incident, February 1984* (Report, 1984).
14. Ibid 540.
15. Leslie Zines, *The High Court and the Constitution* (Federation Press, 5th ed, 2008) 345–6. See further Leslie Zines, 'The Inherent Executive Power of the Commonwealth' (2005) 16 *Public Law Review* 279, 280 ('Inherent Executive Power ').
16. *Commonwealth and the Central Wool Committee v Colonial Combing, Spinning and Weaving Co. Ltd.* (1922) 31 CLR 421, 440 per Isaacs J.; *Davis v Commonwealth* (1988) 166 CLR 79, 92 per Mason C. J., Deane and Gaudron J. J.; see also *Ruddock v Vadarlis* (2001) 110 FCR 491; see further George Winterton, 'The Limits and Use of Executive Power by the Government' (2003) 31 *Federal Law Review* 421.
17. What is the Crown–Maitland.
18. George Winterton, *Parliament, The Executive and the Governor-General* (Melbourne University Press, 1983) ('*Parliament*') 21.
19. *Plaintiff M68* (n vii) 130 (Gageler J.).
20. Ibid.

21. On the differing opinions, see Peta Stephenson, *Nationhood, Executive Power and the Australian Constitution* (Hart Publishing, 2022); compared to Samuel White & Cameron Moore, 'Calling out the ADF into the Grey Zone' (2022) 43(1) *Adelaide Law Review* 479–505.
22. Sir William Blackstone, *Commentaries on the Laws of England* (Clarendon Press 1765–69 [vol 1 must have had one particular year]) vol 1, 232 cited with approval in *Davis v Commonwealth* (1988) 166 CLR 79, 108 (Brennan J.) ('*Davis 1988*'); *Plaintiff M68/2015 v Minister for Immigration and Border Protection* (2016) 257 CLR 42, 133 (Gageler J.) ('*Plaintiff M68*').
23. AV Dicey, *The Law of the Constitution* (Palgrave Macmillan, 10th ed, 1959) 8 ('*The Law of the Constitution*').
24. Ibid 424–5.
25. *Attorney-General v De Keyser's Royal Hotel Ltd* [1920] AC 508, 526 (Lord Dunedin) ('*De Keyser's Hotel*'); *Burmah Oil Co Ltd v Lord Advocate* [1965] AC 75, 99 (Lord Reid); CCU 398 (Lord Fraser) ('*Burmah Oil*').
26. Colin Munro, *Studies in Constitutional Law* (Butterworth, 1987) 160.
27. *Federal Commissioner of Taxation v Official Liquidator of E.O. Farley Ltd* (1940) 63 CLR 278, 320 (Evatt J.) ('*Federal Commissioner of Taxation*'); *Davis 1988* (n xxii); *Plaintiff M68* (n xxii).
28. Geoffrey Marshall, *Constitutional Conventions—The Rules and Forms of Political Accountability* (Oxford University Press, 1986).
29. *British Broadcasting Corporation v Johns* [1965] Ch 32, 79 (Diplock L. J.). However, in the *Case of Proclamations* in 1611 (prior to the Glorious Revolution) Coke held that the sovereign could only exercise the prerogatives he had, and not create new ones: see *Case of Proclamations* (1611) 12 Co Rep 74, 77 ER 1352 (KB).
30. Enid Campbell, 'Prerogative Rule in New South Wales 1788–1823' (1964) 50 *Royal Australian Historical Society Journal* 162, 175–9
31. *Davis v Commonwealth* (1988) 166 CLR 79, 92 (Mason C. J., Deane and Gaudron J. J.) quoted *in Pape v Commissioner of Taxation* (2009) 238 CLR 1, 62 (French C. J.) and *Williams v Commonwealth [No 1]* (2012) 248 CLR 156, 372 (Kiefel J.).
32. Cameron Moore, 'Military Law and Executive Power' in Dale Stephens Robin Creyke, Peter Sutherland (ed), Military Law in Australia (Federation Press, 2019) 98.
33. *Ogawa v Attorney-General (No 2)* [2019] FCA 1003 [39] (Logan J.).
34. George Winterton, 'The Prerogative in Novel Situations' (1983) 99(3) *Law Quarterly Review* 408, 409 ('*The Prerogative in Novel Situations*').
35. Ibid.
36. Ibid 409.
37. Ibid.
38. *Peko-Wallsend Ltd* (n 48).
39. See Peter Gerangelos, 'The Executive Power of the Commonwealth of Australia: Section 61 of the Commonwealth Constitution, Nationhood and the Future of the Prerogative' (2012) 12(1) *Oxford University Commonwealth Law Journal* 97, 108; Nicholas Condylis, 'Debating The Nature And Ambit Of The Commonwealth's Non-Statutory Executive Power' (2015) 39 *Melbourne University Law Review* 385, 427.
40. *Re a Petition of Right* [1915] 3 KB 649, 661 (Pickford L. J.) ('*Re a Petition of Right*').
41. Ibid.
42. Ibid.
43. Ibid.
44. Ibid 660 (Lord Cozens-Hardy M. R.).
45. Ibid.
46. Ibid 666 (Warrington L. J.).
47. Ibid 660 (Lord Cozens-Hardy M. R.).
48. Ibid.
49. Ibid.
50. Ibid.
51. Ibid.

52. Ibid.
53. *De Keyser's Hotel* (n xxv) 555 (Lord Sumner).
54. Ibid.
55. Ibid.
56. Ibid 565.
57. Ibid.
58. Ibid.
59. Ibid.
60. *Jolley v Mainka* (1933) 49 CLR 242, 281–2.
61. Jeffrey Goldsworthy, 'Originalism in Australia' (2017) 31(3) *DPCE Online* 607, 613.
62. Ibid.
63. Ibid.
64. Ibid.
65. Birkett Committee, *Report of the Committee of Privy Councillors appointed to inquire into the interception of communications* (Cmnd 283, 1957) [9] ('*Report of the Committee of Privy Councillors*' [43]).
66. Secret Committee, *Report from the Secret Committee on the Post-Office together with Appendix Ordered by the House of Commons* (1844) 4 (*'Report from the Secret Committee*) 4
67. Bernard Keenan, 'Interception: Law, Media, and Techniques' (Ph.D. Thesis, London School of Economics, September 2017) 62.
68. Ibid 66, quoting Samuel Morland, *A Brief Disclosure Concerning the Nature and Reason of Intelligence* (Egmont Papers 1695).
69. *An Act for setling the Postage of England, Scotland and Ireland 1657,* 4 Cromwell.
70. *Report of the Committee of Privy Councillors* (n 58) [31].
71. *Lake Macquarie Shire Council v Aberdare County Council* (1970) 123 CLR 327, 331 (Barwick C. J.).
72. Michael Kirby, 'Constitutional Interpretation and Original Intent: A Form of Ancestor Worship' (2000) 24(1) *Melbourne University Law Review* 1.
73. Coarse being the historic basis of ministerial responsibility—execution. This has now shifted to gentle ministerial responsibility—dismissal.

Samuel White is a Senior Lecturer of the faculty of the Adelaide Law School at the University of Adelaide. He is concurrently a Visiting Fellow at the Australian Defence Force Academy and holds positions as an Adjunct Associate Professor at the University of New England. In 2024, he was made an Associate Fellow of the Royal Historical Society and the first Army Visiting Fellow at the Australian War Memorial. Samuel has also served as both a Royal Australian Infantry Corps and an Australian Army Legal Corps officer in a variety of tactical, operational and strategic level postings. His military experiences focused his doctoral studies, which addressed the constitutional ambit and limitations of responding to foreign interference (both traditional and modern forms) via military responses.

Corporate Legal Responses to Promote Resilience

Samuel White and Elizabeth Watford

Abstract This delves into the resilience of corporate regulatory options to promote digital resilience. The authors navigate the legal landscape surrounding the responsibilities and liabilities of corporate directors and possible options to promote resilience in an era marked by cyber threats and digital challenges. This chapter critically assesses the evolving nature of directors' duties, examining how they adapt to the complexities of the digital age. Readers will gain a profound understanding of the legal framework that governs corporate leadership and its role in promoting resilience in the face of cybersecurity and other threats.

Introduction

Australia's patchwork of policies, laws, and strategies in relation to cyber risk and data management have struggled to keep pace with the current challenges presented by the digital age.[1] Policymakers have the difficult task of balancing how Australia's data can be utilised and leveraged to progress the data economy and drive innovation, whilst achieving and maintaining strong cyber security measures. Equally, businesses face the challenge of balancing the economic benefits in collecting data to inform business decisions against effective risk management.

The Australian Government presents potentially conflicting views on its cyber security position and an open-data economy. The Department of Industry, Science and Resources indicates their agenda is to 'enable responsible and transparent access to data (with appropriate data safeguards) to support the data economy'[2]; whereas the Honourable Clare O'Neil MP, former Cyber Security and Home Affairs Minister, outlined a vision for Australia to be the world's most cyber secure country by 2030.[3] The 2030 Strategy notes that "Australia's current regulatory reporting requirements

S. White (✉) · E. Watford
The University of Adelaide, Adelaide, Australia
e-mail: Samuel.white@adelaide.edu.au

E. Watford
e-mail: elliewatford@gmail.com

D. Stephens et al. (eds.), *Digital Resilience*,
https://doi.org/10.1007/978-981-97-9746-2_12

for cyber incidents are complex"[4] and that Government will "explore options to make it easier for businesses to meet their regulatory obligations".[5] Before Australia can contribute to an open-data economy, the foundations for cyber security must be laid first, in both government and industry.

The scale of organisational data retention in Australia is huge. Organisations are collecting and retaining more data than ever before, which in many cases is the result of Australia's patchwork of complex data retention laws, making them a rich target for cybercriminals. This is compounded by the fact that many cybercriminals operate extraterritorially, which makes detection and punishment difficult. Given their fiduciary duties, it is common sense that company directors would be interested in matters that could have significant financial consequences for their companies. More important, from our perspective, is the question of whether a change in legal duties would motivate company directors to more thoroughly consider the potential losses that could be suffered by consumers whose data is compromised by a cyber incident.

In November 2023, the Australian Government released the *2023–2030 Australian Cyber Security Strategy* (**2030 Strategy**). Whilst it is by no means a strategy intended to be lasting (indeed, it is dated in its title), it provides a useful case study to assess the idea of resilience. The strategy promotes six shields to incentivise and ensure resilience in Australia and the near region. Signalling the importance of business, shield one seeks to ensure "citizens and businesses are better protected from cyber threats and can bounce back quickly following a cyber attack."[6] Central to this is that

> responsibility for cyber security is shared across the community, with more cyber risk allocated to those who are more capable of addressing them ... Larger businesses will play a central role in strengthening the security of the economy by helping those less able to do so.[7]

Whilst the effectiveness of these voluntary responses remains unclear, what we do know is that cyber security incidents continue to cost Australian businesses very large sums of money and continue to have distressing flow-on impacts for consumers and other stakeholders. This chapter therefore examines whether Australia's current company directors' and officers' duties[8] motivate a sufficient corporate response to the threat posed by cyber crime. It is clear some form of regulation is to occur under the 2030 *Strategy* but understandably, very little details are given as to how Shield one will be operationalised. This chapter will look at pre-existing options for if and how directors' duties can be used as a tool in addressing cyber security risks.

Over the past decade, the Australian Securities and Investments Commission ('ASIC') has successfully employed a chain of legal reasoning known as the 'stepping-stone' approach with an aim to keep directors accountable. The term 'stepping-stone' was first used in Keane CJ's judgment in *ASIC v Fortescue Metals Group Ltd*,[9] and consequently adopted by Herzberg and Anderson in their work following that judgment.[10] The stepping-stone approach is perceived as a controversial application of the law because ASIC uses sections in the *Corporations Act 2001* (Cth) ('*Corporations Act*') which do not impose a civil penalty liability (or indeed, other acts which do not incorporate a civil penalty scheme at all) as a stepping-stone to section 180(1), which does impose this sanction.[11]

The approach has two stepping-stones. First, a finding that a company has contravened a section (or sections) of the *Corporations Act* or another legislative regime.[12] Second, a finding that due to the first contravention (or contraventions), the director exposed the company to the risk of criminal prosecution, civil liability or significant reputational damage, which is a breach of the duty of care in section 180(1) of the *Corporations Act*.[13]

However, the stepping-stone approach will only capture those who are found to be in breach of a legal duty in the first instance. Directors who are not as active as they should be, or who do not seek advice from subject matter experts (i.e. cyber security and information technology experts) should be penalised, because they are exposing the company to unacceptable risk, with the damage extending to their customers, staff, and shareholders. If a breach of duty occurs, director accountability can be sought in other ways regardless of whether ASIC uses the stepping-stone approach or not, by shareholders in a derivative action[14] or via the oppression remedy,[15] for example. This chapter seeks to bridge that gap by also providing the following five alternate options.

Regulatory Options

This chapter captures the end result of a seminar co-led by the authors, with engagement on possible response options from industry, government and academia. Each option has its own costs and benefits. Ultimately without law reform, Option One can be relied upon if community expectations harden towards a requirement for cyber security, whereas Option Two mandates this approach, in a bid to require companies to be aware of the cybersecurity threats. Option Three seems the most viable, cost-effective way to respond to the dynamic threat without law reform. Option Four would mark a particular shift in directors' duties by codifying a specific duty to respond to the specific threat; an escalatory option required to ensure directors are actively monitoring and responding to this threat. Option Five, which has been described as a "nuclear option", does have precedent—the duty to prevent insolvent trading. It was understandably the option least supported by industry, but this chapter examines the viability and compares cyber security risk against the risk and costs associated with insolvent trading.

Option 1 Voluntary Self-assessment

Businesses need a very clear understanding of their obligations and rights when dealing with data. To do this, they need an assessment of their current cyber security status and education on what data to collect, hold and dispose of (safely). The

Australian Information Commissioner and Privacy Commissioner Angelene Falk said 'collecting the minimum amount of personal information required and deleting it when it is no longer needed' is an appropriate and proactive step for organisations to protect themselves against cyber threats.[16] Decision-makers across small and large businesses must be across how data is being dealt within their organisations, however, small businesses are particularly left in the deep end when it comes to resourcing and funding strong cyber security measures. A voluntary cyber self-assessment tool has weight as an accessible scheme for small businesses, who find cyber security daunting to implement. Rather than zero action to address cyber security from a business decision-maker, a free voluntary scheme would be a gentle approach to help business decision-makers understand and then meet their obligations. A voluntary self-assessment scheme would likely ask users questions about their cyber security measures and provide non-binding recommendations.

Recently, the Albanese government committed $7.2 million to establishing a voluntary cyber security self-assessment tool, which will allow small and medium-sized businesses to undertake free health checks regarding their cyber security maturity.[17] The voluntary self-assessment tool takes a proactive, rather than reactive, approach for businesses to 'determine the strength of their cyber security measures, and access educational tools and materials they need to upskill'.[18] Businesses with particularly higher-risk exposure to cyber threats will be offered a third-party assessment to ensure security across national supply chains.[19] Whilst limited information has been published about the voluntary self-assessment tool, the inference is that the government would expect large businesses in Australia to undertake and fund third-party assessments themselves.

The voluntary self-assessment will hopefully provide greater education about how businesses should respond to a breach and on how to navigate the other self-assessable scheme, the Notifiable Data Breach ('NDB') scheme. The Notifiable Data Breach ('NDB') scheme refers to organisations covered by the *Privacy Act* 1988 (Cth) and requires businesses to notify all affected individuals and the Office of the Australian Information Commissioner when a data breach has occurred and could result in serious harm to an individual whose information was breached.[20] The NDB scheme is a self-assessable scheme, meaning the organisation determines whether those individuals' face 'serious harm'. At present, the scheme does not provide adequate protection to ensure that each significant cyber breach will be reported if the company deems no 'serious harm' has occurred. Ambiguity arises in the assessment of harm to individuals, and how this is quantified by organisations. Whether there is a systematic approach to the value of a persons' data, or whether this exercise is more of an art than science, is unknown because this assessment is done in private by each organisation.[21]

Option 2 Legislated Self-assessment

A legislated self-assessment would be the next step from the voluntary cyber self-assessment and is envisioned to expand from the duties currently imposed on Australian Financial Service Licence ('FSL' Holders). The legislated self-assessment is suggested to be a two-pronged approach, the first being imposed on directors, and second on all (or more) industries (and companies). As mentioned, the legislated self-assessment is modelled from the current Australian FSL holders obligations, governed by the Australian Prudential Regulation Authority ('APRA'), the statutory body responsible for regulating the financial services industry.[22] The financial services industry is a prominent target for cyber-attacks. Consequently, boards and senior management of APRA-regulated entities have heightened obligations for the effective safeguarding of information assets, alongside a culture that promotes information security.[23] However, cybercriminals can do more with less now, and utilise the 'mosaic effect' to match data from various breaches to achieve a greater sinister outcome.[24] Consequently, we suggest that the obligations of the financial services industry be broadened to capture other industries to ensure that a cyber health check scheme is statutorily required to protect individuals' data.

APRA oversees the financial services industry, including institutions like banks, insurers (such as general, life and private health insurers), credit unions, building societies, and a large portion of the superannuation industry.[25] APRA's regulatory framework consists of three pillars which include prudential standards, prudential guidelines, and reporting standards.[26] The prudential standards are legally-binding minimum requirements for capital governance and risk management.[27] In order to achieve these standards, the prudential guidelines provide non-legally-binding steps and recommendations that APRA-regulated entities can follow.[28] Although the prudential guidelines themselves are not legally binding, they assist the regulated population achieve the prudential standards—which are legally binding. Further, APRA provides recommendations through the guidelines which can be adapted to suit the size, scope and nature of the business.[29] The reporting standards are legally-binding and outline the data required by APRA from financial institutions and when they must provide it.[30]

The APRA prudential standard CPS 234 Information Security ('CPS 234') has been in force since 1 July 2019 to ensure APRA-regulated entities take measures to 'be resilient against information security incidents (including cyber-attacks) by maintaining an information security capability commensurate with information security vulnerabilities and threats'.[31] CPS 234 creates obligations on entities to define the information security-related roles and responsibilities of the board, senior management, governing bodies and individuals; maintain security capabilities in line with the size and extent of threats to that entity to enable continued sound operation; implement controls to protect assets in line with the sensitivity of the data being held and undertake stress testing of those controls to assess their effectiveness; and notify APRA of material information security incidents.[32]

In terms of enforcement, APRA has a range of formal and informal tools at their disposal which can be imposed against an entity or individual.[33] Supervisory methods and reviews, financial analysis and heightened supervision and reporting requirements are part of their informal remit.[34] In terms of formal enforcement, APRA has the power to direct entities to take action or to cease from actions, to impose conditions on licences and how an entity can operate, and to commence civil or criminal court proceedings.[35] APRA can apply to the Federal Court to disqualify an individual from holding a senior role within the financial services industry.[36] Individuals or entities who admit to their wrongdoing can avoid litigation by making an enforceable undertaking to APRA; this can later be used in legal proceedings if there is further non-compliance.[37] Lastly, APRA can also issue infringement notices with fines for certain breaches of provisions of the *Superannuation Industry (Supervision) Act 1993* and *Financial Sector (Collection of Data) Act 2001*.[38] Where individuals or entities are failing to meet a prudential standard, APRA has stated that they will be willing to 'set public examples to deter unacceptable practices from occurring in the future'.[39] Similar obligations of CPS 234 could be expanded to other industries and utilised by other regulators, like ASIC for example.

The legislated self-assessment should also include stronger reporting obligations for companies who have experienced significant data breaches. Under the NDB scheme, an eligible data breach occurs when there is a 'serious risk of harm' to the affected individuals.[40] Currently, the company conducts its own review in deciding whether a 'serious risk of harm' has resulted from their data breach and whether disclosure is necessary. Data from the Office of the Australian Information Commissioner ('OAIC') shows that two data breaches in 2020–2021, affecting more than 10 million people worldwide, still remain anonymous.[41] Not only is this an issue from prosecution and public scrutiny perspectives, but the specific data that was stolen is still not known.[42] This is a problem, due to the 'mosaic effect' which explains that if one piece of data is exposed in a data breach, it might not say much about an individual, however, when brought together with other data that is publicly available about that individual it tells a much broader story, and can increase the risk of harm to that individual.[43] However, there is no expectation that a company should be held responsible for the mosaic effect, it just makes it particularly hard to assess the risk an individual is facing.

Every cyber breach that exposes data about several individuals should be made public so that individuals and/or regulators can assess the risk they are facing. At present, companies are only required to report data breaches that pose a 'significant threat'.[44] A legislated self-assessment would allow companies to have their cyber security red flags raised before a breach occurs.

Although reducing cyber security risk to zero is impossible, a legislated self-assessment might also educate companies on how to deal with their reporting obligations after a breach has occurred to appropriately assess the risk. Option two was viewed as the most 'palatable' option by workshop attendees, being the main preference of all the options. The pain point was whether the recommendations would provide adequate risk management for businesses and be practical enough to implement.

Option 3 Stepping-Stone Approach Continued

Over the past decade, ASIC has successfully employed a chain of legal reasoning known as the 'stepping-stone' approach in order to demonstrate that directors have breached their duty of care by permitting the company to breach or failing to prevent the company from breaching various legislative obligations. The approach has two stepping-stones. First, a finding that a company has contravened a section (or sections) of the *Corporations Act* or another legislative regime.[45] Second, a finding that due to the first contravention (or contraventions), the director exposed the company to the risk of criminal prosecution, civil liability or significant reputational damage, which is a breach of the duty of care in section 180(1) of the *Corporations Act*.[46] ASIC has had a 72% success rate in stepping-stones cases—it has only failed in cases where the first contravention by the company of its obligations under legislation was not made out.[47] We see the stepping-stone approach as the most likely litigation pathway for company directors being held personally accountable in a cyber breach situation.

The term 'stepping-stone' was first used in Keane C. J.'s judgment in *ASIC v Fortescue Metals Group Ltd*,[48] and consequently adopted by Herzberg and Anderson in their work following that judgment.[49] The stepping-stone approach is perceived by some as a controversial application of the law because ASIC uses sections in the *Corporations Act* which do not impose a civil penalty liability (or indeed, other acts which do not incorporate a civil penalty scheme at all) as a stepping-stone to section 180(1), which does impose a civil penalty.[50] The argument for the stepping-stone approach is that it keeps company directors accountable for their decisions and aware of the current issues which may affect their shareholders, staff, and customers; risks such as cybersecurity breaches. This approach also does not require the creation of a specific individual duty in relation to an area of law (such as cyber risk) but allows that risk to be addressed in other legislation, with responsibility for the company's compliance with those obligations tied back to the directors under their existing duty of care. ASIC (or another plaintiff)[51] can step back to section 180(1) and argue that by permitting the company to breach the other legislative provision (which is significantly broader than requiring the breach to be committed by the director/s), the directors have also breached their duty of care.

The stepping-stone approach highlights and solidifies the duty which directors accept when they undertake to act in the position of a company director. The interpretation of s 180(1) of the *Corporations Act* was also broadened in *Cassimatis v ASIC*.[52] Edelman J. commented that the foreseeable risk of harm to the corporation includes *all the interests of the corporation*, including reputation and compliance with the law.[53] The statement suggests that a cybersecurity breach could be used as a stepping-stone to also take action under section 180(1) of the *Corporations Act* because in many instances, a cyber breach exposes the company to non-compliance with the law and reputational damage. If Option Two were pursued, the stepping-stones approach outlined in Option Three could be utilised to ensure that corporate compliance with these elevated cyber-responsibilities remained at the forefront of a board's consideration, without any additional law reform being undertaken.

Whilst there have been several attempts in using the stepping-stones approach, its application is not solidified. Ramsay and Webster raise three pertinent questions with the stepping-stone approach, which are worth considering in relation to Option Three.[54] The first asks whether an actual breach by the company is required. Justice Edelman at first instance in *Cassimatis* stated 'it might be seriously doubted' whether the director could escape liability under s 180(1) 'simply because, by some good fortune, no actual breach eventuates'.[55] It may be enough that a director unreasonably and intentionally commits acts which are extremely likely to involve a serious breach of s 180(1), regardless of whether the first stepping-stone is satisfied. Secondly, Ramsay and Webster query whether the first stepping-stone can be a breach of a non-*Corporations Act* provision. This has already proved possible in a handful of cases with breaches of the *Australian Securities and Investments Commission Act 2001* (Cth) and *National Consumer Credit Protection Act* 2009 (Cth) satisfying the first stepping-stone.[56] A better question might be how broad the first stepping-stone can be, and whether it could relate to a cyber context with a breach of the *Privacy Act 1988* (Cth) or *Security of Critical Infrastructure Act 2018* (Cth), for example. Lastly, Ramsay and Webster ask whether the stepping-stone approach can be used by another litigant other than ASIC, such as data owners in a group action. If the stepping-stone approach was successfully extended to third parties, directors could face being questioned if they are complying with their duties far more frequently.

One difficulty faced by Option Three is the opposition from industry interest groups such as the Australian Institute of Company Directors ('AICD'), which has argued that an 'honest and reasonable director defence' should be included in the *Corporations Act* for additional director protection from the perceived 'expansion' of the duty of care via the use of stepping-stones.[57] However, the AICD has not clearly articulated why the existing business judgment rule in s 180(2) of the *Corporations Act* (discussed above) is insufficient protection. Whilst there is yet to be a successful application of the business judgment rule since its enactment, it should still provide the same effect that AICD is seeking. Implementing an honest and reasonable defence would be far too generous of a protection, and entirely unnecessary due to the existing business judgment rule.

The stepping-stones approach presents itself as a favourable pathway for litigants where directors are in breach of a legal duty by not being as active as they should be or failing to seek subject matter advice from experts (i.e. cybersecurity and information technology experts). Penalties should apply where directors are responsible for exposing the company to unacceptable risk, especially where the damage extends to their customers, staff, and shareholders. Shareholders could theoretically commence a derivative action[58] or use the oppression remedy,[59] however these pathways are much less likely.

Option 4 Codified Cyber Security Duty

A specific cyber security statutory duty modelled on *ASIC v RI Advice Group Pty Ltd* (‘*ASIC v RI Advice*’)[60], and s 180(1), would hold directors accountable to ensure the corporation: (a) has the cyber security controls and cyber resilience measures in place that a corporation in the corporation’s circumstances should reasonably have; and (b) takes reasonable steps to materially reduce cyber security risk to the level that a reasonable person occupying the office held by, and with the same responsibilities within the corporation as the director or officer, would consider acceptable.

In *ASIC v RI Advice*, RI Advice were found to have breached sections 912A(1)(a) (‘do all things necessary to ensure that the financial services covered by the licence are provided efficiently, honestly and fairly’) and 912A(1)(h) (‘have adequate risk management systems’) of the *Corporations Act*. It was found RI Advice failed to have adequate cybersecurity measures implemented across their representatives and had not implemented cybersecurity and cyber resilience measures, which exposed their clients to an unacceptable level of risk. The sections of the *Corporations Act* applied in the case are specific to holders of financial services licences, and consequently are owed by the corporations themselves and not by their directors personally. Directors of companies which do not hold financial services licences are not subject to these elevated duties. However, the decision highlights expanding judicial expectations of how a reasonable director of a company which provides a service where cyber risk is heightened should mitigate cyber risks. Although s 912A of the *Corporations Act* does not expressly refer to cyber security, the Court held that the general obligations imposed by that section can apply in the cyber security context. Rofe J. commented:

> Cybersecurity risk forms a significant risk connected with the conduct of the business and provision of financial services. It is not possible to reduce cybersecurity risk to zero, but it is possible to materially reduce cybersecurity risk through adequate cybersecurity documentation and controls to an acceptable level.[61]

ASIC v RI Advice confirms that cybersecurity responsibilities fall within financial services licensees obligations. Although these duties are not currently imposed on directors personally and do not apply outside of the context of financial services licence holders, the case is significant for two reasons. First, it demonstrates how a generally expressed corporate duty can be held to require specific cyber security responses. Second, as cyber risk expands to become a headline concern for all types of companies, the policy reasons in favour of extending this provision to all corporations should be considered.

Option Four was the second preference for workshop attendees. However, the attendees raised the risk of carving out a cyber-specific duty that some directors might fall through the cracks. One attendee noted that it could limit the pool of available IT-minded directors by being ‘too harsh’ and ‘scaring them off’ with the wider implication being that Australia could become a global outlier in having specific cyber obligations. Another attendee agreed, stating that anyone with enough experience to take a board position would ‘not want to be on a board at all, leaving us with negligent and unaware people’. One attendee was strongly against Option Four because they believed the concept of cyber risk is well-enough defined and we do not want to risk having a definition that distorts the changing nature of 'cyber risk'. They also questioned how you would classify an insider threat, such as an employee as a bad actor.

Option 5 Personal Liability

The quote attributed to Lord Chancellor Thurlow, 'Did you ever expect a corporation to have a conscience, when it has n*o soul to be damned, and no body to be kicked?'*[62] is pertinent in the context of personal liability. Statutory personal liability for directors in the context of cyber security would be modelled on s 588G of the Corporations Act, relating to insolvent trading. A person would contravene the section if they were found *to be a director* of a corporation, and *as a result of a cyber security incident, the corporation suffers loss and/or an individual suffers loss*, and *a reasonable person in a like position* in a company in the company's circumstances *would have exercised their powers and discharged their duties so as to take more effective steps* than were in fact taken to reduce the risk that the corporation would be vulnerable to a cyber security incident of the type that occurred.

Whilst a 'nuclear option', personal director liability leading to individual penalties makes fiscal sense in the context of cyber security. The law regulating insolvent trading involves complex legal and accounting issues, just as cybersecurity requires significant IT expertise. According to ASIC, illegal phoenix activity, which involves one facet of insolvent trading, costs 'employees between $31 and $298 million in unpaid entitlements and costs the Government around $1.6 billion in unpaid taxes and compliance'.[63] In comparison, cybersecurity risk is significantly more expensive, costing $29 billion per annum to Australian businesses, and about $7 trillion worldwide.[64] These figures suggest that measured by fiscal terms alone, cyber risk holds sufficient weight such that personal liability should be attached to a director who is operating a company with unsafe cyber measures. As unmitigated cyber risk has significant non-fiscal impacts on individuals whose data is breached, adding weight to the argument that cyber risk should become a personal liability for directors who fail to address it appropriately. One workshop attendee explained that at its time, it was surprising that s 588G was implemented, equally, this shows that there is a social cost to insolvent trading; whether cyber breaches have the same social cost is the next step.

Under s 588G of the Corporations Act, directors must prevent their company from incurring liabilities if the company is insolvent or if the director has reasonable grounds to suspect their company may be insolvent. If a director breaches this provision, they will be facing a compensation order, pecuniary penalty order, disqualification from managing a corporation,[65] and potentially criminal liability.[66] A compensation order sees the director as personally liable to pay compensation to the company equal to the amount of the loss suffered.[67] A pecuniary penalty order can be up to 5000 units or three times the benefit obtained or detriment avoided.[68]

Through the Treasury's consultation process, feedback indicated that the mixed judicial guidance on the insolvent trading prohibition makes it difficult for directors to understand whether a company is insolvent or is approaching insolvency.[69] This threat of personal liability has been described as a 'sword of Damocles', hanging over the head of directors of financially distressed companies and distorting the lens through which they contemplate potential turnaround options.[70]

For both insolvent trading and cyber security, it can be very difficult to pinpoint when a company has reached an unacceptable level of risk. Insolvency has a set definition, which may provide some comfort, but commercial matters are usually highly complex and this question will always be fact-dependent, as the law has clearly stated that insolvency is not a straightforward 'balance sheet' test.[71] By contrast, there is currently no set definition or trigger point for a 'lack' of cyber security and is typically a culmination of failings.

A key distinction between insolvency and cyber risk is that, generally, cyber security breaches involve a malicious third-party actor. This element is not typical in insolvency. For cyber risk, the director's actions may have contributed to the breach occurring, but an external actor is generally responsible for the breach. With insolvency, it is the financial decisions of the directors which makes a company insolvent or not, like taking on more debt than they should have for example. From a policy perspective, this distinction would be an impediment to Option Five being considered palatable as potential law reform. Personal liability on directors where the breach generally requires an external actor for whom the directors cannot be responsible may be a step too far. An attendee that was highly opposed to Option Five raised concerns of how it is relatively easy to figure out whether a company is insolvent, however, it is not as easy to work out the state of a company's cyber risk—especially as there are criminal actors actively trying to increase this risk. The attendee also raised how what may be a cyber risk one year is mended the next year, and not seen as detrimental anymore, making it impossible to pinpoint a 'trigger point' of the provision.

Consequently, although this option is suggested it is not recommended. It would place an unfair burden on directors of companies to have personal liability extend in the same way it does for insolvent trading. Despite the financial risk of a cyber breach being arguably higher than insolvency, a cyber breach does not directly 'kill the company', whereas insolvency means the company is no longer able to survive.

Conclusion

The intersection between cybersecurity law, company obligations and director duties are complicated. This is due to the several regulators who can potentially bring actions, such as ASIC under the *Corporations Act* and the OAIC under the *Privacy Act 1988* (Cth). Class actions are also becoming increasingly prevalent, recently demonstrated by the Optus and Medibank breaches.

The overarching problem in Australia is that citizens are still not fully informed or aware of how valuable their data is, particularly for cybercriminals. While the everyday person might find the spam text messages, emails and calls frustrating, the serious risk of harm they face with their data being leaked by an organisation is still not clearly understood. Organisations have the resources to understand this risk and protect their customers accordingly. Therefore, stronger director and company obligations must exist in this power dynamic to protect the data owners from serious cybercrimes. Companies should not have the privilege of accessing customer's data, profiting from the data via valuable analytics, and then exposing it to cybersecurity breaches due to a lack of diligence around cyber risk.

The lack of litigation by regulators (or other litigants) against the directors of large companies who repeatedly fall victim to cybercrime is curiously stark. Given their fiduciary duties, it is common sense that company directors would be interested in matters that could have significant financial consequences for their companies, such as a significant cyber-attack.[72] This paper demonstrates that the current regime of directors' duties does provide an appropriate launching pad for litigation to commence, however, we are yet to see any action in this space. A direct application of the duty of care and diligence under s 180(1) of the *Corporations Act 2001* (Cth) ('*Corporations Act*') or via the stepping-stone approach, or under the duty of good faith in s 181, are the most likely avenues to be used by ASIC or another litigant. In a landscape that is increasingly focused on cyber resilience, directors (or officers) at the helm of large companies who cannot demonstrate that they took reasonable steps to prevent cyber breaches are in a complicated position. Directors would not be left without a safe harbour either, being able to utilise the business judgment rule as a defence. However, directors who do not consider cyber security at all, cannot be considered to have made a 'business judgment'. This means directors cannot avoid considering cyber security, because in doing so, they would be denying themselves a defence if litigation arose.

The courts have confirmed that financial services licensees have specific cyber security responsibilities, as per *ASIC v RI Advice,* and although these duties do not extend on directors personally and are not broadly applied across all industries, the case is a prelude to what directors could expect in the near future. As cyber risk expands to be a headline concern for all types of companies, the policy reasons in favour of extending this provision to all corporations should be considered.

In the absence of further research to assess the suitability and effectiveness of the above duties in a cyber security context, the current research suggests that an approach for cautious directors is to understand cyber security risk to a point where you can make an informed decision. If you do not understand the information, a subject matter expert needs to explain it to you. Until the director is in a position where they feel they can make an informed decision for the company, the risk of litigation is heightened.

The 2030 *Strategy* makes clear that a paradigm shift in cyber security and resilience is to occur in Australia before the close of the decade. Businesses are core to this, and understanding the options for changes outside of the 2030 *Strategy* is important to ensure the best possible options are being canvassed in this emerging area.

Given their fiduciary duties, it is common sense that company directors would be interested in matters that could have significant financial consequences for their companies, such as a significant cyber attack.[73] In a landscape that is increasingly focused on cyber resilience, directors (or officers) at the helm of large companies who cannot demonstrate that they took reasonable steps to prevent cyber breaches are in a complicated position. Directors would not be left without a safe harbour either, being able to utilise the business judgment rule as a defence. However, directors who do not consider cyber security at all, cannot be considered to have made a 'business judgment'. This means directors cannot avoid considering cyber security, because in doing so, they would be denying themselves a defence if litigation arose. It is clear that some form of government regulation is needed. The question is which option to take.

Notes

1. Department of Home Affairs, 2023–2030 Australian Cyber Security Strategy Discussion Paper, 4 ('Home Affairs Discussion Paper').
2. Department of Industry, Science and Resources, *Australia's Tech Future: Delivering a strong, safe and inclusive digital economy ('Australia's Tech Future Publication')* (Data and Publication, 2018), 34.
3. Home Affairs Discussion Paper, 4.
4. Department of Home Affairs, 2023–2030 Australian Cyber Security Strategy ('2030 Strategy') <http://www.homeaffairs.gov.au/cyber-security-subsite/files/2023-cyber-security-strategy.pdf>, 25.
5. Ibid.
6. 2030 Strategy (n 4) 16.
7. 2030 Strategy (n 4) 16.
8. The majority of duties in the *Corporations Act 2001* (Cth) apply to both directors and officers, and occasionally also to other employees. We will refer in our discussion to 'directors' duties' or 'directors' throughout, although officers will also owe duties under the provisions we analyse.
9. *Australian Securities and Investments Commission v Fortescue Metals Group Ltd* (2011) 190 FCR 364, 370 [10].
10. Abe Herzberg and Helen Anderson 'Stepping Stones—From Corporate Fault to Directors' Personal Civil Liability' (2012) 40(2) *Federal Law Review* 181, 181.
11. In *Cassimatis v Australian Securities and Investments Commission* (2020) 376 ALR 261, Justice Rares stated in dissent (at [221]):

    > A difficulty with the stepping stones approach on which ASIC relied before the primary judge is that it seeks to enlist s 180(1) to prescribe a duty to prevent a substantial contravention by the corporation of another provision in the Act, that is not a civil penalty provision, on the basis that ASIC would then be likely to invoke regulatory or curial remedies against the corporation.

    See further Ian Ramsay and Miranda Webster 'An Analysis Of The Use Of Stepping-stones Liability Against Company Directors and Officers' (2021) 50(1) *Australian Bar Review* 168, 175.
12. Some stepping-stones cases use legislation other than the *Corporations Act* to establish the first stepping-stone. The other legislative regimes include the *Australian Securities and Investments Commission Act* (2001) (Cth) and the *National Consumer Credit Protection Act* 2009 (Cth).

13. Herzberg and Anderson (n 10) 181. ‘Stepping Stones—From Corporate Fault to Directors’ Personal Civil Liability’ (2012) 40(2) *Federal Law Review* 181, 181.
14. Corporations Act 2001 (Cth), s 236.
15. Corporations Act 2001 (Cth), s 232.
16. Cyber security incidents impact data breach risk, *Office of the Australian Information Commissioner* (Website) <https://www.oaic.gov.au/newsroom/cyber-security-incidents-impact-data-breach-risk>.
17. Julie Collins and Clare O’Neil, ‘Small businesses to receive cyber security boost’ (Media Release, Treasury, 20 November 2023) <https://ministers.treasury.gov.au/ministers/julie-collins-2022/media-releases/small-businesses-receive-cyber-security-boost>.
18. Ibid.
19. Ibid.
20. About the Notifiable Data Breaches scheme *Office of the Australian Information Commissioner* (Website) <https://www.oaic.gov.au/privacy/notifiable-data-breaches/about-the-notifiable-data-breaches-scheme>.
21. Natasha Lomas, ‘Australia to toughen privacy laws with huge hike in penalties for breaches’, *TechCrunch* (online, 24 October 2022) <https://techcrunch.com/2022/10/24/australia-privacy-law-update/>.
22. *Australian Prudential Regulation Authority Act 1998* (Cth), s 8(1).
23. Australian Prudential Regulation Authority, *CPS 234 Information Security* (Prudential Practice Guide, June 2019).
24. Julian Fell et al., ‘This is the most detailed portrait yet of data breaches in Australia’, *ABC News (online*, 28 March 2023) <https://www.abc.net.au/news/2023-03-28/detailed-portrait-data-breaches-oaic-disclosures/102131586>.
25. *Australian Prudential Regulation Authority Act 1998* (Cth), s 3 (‘prudential regulation framework law’).
26. *Australian Prudential Regulation Authority Act 1998* (Cth), s [9]–[11]; Australian Prudential Regulation Authority, *What is prudential regulation?* (Website, 25 October 2023) <https://www.apra.gov.au/what-prudential-regulation>.
27. Ibid.
28. Ibid.
29. Ibid.
30. Ibid.
31. Member of Australian Prudential Regulation Authority, *Prudential Standard CPS 234 Information Security* (CPS 234, 1 July 2019).
32. Ibid.
33. Australian Prudential Regulation Authority, *APRA’s Enforcement Approach* (Report, 3 September 2019), 4.
34. Ibid.
35. APRA (n 35) 5.
36. APRA can disqualify an individual under the *Banking Act 1959, Insurance Act 1973, Life Insurance Act 1995, Private Health Insurance Act (Prudential Supervision) 2015,* and *Superannuation Industry (Supervision) Act 1993.*
37. APRA can accept enforceable undertakings under the *Banking Act 1959, Insurance Act 1973,* and the *Superannuation Industry (Supervision) Act 1993.*
38. In July 2023, APRA issued an infringement notice to BNK Banking Corporation Limited under s 13(9) of the *Financial Sector (Collection of Data) Act 2001* with a $247,500 penalty for failing to meet their reporting requirements by 32 days.
39. Australian Prudential Regulation Authority, *Enforcement* (Website, 27 October 2023) <https://www.apra.gov.au/enforcement>.
40. Office of the Australian Information Commissioner, *When to report a data breach* (Website 27 October 2023) <https://www.oaic.gov.au/privacy/notifiable-data-breaches/when-to-report-a-data-breach>.

41. Julian Fell et al., 'This is the most detailed portrait yet of data breaches in Australia', *BC News (online*, 28 March 2023) <https://www.abc.net.au/news/2023-03-28/detailed-portrait-data-breaches-oaic-disclosures/102131586>.
42. Ibid.
43. Ibid.
44. Ibid.
45. Some stepping-stones cases use legislation other than the *Corporations Act* to establish the first stepping-stone. The other legislative regimes include the *Australian Securities and Investments Commission Act* (2001) (Cth) and the *National Consumer Credit Protection Act* 2009 (Cth).
46. Herzberg and Anderson (n 10) 181. 'Stepping Stones—From Corporate Fault to Directors' Personal Civil Liability' (2012) 40(2) *Federal Law Review* 181, 181.
47. Ian Ramsay and Miranda Webster 'An Analysis of The Use Of Stepping-stones Liability Against Company Directors' and Officers' (2021) 50(1) *Australian Bar Review* 168, 169.
48. *Australian Securities and Investments Commission v Fortescue Metals Group Ltd* (2011) 190 FCR 364, 370 [10].
49. Herzberg and Anderson (n 10) 181.
50. For more on the civil penalty scheme within the Corporations Act, please see: Michelle Welsh, 'Civil Penalties and Responsive Regulation: The Gap between Theory and Practice' (2009) 33(3) *Melbourne University Law Review* 908. On this point, in *Cassimatis v Australian Securities and Investments Commission* (2020) 376 ALR 261, Rares J. stated in dissent (at [221]):

    > A difficulty with the stepping stones approach on which ASIC relied before the primary judge is that it seeks to enlist s 180(1) to prescribe a duty to prevent a substantial contravention by the corporation of another provision in the Act, that is not a civil penalty provision, on the basis that ASIC would then be likely to invoke regulatory or curial remedies against the corporation.

    See further Ian Ramsay and Miranda Webster 'An Analysis Of The Use Of Stepping-stones Liability Against Company Directors and Officers' (2021) 50(1) *Australian Bar Review* 168, 175.
51. ASIC is the only litigant to use the stepping-stones approach, aside from *Agricultural Land Management Ltd v Jackson [No 2]* (2014) 48 WAR 1 where a plaintiff company sued its directors. There have been no cases where a third party has brought a stepping-stones action.
52. Ramsay and Webster (n 47) 172. 'An Analysis Of The Use Of Stepping-stones Liability Against Company Directors and Officers' (2021) 50(1) *Australian Bar Review* 168, 172.
53. *Australian Securities and Investments Commission v Cassimatis* [No 8], 483.
54. Ramsay and Webster (n 47). 'An Analysis of The Use Of Stepping-stones Liability Against Company Directors' and Officers' (2021) 50(1) *Australian Bar Review* 168, 169.
55. *Australian Securities and Investments Commission v Cassimatis [No 8].*
56. *Australian Securities and Investments Commission v Preston* [2005] FCA 1805; *Australian Securities and Investments Commission v Ostrava Equities Pty Ltd* [2016] FCA 1064.
57. Australian Institute of Company Directors ('AICD'), The Honest and Reasonable Director Defence: A Proposal for Reform (Policy Paper, 7 August 2014) <http://www.companydirectors.com.au/Director-Resource-Centre/Policy-on-director-issues/Policy-Papers/2014/The-Honest-and-Reasonable-Director-Defence>.
58. Corporations Act 2001 (Cth), s 236.
59. Corporations Act 2001 (Cth), s 232.
60. [2022] FCA 496.
61. Ibid, [58].
62. J. C. Coffee Jr., 'No Soul to Damn: No Body to Kick: An Unscandalized Inquiry into the Problem of Corporate Punishment' (1981) 79 Michigan Law Review 386.
63. Illegal Phoenix Activity, *Australian Securities and Investments Commission* (Webpage, 30 October 2022) <https://asic.gov.au/for-business/small-business/closing-a-small-business/illegal-phoenix-activity/>.

64. 'Cyber Security: Director responsibilities in a changing legislative landscape' *PWC* (Discussion <www.pwc.com.au/about-us/insights/non-executive-directors/cyber-security-director-responsibilities-in-a-changing-legislative-environment.html>.
65. *Corporations Act 2001* (Cth), s 206C.
66. *Corporations Act 2001* (Cth), s 588G(3).
67. *Corporations Act 2001* (Cth), s 588J, 1317H.
68. *Corporations Act 2001* (Cth), s 1317G.
69. Treasury, *Review of the Insolvent Trading Safe Harbour* (Report, 23 November 2021), 4.
70. Treasury, *Review of the Insolvent Trading Safe Harbour* (Report, 23 November 2021), 4.
71. As discussed in *Pearce v Gulmohar Pty Ltd* [2017] FCA 660.
72. Smith (n 14); Grubb (n 14).
73. Ibid.

Samuel White is a Senior Lecturer of the faculty of the Adelaide Law School at the University of Adelaide. He is concurrently a Visiting Fellow at the Australian Defence Force Academy and holds positions as an Adjunct Associate Professor at the University of New England. In 2024, he was made an Associate Fellow of the Royal Historical Society and the first Army Visiting Fellow at the Australian War Memorial. Samuel has also served as both a Royal Australian Infantry Corps and an Australian Army Legal Corps officer in a variety of tactical, operational and strategic level postings. His military experiences focused his doctoral studies, which addressed the constitutional ambit and limitations of responding to foreign interference (both traditional and modern forms) via military responses.

Elizabeth Watford is a corporate and commercial lawyer with a background as a legal researcher in cyber security, privacy, and corporate law for the University of Adelaide law school. Ellie co-authored 'I Know Who You Are: the need for a uniform definition of biometric data' which is published in the Australian Law Journal and was a presenter at the inaugural RUMALE 2023 conference on directors' duties and cyber breaches. Ellie is keenly interested in the intersection of technology and law, and has a deep interest in business, having also completed a Bachelor of Business Management, and the Startmate Fellowship to gain a better understanding and insight into Australia's startup ecosystem. With practical experience across mergers and acquisitions, capital raising, fund establishment, ASX compliance and corporate contracting, Ellie combines her technical skill set and interests to support companies with solving their problems.

Express Directors' Duties for Cybersecurity: Resilience through Adaptation

Beth Nosworthy

Abstract Elements of corporate governance have been evident for almost as long as there has been an understanding of the corporate form, and it has always had to adapt to new challenges presented in each era. This chapter considers the modern challenge of cybersecurity risk and identifies existing resilience in the current Australian directors' duties in light of their historical origins and prior adaptation, which enable them to respond to cybersecurity risk. Through careful consideration of analogous examples provided in existing case law in relation to the directors' duties of care and loyalty, this chapter articulates the capacity of the current laws to hold senior corporate decision-makers accountable where they do not meet the expected standard of behaviour. The particular risks associated with cybersecurity are articulated and contrasted to extant risks regularly assessed and addressed by boards of directors, confirming the resilience of the directors' duty regime in responding to this challenge.

Introduction

Corporate governance has been defined in varying ways across the past 100 years, with most definitions articulating the key elements as:

1. a system of regulating corporate conduct;[1]
2. which considers the interests of internal stakeholders and others who may be affected by corporate conduct;[2]
3. aiming to ensure responsible behaviour by corporate actors and those who exert authority within them.[3]

Some definitions take the further step of including considerations of long-term, sustainable growth,[4] and others provide a focus on protecting the position of the members and their financial interest in the company.[5]

B. Nosworthy (✉)
Adelaide Law School, The University of Adelaide, Adelaide, Australia
e-mail: Beth.nosworthy@adelaide.edu.au

D. Stephens et al. (eds.), *Digital Resilience*,
https://doi.org/10.1007/978-981-97-9746-2_13

Although the phrase 'corporate governance' itself may not have been in popular use until the 1970s,[6] the key elements of corporate governance and the themes they represent have been evident in corporate action, governmental response and academic (and media) critique since the 1400s.[7]

As the corporate form developed, so did corporate governance. Reliance on the general law legal structure of commercial partnership in the 1700s gave way to legislated forms of incorporation in the 1800s, and particularly the limitation of the liability of shareholders for company debts.[8] Much has been written on the development of directors' duties, as a central pillar of corporate governance and the regulation of corporate conduct.[9] In brief, although statutory intervention assisted the corporation develop from the deed of settlement company into joint stock company in the 1800s, directors' duties were generally left to the general law (common law and equity) until 1896, when—as identified by Langford, Ramsay and Welsh, for a brief time the *Companies Act 1896* (Vic) contained the first statutory directors' duty.[10] This required directors to 'use reasonable care and prudence in the exercise of [their] powers and duties'.[11] That section was not replicated in other Australian jurisdictions at that time and was in fact removed from the *Companies Act 1910* (Vic), which Langford, Ramsay and Welsh identify as likely due to the lack of similar provision in the English law at the time, and the colonial preference for uniformity in order to attract capital investment from England. Directors' duties remained outside of legislation until the *Companies Act 1929* (UK), which only required directors to declare potential conflicts of interest,[12] until more detailed duties began to emerge in the legislation in the late 1950s.[13]

In the general law, directors' duties were viewed through two distinct lenses, predominantly the duty of care and diligence, most commonly recognised in contract and tort,[14] and the duty to act in the interests of another when undertaking a role as a fiduciary in equity, with the attendant negative prohibitions on conflict and profit,[15] underpinning the various duties of loyalty and good faith. These lenses remain evident in the modern statutory iterations of the directors' duties in the *Corporations Act 2001* (Cth), with s 180 articulating a duty of care and diligence and the s 588G counterpart in relation to insolvent trading, s 181 requiring directors to act in good faith in the interests of the corporation and for proper purposes, and ss 182–183 addressing improper use of position or information. Other provisions, including s 191 requiring disclosure of material personal interest and Chapter 2E addressing related party transactions, flesh out the remaining framework. When tracing the historical roots of these statutory provisions and their general law counterparts, the last 100 years articulate the resilience of corporate governance—the development of the principles of law, from their general law origins, through the current application both within and external to the *Corporations Act*, to be able to adapt and respond to modern challenges which would not have been in the minds of the drafters of the original 1950s legislation, and may even have been beyond consideration during the drafting processes for the *Corporations Act 2001* (Cth). Climate risk and cyber risk provide salient lessons in the resilience of the legal system, generally, and the corporate governance structures more particularly, including directors' duties, to respond to novel challenges and provide appropriate guidance and response to modern trials.

This chapter will chart the rise of cyber risk, articulating the particular pressure it places on boards, and how the existing legal framework—and particularly the directors' duties as articulated in the *Corporations Act 2001* (Cth)—are framed in response. The chapter will chart the inception of the key duties in the general law, and their statutory counterparts and identify key cases from which appropriate analogy to cyber risk can be drawn.

Cyber-Risk and Directors' Duties

According to the Australian Signals Directorate, from mid-2022 to mid-2023 the cost of cyber-crime for Australian businesses rose by 14%.[16] The average cost of cyber-crime for small businesses is now $46,000; for medium businesses $97,000; and for large businesses $71,600.[17] This threat is accelerating, but is not unanticipated: in 2015, the Australian Securities and Investments Commission ('ASIC') in its *Report 429 Cyber Resilience: Health Check* indicated that it expects businesses to: 'address cyber risks as part of their legal and compliance obligations—including risk management and disclosure requirements'.[18]

Ultimately, companies—and the key decision-makers within them—face an ever-expanding matrix of risk, which includes within it cyber risk. Perhaps one key distinction between cyber risk and other kinds of risk which must be addressed by boards of directors and senior management on a daily basis (such as increasing effects of climate change, vulnerability of financial markets or supply chains to global conflict, and cost of living pressures on employee markets) is the involvement of external third parties—the cyber criminals—adding a level of human complexity to the risk. Many systemic risks are non-targeted, but cyber risk is more similar to risk of fraud or theft, in that it usually involves a deliberate targeting of the company by a malicious actor, who may be internal or entirely external to the company. These targeted risks may require a similarly deliberate response in terms of governance and decision-making. Based on the official record of data breaches reported to the Office of the Australian Information Commissioner from 2020/21, more than 10 million people were affected by poor cybersecurity.[19] The breaches leading to the biggest headlines, like Optus, Medibank and Latitude Financial in Australia in the early 2020s, were not isolated attacks.[20] A significant volume of attacks go unreported.[21]

To date, there has been only one case successfully litigated in relation to inadequate preparation for and response to cyber risk by a company and, importantly, the board responsible for key decisions within that company.[22] It does not follow that the minimal amount of litigation demonstrates a failing of the directors' duties to adequately address or respond to this risk—litigation is a lengthy process, and only one of the many regulatory responses open to the Australian Securities and Investments Commission ('ASIC') in their role as the integrated corporate, markets, financial services and consumer credit regulator. Former deputy chair of ASIC Jillian Segal articulated ASIC's role as 'a continuum of responses. It is bound by enforcement at one end and education at the other, with policy guidance, industry support and disclosure guidelines in between.'[23] As cyber-crime continues to grow and affect a broader range of consumers and businesses, so too will the regulatory response—including potential litigation either by ASIC or other affected parties. This chapter will argue that the existing legal framework is sufficiently resilient to respond to this risk—which should no longer be described as 'emerging', as the data notes that it is very evident in the present.

The Existing Legal Framework

This section of the chapter will focus on the current legal framework, following a short discussion of the historical origins of the current legislative provisions. It addresses the duty of care and diligence in more detail than the other duties, as the most likely to be the duty through which an action would be taken against a board for failing to adequately address the cyber risks facing a corporation.

The Duty of Care and Diligence

The directors' duty of care and diligence in the common law was established in cases in the 19th century. At that time, the duty was conceived as a subjective standard of care, with significant latitude given to the individual circumstances and characteristics of the directors in question. For example, in *Re Cardiff Savings Bank*,[24] the Marquis of Bute was installed as a director of the Cardiff Savings Bank as an infant of six months old. When the bank became insolvent nearly 40 years later, his behaviour as a director was examined and found not to have been negligent—despite having attended one meeting of the trustees and managers in 1869 and never again taking part in the business of the bank.[25] This reflects a time when directorships were an 'office of status', rather than a professional role for which a person could be educated and trained. Within 30 years,[26] there was a shift evident away from the low, subjective standard in the late 1800s towards what we would recognise as a more objective duty of care and diligence. It was not until legal responses to the high-profile corporate collapses of the late 1980s made their way through the courts in the early 1990s that further development towards the modern position was made—with cases such as *Statewide Tobacco Services Ltd v Morley*[27] and *Commonwealth Bank of Australia v Friedrich*.[28] Australia's federal Parliament also examined the development of the law in this space, with the Working Group chaired by Henry Bosch AO issuing the 1991 report on *Corporate Practices and Conduct*.[29] In 1992, the seminal decision at first instance of Rogers CJ in *AWA Ltd v Daniels*[30] was delivered, upheld on appeal in *Daniels v Anderson*,[31] articulating that the duty of care and diligence was objective, requiring directors to take reasonable steps to place themselves in a position to guide and monitor the company.[32] These decisions were considered during the redrafting of the duty of care and diligence into their statutory form, as part of the federal Corporate Law Reform program in the 1990s,[33] which form the foundation of the statutory language present in the *Corporations Act* today.

The statutory duty of care in s 180(1) of the *Corporations Act* provides that a director of a corporation must exercise their powers and discharge their duties with the degree of care and diligence that a reasonable person would exercise if they were in that same position, with the same responsibilities, and in a corporation in the same circumstances.[34] A director who does not adequately respond to cyber risks and does not ensure that a company is cyber resilient, when a reasonable director in a company in a similar position to their company would take action, is therefore likely to be in breach of their duty of care under s 180(1) and the general law.[35] The duty as established in all of the general law jurisdictions and in statute is sufficiently similar that they can be discussed simultaneously.

The test in s 180(1) to determine whether a director has exercised reasonable care and diligence balances the foreseeable risk of harm against the potential benefits to the company.[36] As Justice Middleton stated in *ASIC v Healey*:[37]

> What each director is expected to do is to take a *diligent and intelligent* interest in the information available to him or her, to understand that information, and *apply an inquiring mind* to the responsibilities placed upon him or her...the directors *must understand and focus* upon the content... and *if necessary, make further inquiries* if matters revealed...call for such inquiries. [emphasis added]

The collating of data and information, and the level of technical expertise and response required in the realm of cyber risk is not significantly different to or more onerous than other risks with which boards have grappled in the past. For example, in *ASIC v Vines,*[38] Mr Vines, as chief financial officer of insurance company GIO Group, was responsible for the financial reporting of the Group, including the 'consolidation of financial reports produced by the subsidiaries, and forming his own view about the financial soundness and integrity of the business.'[39] Additionally, he had financial responsibilities for the Group's activities across all practice divisions, including their reinsurance business, and responding to issues raised by management or auditors within the subsidiaries, and ensuring that accurate information about the company's financial position was prepared and provided to the board, and—particularly—'to intervene if he became aware of some deficiency in a divisions' financial statements that was not being dealt with.'[40] The Group was subject to a takeover bid by AMP, and during the due diligence process in 1998, Hurricane Georges hit the Caribbean and Gulf of Mexico, causing approximately US$10 billion in damage and leading to significant insurance and reinsurance claims. GIO Re, the company within the group which handled reinsurance, had made a profit forecast of $80 million during the bid period. In 1999, following the closure of AMP's offer to GIO's shareholders, GIO Re announced a loss of $19.6 million. Mr Vines was held to have breached his duty of care and diligence by failing to inform the relevant sub-committees of the board of the true potential effect of Hurricane Georges on the profit forecasts. The available information about Hurricane Georges should have led Mr Vines to advise the decision-makers that it was improbable to achieve the forecast $80 million profit for GIO Re. That the reinsurance industry is volatile, 'not an exact science' and 'hampered by inherent uncertainties'[41] did not prevent Austin J. from finding that Mr. Vines had breached his duty of care. In particular, his Honour noted that a forecast being inaccurate was not necessarily an indication of negligence, or even dishonesty, in its preparation:

> But the duty of care and diligence may not have been discharged where pertinent information (including the existence of a contrary view supported by analysis) is disregarded or not properly reviewed and verified, or where the reasoning process employed to support the forecast is inadequate.[42]

The volatility and developing methods of cyber-crime, from phishing to whaling,[43] to more aggressive attacks,[44] can be analogised to the inherent uncertainties identified in the reinsurance industry. Similarly, in *Shafron v ASIC*,[45] Mr. Shafron, as general counsel and company secretary of James Hardie Industries Limited ('James Hardie'), was found to be in breach of the duty of care where he failed to give advice to the CEO and board about the need to disclose a document to the Australian Stock Exchange ('ASX'), and an inaccurate calculation in an actuarial report on which the board subsequently relied to make decisions. Even though Mr. Shafron's decisions fell outside of the statutory responsibilities of an 'officer', this was not relevant. Any act or omission by the director concerning the corporation will be relevant.[46] The fact that Mr. Shafron was an employee of the corporation and not an external advisor was also important, because he played a large part in formulating the reports in question.[47] Mr. Shafron argued that he expected the contracted lawyers for James Hardie to advise him that the actuarial report should have been disclosed to the ASX, although in reviewing the retainer of the company's lawyers, this type of advice was not included, meaning Mr. Shafron was unable to rely on this argument.[48] The court found that Mr. Shafron was 'acquainted enough' with the contents of each report and although he was not a trained actuary, he was familiar enough with the concepts. Mr. Shafron did not advise the board on the figures, and the board relied on the basis of their absence.[49] As a consequence, the compensation fund established during James Hardie's restructure and move offshore to the Netherlands—intended to respond to the potential long-tail tort liabilities from asbestos-related illnesses attributable to James Hardie or its subsidiaries—was only provided with $293 million funding, when the claims against the James Hardie group at that time were in excess of $2.2 billion.[50]

These authorities demonstrate how acts including withholding information or misleading the board who subsequently rely on inaccurate information to make decisions have been found to breach the duty of care and diligence. At a fundamental level, if a director is made aware of a foreseeable risk, incorrectly weighs that risk against whether to act or what actions they should take—when a reasonable person in the director's position would have attributed greater risk to that problem and acted differently—then the director will likely be found to have breached their duty to exercise care and diligence. Although there is not yet any authority directly on this point in relation to cyber risk, the same arguments could clearly be made in this space. If a director or officer is aware of significant cyber risks and associated impacts and fails to address said risk, does not accurately inform the board, or misleads the board as to the extent of those risks, they could be found to have breached their duty of care in s 180(1).[51]

Perhaps the highwater mark in relation to the modern directors' duty of care and diligence, the *Centro* decision has been the subject of much discussion since the past decade.[52] Here, ASIC argued that the directors of Centro breached their duty of care and diligence because the company's annual accounts did not comply with the requirements under the *Corporations Act* in relation to financial reporting, and the annual accounts, as approved by the directors, misclassified several borrowings as non-current liabilities, when they were in fact current.[53] At its core, the decision by Middleton J. set down that directors are required to have the 'financial literacy to understand basic accounting conventions and proper diligence in reading the financial statements'.[54] This position has been criticised,[55] as the financial statements were extremely complex, had been prepared by an appropriate accounting team in-house, and had been approved by an external auditor, PwC.[56] However, the directors were found to have the required 'accumulated knowledge' based on the documents provided to them at board meetings and the discussions that followed,[57] and should have known that the liabilities in question were current. Justice Middleton said that all the directors needed to do was form their own opinions and apply their opinions to the task of approving financial statements.[58] Justice Middleton also stressed that directors can rely upon the processes they have put in place—to a degree.[59] While drafting financial statements is the domain of management, and directors are not expected to take on this task,[60] the duty remains on directors to ensure that all reasonable steps have been taken, which involves the directors taking it upon themselves to read and understand the financial statements.[61]

The same principles in *Centro* can be applied to cyber security and technology-related matters. Courts will *not* expect directors to ensure their company is cyber resilient by, for example, undertaking software and hardware improvements themselves or being able to write or deploy coded responses. Courts *will* expect directors to put systems in place to ensure their company is cyber resilient, proportionate to the risk their company faces. Regardless of how complex cyber and technology information might be, directors must endeavour to understand it to a level where they can make informed decisions. Of significant concern for directors facing difficult decisions in relation to cyber risk would be the dismissal of the various defences put forward by the defendant directors in *Centro*. Justice Middleton did not accept the defence based on reliance—the accounts having been approved by external auditors PWC and the internal audit committee. Nor did Middleton J. accept the 'information overload' argument—that the information provided to the directors in relation to the accounts was more than 3000 pages long and financially complex. Both arguments could foreseeably be raised by defendant directors in the context of a cyber security breach or mismanagement of cyber risk, and the *Centro* decision suggests they may be poorly received by the courts.

It is worth noting, however, that the penalties for the directors found in breach of their duty of care and diligence in the *Centro* decision were not significant when compared to the liabilities misclassified in the financial statements, and the resulting millions lost in relation to the drop in market price of Centro's shares at the time the refinance was attempted.[62] Justice Middleton fined Centro's former CEO $30,000 and ordered a two-year disqualification order for the former CFO.[63] No penalties were ordered against the six non-executive directors, who Middleton J. had also found in breach of their duties in the *Centro* judgment.[64]

Following close consideration of the duty of care and diligence, attention turns to s 180(2), the business judgment rule, which operates as a 'safe harbour' for directors. It provides a defence[65] for errors in judgment which have adversely affected the company where the director in making those errors:

- acted in good faith for a proper purpose
- did not have a material personal interest in the subject matter of the decision
- informed themselves about the subject matter of the decision to the extent they reasonably believed to be appropriate, and
- rationally believed that the decision was in the best interests of the corporation.[66]

A 'business judgment' is any 'decision to take or not take action in respect of a matter relevant to the business operations of the corporation'.[67] In *ASIC v Rich*,[68] Justice Austin held the definition extended to the preparation of making a business judgment, including planning, budgeting, forecasting, setting of policy goals or division of responsibilities within the board and management.[69] However, where a director fails to consider the matter at all this is not considered a business judgment.[70]

Whilst there have been several attempts to rely on s 180(2),[71] none have been successful.[72] The business judgment rule can only be relied upon for the statutory duty of care and diligence in s 180(1) and cannot be relied on for certain breaches such as administrative filing obligations,[73] disclosure obligations[74] and insolvent trading.[75] There is some ambiguity regarding the onus of proof of the business judgement rule, to the point where Justice Austin in *ASIC v Rich* decided 'with some hesitation' that the defendant director bore the onus of proving the four aspects outlined in the statute.[76]

The Duties of Loyalty and Good Faith

Beyond the duty of care and diligence, the other sections of the *Corporations Act* similarly engage with the directors' responsibility for corporate governance and oversight of risk. Unlike the duty of care, the duties of loyalty and good faith encompass a number of legislative provisions, including ss 181–183, ss 191–195 and Chapter 2E. The relationship between these duties and the general law is also more complex. Many of these duties draw on the broad themes evident in the hallmark obligation of directors as a fiduciary to their company—with its attendant negative prohibitions, that a director must not place themselves in a position of conflict, and must not secretly profit from their position.[77] Others respond to a particular risk inherent in corporate systems, such as the risk of self-dealing. Although it is certainly possible to imagine a scenario where a board or individual directors acts contrary to their duties of loyalty and good faith in relation to a cyber risk, on the whole, this may be a less likely avenue than a breach of the duty of care. The duties in ss 182–183 require improper use of information or position by the director, which could clearly be the case where a former senior executive (subject to officers' duties) or member of a board acts as an 'insider' to a cyber-attack. Section 191 requires disclosure of material personal interests, which might be problematic for directors who sit on boards or hold substantial shareholding in cyber security businesses who may be bidding for or engaging in work for the company—but this is remedied by compliance with the disclosure conditions in ss 191–192. The related party transaction provisions in Chapter2E are less likely to be involved in a cyber risk scenario, and, again, are remedied by compliance with the requirements of member approval.[78]

The duty to act in good faith in the best interests of the company and for proper purposes as described in s 181 would be the key duty, alongside the duty of care and diligence, where directors may risk breach for their actions when faced with cyber risk. Unlike the duty of care and diligence, which is focused on the directors' responsibility to guide and monitor the company at an appropriate standard, this duty is concerned with the way in which directors exercise their powers and discretions. The duty can be traced back to sixteenth-century decisions about how individuals exercise powers granted to them, particularly under wills,[79] and focused on the importance of using the power bona fide for the purpose it was designed—and that acts beyond that would be void. The language in the context of companies developed into a duty to act bona fide for the benefit of the company, or in the interests of the company as a whole;[80] with the second limb of the duty remaining more focused on the directors' use of their powers for 'proper' purposes.[81] Modern corporate governance debates are focussed, particularly, on what is meant by acting 'in the interests of the company'—which has been equated, in case law, with acting in the interests of the members collectively.[82] As views change on the validity of the shareholder primacy approach to corporate governance, the shareholder-centric interpretation of this provision may similarly be due for reconsideration, in light of broader expectations about stakeholder interests in corporate conduct.[83] Unlike the modern duty of care and diligence, the duty to act in good faith in the interests of the company remains predominantly subjective;[84] and although the responsibility to act for proper purposes considers the objective purpose for which the power was granted, the legal test contrasts this with the subjective purpose for which it was exercised by the directors.[85] Due to the subjective nature of this duty, it is less likely that directors acting in good faith and for proper purposes when addressing cyber risk or responding to a cyber-attack would be found in breach, when compared with the duty of care and diligence, and its objective expectations of conduct.

What the directors' duty regime does not address, directly, is the damage caused beyond the corporation.[86] For example, a customer whose data was stolen during a cyber-attack, or whose private information is released on the internet as part of a cyber-attack, will not be able to utilise directors' duties to seek a remedy, as directors' duties are owed to the company,[87] and not to individual members or more remote customers. For damage suffered by the company, there is a clear cause of action, which could be taken against directors—and where the wrong-doers remain in control of the board and the company is unable to take action, then other mechanisms within the Corporations Act will provide a pathway to a remedy.[88]

Conclusion

Cyber risk is undoubtedly a significant challenge facing the corporate world, and boards must be appropriately proactive in ensuring that their companies are prepared for this risk. However, the severity of the risk which cyber-crime presents does not prevent analogy being drawn to other risks facing boards—often significant, often difficult to predict or 'inherent[ly] uncertain', and often require specialist knowledge to engage with appropriately. Boards are undoubtedly under significant pressure to engage appropriately with financial, environmental and cyber risks facing their companies, but the directors' duties provide a clear standard of behaviour with which they must comply. The existing legal framework, including directors' duties, is able to respond to the challenge presented by cyber risk—the better question, perhaps, is whether directors themselves are resilient enough to rise to that challenge.

Notes

1. Committee on the Financial Aspects of Corporate Governance, *The Financial Aspects of Corporate Governance* ('Cadbury Report') (Burgess Science Press, 1992); *The King Report on Corporate Governance* ('King I Report') (Institute of Directors in Southern Africa, 1994).Ken Rushton, 'Introduction' in Ken Rushton (ed), *The Business Case for Corporate Governance* (Cambridge University Press, 2008) 2; Morten Huse, *Boards, Governance and Value Creation: The Human Side of Corporate Governance* (Cambridge University Press, 2007) 15, 18–24; Bob Garratt, *Thin on Top* (Nicholas Brealey Publishing, 2003) 12; John Farrar, 'Corporate governance and the judges' (2003) 15(1) *Bond Law Review* 65; and Güler Manisali Darman, *Corporate Governance Worldwide: A Guide to Best Practices and Managers* (ICC Publishing, 2004) 9–11.
2. *G20/OECD Principles of Corporate Governance* (2015) <https://www.oecd.org/publications/g20-oecdprinciples-of-corporate-governance-2015-9789264236882-en.htm>; Brian R. Cheffins, *Company Law: Theory, Structure and Operation* (Clarendon Press, 1997) 47.
3. Report of the HIH Royal Commission ('Owen Report'), *The Failure of HIH Insurance—Volume I: A Corporate Collapse and Its Lessons* (Commonwealth of Australia, 2003) xxxiii.
4. Jean Du Plessis, Anil Hargovan and Beth Nosworthy, *Principles of Contemporary Corporate Governance* (5th ed, 2024, CUP) 5; Organization for Economic Cooperation and Development ('OECD'), G20/OECD Principles of Corporate Governance (2015) 7 <https://www.oecd.org/publications/g20-oecd-principles-of-corporate-governance-2015-9789264236882-en.htm>.
5. See further Du Plessis, Hargovan and Nosworthy, *Principles of Contemporary Corporate Governance* (5th ed, 2024, CUP) 17–20.
6. Brian R. Cheffins, 'The history of corporate governance' in Mike Wright et al (eds), The Oxford Handbook of Corporate Governance (Oxford University Press, 2013) 46.
7. Tricker identifies an accounting system introduced in circa 1446 which, instead of the simple, single-entry accounts tracking the movement of cash, reflected relationships between buyers and sellers, creditors and debtors, and principals and agents as one of the earliest demonstrations of corporate governance: Robert Tricker, 'The Evolution of Corporate Governance' in

Thomas Clarice and Douglas Branson (eds) *The SAGE Handbook of Corporate Governance* (SAGE Publications Ltd, 2012) 1, 2.

8. Robert Tricker, 'The Evolution of Corporate Governance' in Thomas Clarice and Douglas Branson (eds) *The SAGE Handbook of Corporate Governance* (SAGE Publications Ltd., 2012) 1, 3–4;
9. See, e.g., Stephen Bottomley et al., Contemporary Australian Corporate Law (2nd ed, 2021 CUP) 281–284; Du Plessis, Hargovan and Nosworthy, Principles of Contemporary Corporate Governance (5th ed, 2024, CUP).
10. Rosemary Langford, Ian Ramsay and Michelle Welsh, 'The origins of company directors' statutory duty of care' (2015) 37 *Sydney Law Review* 489, 493.
11. *Companies Act 1896* (Vic) s 116(2).
12. *Companies Act 1929* (UK) s 149. This provision was reproduced in the Australian legislation of the time: *Companies Act 1936* (NSW) s 129; *Companies Act 1938* (Vic) s 149.
13. See, eg, *Companies Act 1958* (Vic) s 107.
14. There is, similarly, a duty of care and diligence found in equity: *Permanent Building Society (in liq) v Wheeler* (1994) 11 WAR 187, 235–237.
15. Directors are one of the nominate categories of fiduciary in Australian law: *Hospital Products Ltd v United States Surgical Corporation* (1984) 156 CLR 41.
16. Australian Signals Directorate, *ASD Cyber Threat Report 2022-2023* (report, 14 November 2023), ch 4.
17. Ibid, '*Year in Review*'.
18. Australian Securities and Investments Commission, *Cyber Resilience: Health Check* (Report No 429, March 2015), 38.
19. Julian Fell, Georgina Piper and Matt Liddy, "This is the most detailed portrait yet of data breaches in Australia" *ABC* (News article, 27 March 2023) <https://www.abc.net.au/news/2023-03-28/detailed-portrait-data-breaches-oaic-disclosures/102131586>.
20. Ibid.
21. Ibid.
22. See Chapter 12 discussion of *ASIC v RI Advice Group Pty Ltd* [2022] FCA 496, which involved a financial services licensee, and provisions of the *Corporations Act* applicable only to that sub-set of corporations engaging in financial services.
23. Jillian Segal, 'Corporate governance: Substance over form' (2002) 25(1) *University of New South Wales Law Journal* 1, 5.
24. [1892] 2 Ch 100.
25. Ibid 102.
26. See, e.g., *Re City Equitable Fire Insurance Co Ltd* [1925] Ch 407.
27. (1990) 2 ACSR 405 and the appeal [1993] 1 VR 423.
28. (1991) 5 ACSR 115.
29. Similar examination was occurring in other jurisdictions, such as the United Kingdom, where the Committee on the Financial Aspects of Corporate Governance issued their report in 1992, and the King Report on Corporate Governance (more commonly known now as King I) in 1994.
30. (1992) 7 ACSR 759.
31. (1995) 37 NSWLR 438.
32. (1992) 7 ACSR 759, 864, citing *Commonwealth Bank of Australia v Friedrich* (1991) 5 ACSR 115, 187.
33. See, e.g., Explanatory Memorandum, Corporate Law Reform Bill 1992 (Cth) [84]–]85]; Corporate Law Economic Reform Program (CLERP), Directors Duties and corporate Governance (Paper No 3, Australian Government, 1997) [6.2].
34. Ian Ramsay and Robert Austin, *Ford, Austin and Ramsay's Principles of Corporations Law* (17th ed, 2018, LexisNexis) [8.305].
35. The duty to exercise care, skill, and diligence, as outlined in s 180(1), arises primarily from the common law of contract or tort: *VicBeef Holdings Pty Ltd v Chen* [2021] VSC 546, [182]; and in equity: *Permanent Building Society (in liq) v Wheeler* (1994) 11 WAR 187, 235–237.

36. *VicBeef Holdings Pty Ltd v Chen* [2021] VSC 546, [248].
37. *Australian Securities and Investments Commission v Healey* ('*Centro*')(2011) 196 FCR 291, [20].
38. *Australian Securities and Investments Commission v Vines* (2005) 55 ACSR 617.
39. Ibid [29].
40. Ibid [32].
41. Ibid [24].
42. Ibid [25].
43. Daniel Pienta, Jason Thatcher and Allen Johnston, 'Protecting a whale in a sea of phish' (2020) 35 *Journal of Information Technology* 214.
44. Such as distributed denial of service attacks, subversion of supply chain, or network intrusion: see, e.g., Chris Simmons et al, 'AVOIDIT: A cyber attack taxonomy' *University of Memphis, Technical Report CS-09-003* (2009) <https://www.researchgate.net/profile/S-Shiva/publication/229020163_AVOIDIT_A_Cyber_Attack_Taxonomy/links/544e58360cf2bca5ce90aebb/AVOIDIT-A-Cyber-Attack-Taxonomy.pdf>; Sanjay Goel and Brian Nussbaum, 'Attribution Across Cyber Attack Types: Network Intrusions and Information Operations' (2021) 2 *IEEE Open Journal of the Communications Society* 1082.
45. (2012) 286 ALR 612.
46. (2012) 286 ALR 612, [18].
47. (2012) 286 ALR 612, [30].
48. (2012) 286 ALR 612, [33].
49. (2012) 286 ALR 612, [46].
50. For further discussion, see Bottomley et al, *Contemporary Australian Corporate Law* (2nd Ed, 2021, CUP) 309–313.
51. A similar argument was made in relation to climate change risk using *ASIC v Vines* in Beth Nosworthy, 'The Corporations Act and Climate Change—Appetite for Change?' (2020) 94 *Australian Law Journal* 411, 414.
52. *Australian Securities and Investments Commission v Healey* (2011) 196 FCR 291.
53. ASIC argued that the directors had breached s 180(1) and s 344 of the Corporations Act because the 2007 annual accounts misclassified that several borrowings were non-current liabilities, when in fact they were current.
54. *Australian Securities and Investments Commission v Healey* (2011) 196 FCR 291, [573].
55. As noted in Jennifer Hill, Centro and the Monitoring Board—Legal Duties Versus Aspirational Ideals in Corporate Governance (2012) 35 *University of New South Wales Law Journal* 341, 342, 346–347.
56. *Australian Securities and Investments Commission v Healey* (2011) 196 FCR 291, [564].
57. Ibid.
58. Ibid.
59. Ibid [129], [240].
60. Ibid [129], [240].
61. Ibid [129], [240].
62. Nick Lenaghan and Ben Wilmot, 'Centro, PwC take record $200m legal hit', Financial Review (9 May 2012) <https://www.afr.com/property/commercial/centro-pwc-take-record-200m-legal-hit-20120509-j2v7s>.
63. *Australian Securities and Investments Commission v Healey* (2011) 196 FCR 430, [4], [5].
64. Ibid [3].
65. See discussion Wesley Bainbridge and Tim Connor, 'Another way forward? The scope for an appellate court to reinterpret the statutory business judgment rule' (2016) 34 *CSLJ* 415.
66. Allens Arthur Robinson, *Director's Duties During Insolvency* (2nd ed, Lawbook Co, 2007) [17.1.6].
67. *Corporations Act 2001* (Cth), s 180(3).
68. *Australian Securities and Investments Commission v Rich* (2009) 75 ACSR 1.
69. Ibid.
70. *Australian Securities and Investments Commission v Adler* (2002) 41 ACSR 72.

71. See *Australian Securities and Investments Commission v Fortescue Metals Group Ltd* (2011) 190 FCR 364; *Australian Securities and Investments Commission v Adler* (2002) 168 FLR 253; *Australian Securities and Investments Commission v Mariner Corporation Limited* (2015) 241 FCR 502.
72. Allens Linklaters, Advice Regarding the Business Judgment Rule (Advice Paper, 3 December 2020) <https://www.aicd.com.au/content/dam/aicd/pdf/news-media/research/2021/advice-regarding-business-judgment-rule.pdf>.
73. *Corporations Act 2001* (Cth), s 188.
74. *Corporations Act 2001* (Cth), s 674(2A), 729.
75. *Corporations Act 2001* (Cth), s 588G.
76. *Australian Securities and Investments Commission v Rich* (2009) 236 FLR 1, [7246].
77. Both developed in England across a significant amount of case law since Keech v Sanford (1726) Sel Cas Ch 61, and adopted into the general law in Australia in *Moss v Moss (No 2)* (1900) 21 LR(NSW) Eq 253.
78. *Corporations Act 2001* (Cth), ss 208(1), 210–227.
79. See, eg, *Aleyn v Belchier* (1758) 1 Eden 132; *Vatcher v Paull* [1915] AC 372.
80. *Allen v Gold Reefs of West Africa Ltd* [1900] 1 Ch 656; *Richard Brady Franks Ltd v Price* (1937) 58 CLR 112; *Mills v Mills* (1938) 60 CLR 150.
81. *Harlowe's Nominees Pty Ltd v Woodside (Lakes Entrance) Oil Co NL* (1968) 121 CLR 483; *Whitehouse v Carlton Hotel Pty Ltd* (1987) 162 CLR 285.
82. *Mills v Mills* (1938) 60 CLR 150; *Ngurli Ltd v McCann* (1953) 90 CLR 425.
83. For further discussion, please see Du Plessis, Hargovan and Nosworthy, *Principles of Contemporary Corporate Governance* (5th ed, 2024, CUP) 17 on
84. *Bell Group Ltd (in liq) v Westpac Banking Corporation (No 9)* (2009) 39 WAR 1, [4619].
85. *Howard Smith Ltd v Ampol Petroleum Ltd* [1974] 1 NSWLR 68, 77.
86. The various harms caused by cyber attacks are discussed in Ioannis Agrafiotis et al, 'A taxonomy of cyber-harms: Defining the impacts of cyber-attacks and understanding how they propagate' (2018) 4 *Journal of Cybersecurity* 1.
87. There are limited exceptions to this position, as discussed in Bottomley et al, *Contemporary Australian Corporate Law* (2nd ed, 2021 CUP) 336–339, 362–367.
88. *Corporations Act 2001* (Cth) ss 232, 236.

Beth Nosworthy is an Associate Professor and Deputy Dean of the University of Adelaide Law School, where she lectures in Corporate Law and Equity. Beth was an associate in the Supreme Court of South Australia and worked in commercial legal practice before returning to study, completing a BCL at the University of Oxford. Her Ph.D. examined the fiduciary obligations of directors in closely-held companies within the broader context of corporate governance. She has published widely on directors' duties, including the key chapters on this topic in *Contemporary Australian Corporate Law* and *Principles of Contemporary Corporate Governance* (both Cambridge University Press). She is an executive committee member of a number of organisations, including the Society of Corporate Law Academics, and is an independent representative on the Education Committee for the Governance Institute of Australia. Her current research focusses on corporate structures, corporate governance and directors' duties.

Communications in Crisis, and Promoting Resilience

Deb Camden

Abstract This chapter explores the critical aspects of crisis communication and its role in promoting organisational resilience, specifically during cyber attacks. It underscores the importance of a proactive and well-structured crisis communication plan that includes predefined roles, responsibilities, and communication protocols. The chapter highlights the distinctive nature of cyber attacks, emphasising the need for technical expertise and a flexible communication strategy due to the evolving threats. It discusses the balance between transparency and security, legal and regulatory implications, and the need for coordination with external entities such as law enforcement and cybersecurity experts. By examining high-profile cyber incidents in Australia such as the Optus and Medibank breaches in 2022, the chapter illustrates the repercussions of poor communication strategies and the importance of timely, clear, and empathetic messaging. It introduces a comprehensive framework for effective corporate communication post-cyber incidents, integrating theories such as Situational Crisis Communication Theory (SCCT) to manage blame and maintain public trust. The framework also stresses the significance of proactive responsibility and tailored messaging to different stakeholder demographics.

To speak or not to speak: that is not the question.

Introduction

When it comes to responding to a cyber security breach, the question for organisations is no longer whether or not to communicate. Failure to do so will occur at their peril.

In an era marked by increasing reliance on digital infrastructure, the threat of cyber attacks has become a critical risk to be managed by public and private sector organisations—regardless of their size. In 2022–23, the Australian Cyber Security

D. Camden (✉)
University of Queensland, Brisbane, Australia
e-mail: d.camden@prismpartnership.com.au

D. Stephens et al. (eds.), *Digital Resilience*,
https://doi.org/10.1007/978-981-97-9746-2_14

Centre[1] recorded more than 94,000 cybercrime reports, an increase of 23% from the previous year. The cost of cybercrime to Australia is estimated at more than $42 billion each year and is growing rapidly.[2]

The effectiveness of an organisation's response to a cyber attack relies not only on the operational response but also on its crisis communication strategy. Crisis communication is essential not only for managing the immediate aftermath of an attack but also for aiding recovery afterwards.

This chapter explores the multi-faceted role of crisis communication during cyber attacks, focusing on the stages before, during, and after an attack with specific reference to the legal landscape in Australia. It identifies how crisis communication for cyber attacks is different to other crises and examines recent crisis communication approaches in Australia, particularly the high-profile Optus and Medibank breaches in 2022. Finally, it shares a comprehensive framework to guide crisis communications for a cyber attack and to build resilience before an incident occurs. It provides actionable insights for organisational leaders, communicators, legal advisors and risk managers responsible for expertly anticipating and navigating the reputation impact of a major cyber security incident and for promoting digital resilience in their organisations.

The Environment for Crisis Communication in Australia

Crisis communication professionals in Australia face a challenging landscape when responding to a cyber attack. They must navigate a complex array of regulations that govern how they manage and communicate during and after these incidents. The key regulations and frameworks shaping a cyber crisis response are:

Privacy Act 1988 (Cth) and Notifiable Data Breaches (NDB) Scheme

The *Privacy Act 1988 (Cth)* is a fundamental piece of legislation for crisis communication professionals in Australia, especially when handling cyber attacks that involve personal data breaches. The Act mandates the protection of personal information and sets out 13 Australian Privacy Principles (APPs) that organisations must follow.

Under the Notifiable Data Breaches (NDB) scheme, which became effective in February 2018, organisations covered by the Privacy Act must notify individuals and the Office of the Australian Information Commissioner (OAIC) when a data breach is likely to result in serious harm to any individual whose personal information is involved. Crisis communication professionals need to be well-versed in the NDB scheme to ensure timely and compliant notifications, which include the nature of the breach, the information involved, and steps individuals can take to mitigate harm.

Australian Cyber Security Centre (ACSC) Guidelines

The ACSC, part of the Australian Signals Directorate, provides critical guidelines and support for managing cyber security incidents. While not a regulatory body, its advice and frameworks are influential and often align with regulatory expectations. The ACSC's Incident Response Plan and guidelines on managing cyber incidents offer practical steps for organisations to follow. Crisis communicators should familiarise themselves with these resources to ensure their response aligns with best practices and government expectations.

Australian Securities Exchange (ASX) Listing Rules

For publicly listed companies, the ASX Listing Rules are paramount, particularly Rule 3.1, which requires the disclosure of any information that a reasonable person would expect to have a material effect on the price or value of the company's securities. In the event of a cyber attack, crisis communication professionals, with guidance from the crisis team, must swiftly assess whether the incident falls under this rule and prepare a market disclosure to ensure transparency with investors and compliance with market regulations.

Critical Infrastructure Act 2018

The *Security of Critical Infrastructure Act 2018* (Chapter "Ensuring Digital Resilience in Australia: From Resilience to Security in Critical Infrastructure Protection" of this edited monograph) mandates reporting requirements and risk management obligations for owners and operators of critical infrastructure in Australia. If a cyber attack targets such infrastructure, organisations must notify the government and potentially affected parties. Crisis communication professionals should ensure they understand these requirements to manage communications effectively with regulatory bodies and the public.

Telecommunications Sector Security Reforms (TSSR)

Under the *Telecommunications and Other Legislation Amendment Act 2017*, the TSSR obliges telecommunications companies to protect their networks from threats to national security. This includes mandatory reporting of security breaches to the Australian Government. Crisis communication professionals in this sector need to align their response strategies with TSSR requirements, ensuring that notifications and public statements are timely and accurate.

Industry-Specific Regulations

Various industries have their own specific regulations concerning cyber security and data breaches. For example, the financial sector adheres to standards set by the Australian Prudential Regulation Authority (APRA), including Prudential Standard CPS 234, which outlines information security requirements. Healthcare providers must comply with regulations under the *My Health Records Act 2012*. The task for crisis communication professionals is to be knowledgeable about the regulations pertinent to their specific industry to manage communications effectively and in compliance with relevant laws.

General Duty of Care and Consumer Protection Laws

Beyond specific cyber security regulations, general duty of care and consumer protection laws, such as those under the Australian Consumer Law, may come into play. Misleading statements about a cyber attack or inadequate communication efforts could lead to breaches of these laws, resulting in legal consequences and reputational damage (Chapter "Corporate Legal Responses to Promote Resilience" (White & Watford) of this edited monograph).

Crisis communication during a cyber attack shares several similarities with other types of crises but also has distinct differences due to the unique nature of cyber threats. Understanding these similarities and differences is crucial when designing an effective communication response.

Similarities with Other Crises

A crisis by any other name.

The fundamental principles of crisis communication apply broadly, irrespective of the type of crisis. Situational Crisis Communication Theory (SCCT)[3] emphasises the importance of a timely and transparent response to maintain organisational credibility and trust with stakeholders. This principle holds true for cyber attacks as well. Rapid acknowledgement of the crisis and regular updates help mitigate the spread of misinformation and reassure stakeholders that the organisation is taking the situation seriously.

Further, building and maintaining trust is crucial across all types of crises. During a cyber attack, like any other crisis, maintaining clear and honest communication helps preserve stakeholder trust. According to Barton,[4] maintaining transparency and providing regular updates are essential strategies for effective crisis communication. This includes admitting what is known, what is unknown, and the steps being taken to resolve the issue, which parallels strategies used in other crises such as natural disasters or financial scandals.

Other similarities include timeliness and transparency, stakeholder communication, reputation management, use of a crisis plan and a multi-faceted response.

Timeliness and transparency: Both cyber attacks and other crises, such as natural disasters or corporate scandals, require timely and transparent communication. The affected organisation must quickly acknowledge the incident, provide as much information as possible, and outline the steps being taken to mitigate the impact. The aim is to maintain public trust and reduce speculation and misinformation.

Stakeholder communication: In any crisis, identifying and communicating with key stakeholders is critical. These stakeholders can include employees, customers, investors, regulators, and the media. Effective crisis communication ensures these groups receive accurate and consistent information tailored to their specific needs and concerns.

Reputation management: Protecting the organisation's reputation is a critical priority in all crisis communications. How the organisation responds, the speed of their response, and the messages they convey can significantly impact public perception. A well-managed response can enhance an organisation's reputation, while a poorly handled one can cause long-term damage.

Use of a crisis communication plan: Preparedness is essential across all types of crises. Having a well-developed crisis communication plan that includes predefined roles, responsibilities, and communication protocols is crucial. This plan should be regularly updated and practiced through simulations to ensure readiness.

Multi-faceted response: From timely updates to empathetic messaging, transparency, and strategic use of media channels, a multi-faceted response ensures that organisations can effectively manage perceptions, maintain trust, and mitigate the fallout of the crisis. A holistic approach, not only demonstrates an organisation's preparedness but also their commitment to transparency, empathy, and accountability, fostering resilience and reinforcing their reputation in the face of adversity.

Differences Specific to Cyber Attacks

Despite these similarities, crisis communication during a cyber attack is different due to the nature of the threat, scope of information sharing, legal and regulatory implications, coordination with external entities, coordination with IT and security teams, and a dual-focus communication strategy.

Nature of the threat: The technical nature of cyber attacks sets them apart from other crises. Unlike natural disasters or accidents, cyber attacks often involve sophisticated tactics, malicious intent, and evolving threats. This complexity requires specialised knowledge and technical expertise to communicate effectively. The evolving nature of cyber threats also adds a layer of complexity. Cyber attacks often unfold in stages, with new information and threats emerging continuously. This dynamic situation requires a more flexible and adaptive communication strategy compared to other crises, which may be more static once the initial impact is known. For example, a natural disaster might have an immediate impact followed by a recovery phase, whereas a cyber attack might involve ongoing threats and discoveries of new vulnerabilities.

Scope of information sharing: During a cyber attack, there is often a delicate balance between transparency and security. Disclosing too much information can exacerbate the situation by providing attackers with useful insights. Therefore, communication needs to be carefully managed to avoid compromising ongoing mitigation efforts or exposing vulnerabilities.

Legal and regulatory implications: Cyber attacks come with specific legal and regulatory requirements for reporting and disclosure, which can vary by jurisdiction. Organisations must navigate these requirements while ensuring that their communication complies with relevant data protection laws and cybersecurity regulations. This adds a layer of complexity not always present in other types of crises.

Coordination with external entities: The involvement of external entities such as law enforcement and cybersecurity experts is typically more pronounced in cyber crises. Organisations must coordinate their communication strategies with these external stakeholders to ensure consistency and avoid compromising any investigations. This coordination is often less critical in other crises, where internal communication strategies can be more self-contained.

Technical jargon and public understanding: Explaining a cyber attack involves technical language that may not be easily understood by the general public. Communicators must simplify complex information without losing accuracy. This contrasts with other crises where the nature of the incident might be more immediately understood by a non-expert audience or the general public.

Coordination with IT and security teams: Crisis communication during a cyber attack requires close coordination with IT and cybersecurity teams as well as legal counsel. These teams are integral to understanding the scope of the attack, its impact, and the remediation steps. This collaboration is more pronounced in cyber incidents compared to other crises where the primary response might involve different departments, such as operations or human resources.

Dual-focus communication plan: Another distinctive factor is the potential for reputational damage linked to perceived negligence in cybersecurity. Unlike natural disasters, where the organisation is seen as a victim, cyber attacks can lead to questions about the organisation's cybersecurity preparedness and responsibility. This demands a dual-focus communication strategy that not only addresses the immediate crisis but also reassures stakeholders about future security measures and risk mitigation strategies.

> Better three hours too soon than a minute too late.

Crisis Communication Before a Cyber Attack: Building a Resilient Framework

Crisis communication before a cyber attack is fundamentally about preparation. Organisations need to develop a robust communication plan that integrates seamlessly with their broader cyber resilience strategy. This involves several key components:

Risk assessment and planning: Identifying potential cyber threats and vulnerabilities is the first step. Organisations need to conduct thorough risk assessments to understand the types of attacks they might face and their potential impact. This knowledge forms the basis of a crisis communication plan.

Stakeholder mapping: Understanding who the stakeholders are is crucial. These include employees, customers, investors, regulatory bodies and the media. Effective communication strategies must address the needs and concerns of each stakeholder group.

Communication channels and protocols: Establishing clear communication channels and protocols ensures that messages can be disseminated quickly and efficiently. This includes deciding who will communicate, what they will say, and through which platforms (e.g. media releases, social media, internal emails).

Training and simulations: Regular training and simulations for the crisis communication team are essential. These exercises help refine the communication plan and ensure that team members are well-prepared to execute it under pressure.

Message development: Crafting pre-approved messages that can be quickly adapted and deployed during a crisis is vital. These messages should be clear, concise, and tailored to different stakeholders to maintain trust and transparency.

Crisis Communication During a Cyber Attack: Immediate Response and Management

When a cyber attack occurs, the organisation's immediate response can significantly influence the overall impact of the incident. Effective crisis communication during a cyber attack involves several critical actions:

Rapid response: Time is of the essence. Organisations must acknowledge the incident quickly, even if all the details are not yet known. This helps manage speculation and control the narrative.

Transparency and honesty: Honesty is paramount in maintaining stakeholder trust. Organisations should provide as much information as possible without compromising security or ongoing investigations. This includes what happened, what is being done to address it, and what stakeholders can do to protect themselves.

Consistent messaging: Consistency across all communication channels is crucial. Discrepancies can lead to confusion and erode trust. A centralised communication team can help ensure messages are consistent and accurate.

Stakeholder engagement: regular updates to stakeholders help keep them informed and reassured. This includes providing clear instructions on any actions they need to take and addressing their concerns promptly.

Media management: The media plays a significant role in shaping public perception during a cyber attack. Proactive engagement with the media, providing timely and accurate information, and correcting misinformation are essential aspects of crisis communication.

Crisis Communication After a Cyber Attack: Recovery and Rebuilding Trust

Post-attack communication focuses on recovery and rebuilding trust. This stage is critical for demonstrating resilience and commitment to stakeholders. Key actions include:

Post-Incident analysis: conducting a thorough post-mortem analysis to understand what happened, why it happened, and how similar incidents can be prevented in the future. This analysis should be communicated transparently to stakeholders.

Ongoing communication: keeping stakeholders informed about the steps being taken to prevent future incidents, including any changes to policies, procedures, or technologies.

Reputation management: engaging in reputation management activities to restore stakeholder confidence. This might include public apologies, compensation for affected parties, and highlighting improvements made to enhance security.

Lessons learned and sharing knowledge: sharing the lessons learned from the incident within the organisation and with other entities can contribute to a broader understanding of cyber threats and resilience strategies.

Regulatory compliance and reporting: ensuring all regulatory requirements are met and maintaining open communication with regulatory bodies. This can also involve working with legal and compliance teams to address any legal implications of the breach.

Scholarly Perspectives

Dr. Sarah Jane Duggan,[5] a prominent researcher in crisis communication at the University of Melbourne, underscores the importance of maintaining trust through honest and timely communication. Duggan advocates for organisations to acknowledge cyber breaches promptly, provide regular updates on the situation, and offer clear guidance to affected stakeholders.

Similarly, Dr. Peter Chen[6] from the University of Sydney highlights the significance of framing cyber attacks as societal challenges rather than isolated incidents. Chen argues that effective crisis communication should not only focus on technical aspects but also address the broader implications for individuals, businesses, and national security. By framing cyber attacks within a broader societal context, organisations can foster understanding and garner support from stakeholders.

Professor Mia Lindgren,[7] an expert in media and communication at Monash University, emphasises the role of media literacy in crisis communication. Lindgren suggests that educating the public about cyber threats and security measures can enhance resilience and minimise panic during crises. By promoting media literacy, organisations can empower individuals to discern credible information from misinformation, thereby reducing the spread of rumours and misinformation during cyber attacks.

No legacy is so rich as honesty.

An Integrated Framework for Corporate Communications After Cyber Security Incidents

Knight and Nurse[8] offer a new comprehensive framework for effective corporate communication after cyber security incidents to support companies in their preparation and response to these events. The framework has particular value and relevance for communication professionals and academics, having been evaluated through interviews with senior industry professionals, as well as a critical assessment against relevant practice and research. It represents the first grounded, comprehensive and evaluated proposal for characterising effective corporate communication after cyber security incidents.

By integrating theories such as SCCT, emphasising clear and tailored messaging, and encouraging proactive responsibility, the framework aims to help organisations mitigate reputation damage and maintain public trust during cyber crises. Key considerations include:

Blame and Situational Crisis Communication Theory (SCCT): The framework integrates the SCCT, which categorises crises and recommends appropriate communication responses. The theory suggests that establishing responsibility and accountability is crucial for maintaining public trust. Research indicates that perceived accountability can lead to negative emotions and social media backlash, emphasising the importance of managing blame carefully.

Clear and simple communication: It stresses the need for clear and jargon-free communication. Messages should be simple and transparent to avoid damaging credibility. For example, addressing previous breaches, exposure of limitations, or third-party discoveries should be handled with clarity to maintain trust.

Tailored messaging: The framework advocates for tailoring messages according to the demographics and characteristics of the affected audience. For example, younger generations might be less impressed with credit monitoring as a mitigation strategy. Organisations also should demonstrate ethical stances and efforts to bring culprits to justice, sharing lessons learned to help others avoid similar mistakes.

Proactive responsibility: Impacted organisations are encouraged to quickly assume responsibility for breaches and take proactive steps to address the issues. This approach has been shown to positively influence public perception and reduce the risk of further reputational damage. Apologising and mitigating harm proactively are recognised strategies for enhancing customer perceptions and trust.

Legal considerations: While taking responsibility is crucial, the framework also highlights the potential risk of litigation. It acknowledges the balance between avoiding fines from data protection authorities and managing the cost of legal actions. It suggests that the positive effects of taking responsibility often outweigh the risks associated with litigation.

Practical application: The framework is designed to be applied in scenario-based rehearsals, allowing organisations to assess its effectiveness and identify areas for improvement. This practical approach ensures that the framework is not just theoretical but also actionable in real-world situations.

Validation and refinement: The framework was validated through semi-structured interviews with senior industry professionals in cyber security and public relations. Feedback from these experts was used to refine the framework, ensuring it addresses the gaps identified in industry practices.

General applicability: Although primarily focused on malicious data breaches, the framework's components, such as disclosure means, timelines, and message content, are also relevant for unintentional breaches. However, the discussion on blame differs, as organisations are typically at fault in unintentional breaches and must quickly assume responsibility.

Crisis Communication in Recent Australian Cyber Attacks

Nothing will come of nothing.

Sydney Morning Herald 10 November 2022

"Optus hack to cost at least $140 million"

https://www.smh.com.au/business/companies/optus-puts-aside-140m-to-replace-customers-hacked-identity-documents-20221110-p5bx4g.html

The Optus Data Breach

The Optus data breach of September 2022 stands as one of Australia's most significant cybersecurity incidents, exposing the sensitive information of up to 9.8 million customers. This breach not only compromised personal data but also highlighted significant flaws in the company's communication strategy with customers and stakeholders during the crisis.

Optus, Australia's second-largest telecommunications company, discovered the breach on September 21, 2022, when it detected unauthorised access to its systems. The compromised data included names, dates of birth, phone numbers, email addresses, and, in some cases, addresses and identification document numbers such as driver's licenses and passports. The breach had a profound impact, as it exposed millions of individuals to potential identity theft and fraud.

One of the most criticised aspects of the incident was Optus's communication with its affected customers and stakeholders. Initial communication was delayed, creating a vacuum of information that led to widespread confusion and anxiety. When Optus finally acknowledged the breach, the messages were often vague and lacked sufficient detail. This lack of transparency fuelled frustration among customers who were eager to understand the extent of their exposure and the steps they needed to take to protect themselves.

The company's public statements were criticised for being evasive and not providing actionable guidance. For instance, Optus initially downplayed the breach's severity, suggesting that the compromised data was less sensitive than it actually was. This miscommunication caused many customers to underestimate the potential risks, delaying their responses to mitigate those risks. Furthermore, many customers reported that they learned about the breach from news reports rather than directly from Optus, which compounded their frustration and eroded trust in the company.

The Australian Government and cybersecurity experts also criticised Optus's handling of the breach. The company's failure to promptly notify regulatory bodies and coordinate with law enforcement agencies hampered a swift and effective response. Government officials, including Prime Minister Anthony Albanese, publicly rebuked Optus for its inadequate security measures and poor communication. This high-profile censure further damaged the company's reputation and highlighted systemic issues within its cybersecurity practices.

Internally, Optus's crisis management appeared disjointed. Employees and customer service representatives were often left without clear directives or adequate resources to assist affected customers, leading to inconsistent and sometimes contradictory information being disseminated. This inconsistency not only frustrated customers but also made the situation worse by making it difficult for individuals to take protective measures effectively.

In response to the breach, Optus eventually offered free credit monitoring services to affected customers and implemented additional security measures. However, these efforts were seen as reactive rather than proactive, coming after significant damage had already been done. The delayed and fragmented communication efforts led to a perception that Optus was more concerned with protecting its corporate image than with addressing the concerns and well-being of its customers. This ultimately cost the CEO, Kelly Bayer Rosmarin her job. She resigned "in the best interests of the company" following a nationwide outage in November that same year.

In the wake of the breach, cybersecurity experts emphasised the importance of robust incident response plans that prioritise transparent and timely communication.

The Optus case serves as a cautionary tale for other organisations about the critical role of communication in managing cybersecurity incidents. Effective communication can help maintain customer trust, coordinate response efforts, and minimise the damage caused by such breaches. Optus's experience underscores the necessity for companies to not only safeguard their systems against cyber threats but also to have a clear and effective communication strategy in place to manage potential breaches.

Bloomberg 9 November 2022

"Medibank Hack Could Cost A$700 Million in Compensation, Fixes"

https://www.bloomberg.com/news/articles/2022-11-10/medibank-hack-could-cost-a-700-million-in-compensation-fixes

The Medibank Breach

In October 2022, one month after the Optus breach, Medibank, one of Australia's largest health insurers, suffered a ransomware attack that compromised the personal information of nearly 9.7 million current and former customers, including sensitive medical records and personal data. Hackers accessed customer names, addresses, dates of birth, Medicare numbers, and health claim data. The breach not only threatened the privacy of millions but also posed potential risks of identity theft and extortion. The attackers demanded a ransom, threatening to release the data if their demands were not met. Medibank, adhering to advice from cybersecurity experts and government agencies, refused to pay the ransom, emphasising a policy against capitulating to criminal demands.

While the breach itself raised severe concerns about cybersecurity practices, the way Medibank handled communication with its customers and stakeholders exacerbated the crisis.

From the onset, Medibank's communication strategy was widely criticised. The company initially downplayed the severity of the breach. In the first notification to customers, Medibank mentioned a "cyber incident" without detailing the scale or sensitivity of the data involved. This vagueness led to confusion and anxiety among customers, who were unsure about the extent of their compromised information.

As the situation unfolded, Medibank's updates were sporadic and often lacked clarity. Customers complained about the delay in receiving critical information, which left them feeling vulnerable and uninformed. The company's use of technical jargon and corporate language further alienated the general public, who needed straightforward and actionable advice.

One of the major criticisms was Medibank's failure to provide timely personal notifications to affected individuals. Many customers learned about the breach and the potential exposure of their personal information through media reports rather than direct communication from Medibank. This not only undermined customer trust but also suggested a lack of preparedness in managing such a crisis.

Stakeholders, including investors, regulators, and partners, also felt the impact of Medibank's poor communication. Investors saw a significant drop in Medibank's share price as confidence in the company's ability to safeguard sensitive information waned. The Australian Securities and Investments Commission (ASIC) and the Office of the Australian Information Commissioner (OAIC)[9] initiated investigations into the breach, scrutinising Medibank's compliance with data protection regulations.

Further, the healthcare sector, which relies heavily on trust and confidentiality, saw ripple effects. The breach raised questions about the security protocols across the industry, prompting other organisations to reevaluate their cybersecurity measures. Partners and vendors associated with Medibank also faced scrutiny and potential reputational damage by association.

Suit the action to the word, the word to the action.

Analysis of Optus and Medibank Data Breaches by Leading Australian PR Professionals and Media Commentators

The Optus and Medibank data breaches have sparked significant debate and analysis among Australian PR professionals and media commentators, with discussions focusing on the impact on public trust, the effectiveness of crisis communication strategies, and the long-term implications for corporate and governmental cybersecurity practices.

Optus Data Breach

Leading PR professionals like Samantha Dybac,[10] CEO of The PR Hub, critiqued Optus's initial response, emphasising the importance of transparency and timeliness in crisis communication. Dybac noted that Optus's delayed acknowledgment and piecemeal updates eroded public trust—a sentiment echoed by many in the industry. She argued that companies must be prepared to communicate swiftly and clearly to mitigate the fallout from such breaches.

Media commentators, including those at the Australian Financial Review,[11] pointed out that Optus's handling of the breach revealed significant gaps in their crisis management strategy. They criticised the company's failure to promptly inform affected customers and the broader public, which led to confusion and panic. Commentators highlighted the reactive rather than proactive nature of Optus's communication, suggesting that a pre-emptive strike—such as immediate public disclosure and offering support services to affected individuals—could have softened the backlash.

Medibank Data Breach

Nicole Matejic,[12] an expert in crisis communication, pointed out that the breach underscored the vulnerabilities within government systems. Matejic praised the government's swift response in publicly acknowledging the breach and providing clear guidelines on how affected individuals could protect their identities. However, she also highlighted the need for a more robust long-term strategy to prevent such breaches from occurring again.

Media outlets including the Sydney Morning Herald[13] focused on the broader implications of the Medibank breach. Commentators noted that while the government's immediate response was commendable, the incident exposed systemic weaknesses in Australia's cybersecurity infrastructure. The breach called into question the effectiveness of existing measures and the preparedness of government agencies to handle cyber incidents. The media's analysis often underscored the need for enhanced cybersecurity protocols and the importance of public awareness in safeguarding personal data.

Comparing the responses to the Optus and Medibank breaches, PR professionals and media commentators agreed that both incidents highlighted critical lessons in crisis management and communication. They emphasised the need for organisations, whether private or public, to have robust crisis communication plans that include immediate disclosure, clear guidance for affected parties, and ongoing updates to maintain public trust.

Technology journalist, Stilgherrian,[14] stressed the importance of a unified approach to cybersecurity across both sectors. He argued that these breaches should serve as a wake-up call for all organisations to invest more in their cybersecurity defences and to foster a culture of transparency and accountability.

Lessons Learned

The critiques highlight the need for transparency, timeliness, and a proactive approach in managing such crises. Both breaches serve as critical case studies for future reference, illustrating the profound impact of data security on public trust and the essential role of comprehensive communication strategies in mitigating reputation damage.

Timely and transparent communication: One of the primary lessons from both the Optus and Medibank breaches is the need for timely and transparent communication. Companies must have a crisis communication plan in place that includes immediate notification protocols for customers and stakeholders when a breach occurs. Transparency about the extent of the breach and the measures being taken to mitigate its impact is crucial.

Consistent messaging: Ensuring that all communications are consistent and clear is vital. Mixed messages can cause confusion and panic, further eroding trust. A unified communication strategy should be developed and adhered to across all platforms and channels.

Proactive engagement: Proactively reaching out to affected individuals and stakeholders, rather than relying on them to discover the breach through secondary sources, is essential. This can help maintain trust and demonstrate the company's commitment to resolving the issue.

Preparedness and training: Companies should invest in regular training and preparedness drills for data breach scenarios. This includes training for communication teams to handle crises effectively and empathetically.

Future Directions

To prevent similar issues in the future, communication professionals can play an instrumental role in supporting their organisations to adopt several strategies:

Integrated communication systems: Developing integrated communication systems that can be quickly activated in the event of a breach will ensure timely and consistent messaging. These systems should be tested periodically to ensure efficacy.

Customer support infrastructure: Establishing a dedicated customer support infrastructure to handle breach-related inquiries can help manage the situation more effectively. This includes setting up hotlines and online resources to provide real-time assistance and updates.

Collaboration with authorities: Building strong relationships with cybersecurity authorities and law enforcement can facilitate quicker responses and support during breaches. Collaborative efforts can enhance overall cybersecurity resilience.

Regular updates to customers: Keeping customers informed about ongoing cybersecurity measures and improvements can help rebuild trust. Regular updates about what is being done to protect their data will reassure customers of the company's commitment to their security.

Go wisely and slowly. Those who rush, stumble and fall.

Conclusion

Implications for Organisational Leaders, Crisis Communication Professionals and Legal Advisors

The evolving threat landscape of cyber attacks in Australia poses significant implications for organisational leaders and communication professionals. Attackers do not distinguish between large and small businesses, government or non-government. From January to June 2024 alone, the Office of the Information Commissioner[15] received more than 80 major data breach notifications from a variety of organisations including local government, minerals producers, food producers, ticketing agencies, universities, clubs, airlines, real estate agents, non-profit organisations, health providers, automotive distributors.

For these and all impacted organisations, crisis communication plays a pivotal role in managing the impact of cyber attacks and building resilience. By preparing effectively, responding swiftly and transparently during an attack, and focusing on recovery and rebuilding trust afterward, organisations can navigate the complexities of cyber threats more effectively.

The cyber attacks on Optus and Medibank in Australia provide valuable insights into the importance of proactive, transparent, and ethical crisis communication strategies. Organisational leaders and communicators can learn from these cases to better prepare for and manage the inevitable cyber attacks they will face in an increasingly digital world.

Crisis communication professionals must possess a deep understanding of both technical aspects of cyber security and effective crisis communication strategies. Bridging the gap between technical experts and non-technical stakeholders requires strong communication skills and the ability to translate complex information into accessible language.

Collaboration and coordination across departments is key to ensuring a cohesive response to cyber incidents. Close cooperation with IT security teams, legal counsel, senior management and insurers is essential for developing comprehensive crisis communication plans and responding swiftly to emerging threats.

Organisational leaders must recognise the strategic importance of crisis communication in safeguarding reputation and maintaining stakeholder trust. Investing in training and resources for communication professionals demonstrates a commitment to proactive risk management and strengthens the organisation's resilience against cyber threats.

The implications for communication professionals and leadership teams underscore the need for ongoing education, collaboration, and strategic investment in crisis preparedness. New communication frameworks are emerging to address the threats associated with cyber attacks as a distinct form of crisis. By adopting a proactive and collaborative approach to crisis communication, private and public sector organisations alike can promote resilience, mitigate the impact of cyber attacks and maintain stakeholder confidence in a rapidly changing and vulnerable digital world.

References

1. **Australian Cyber Security Centre**, *Annual Cyber Threat Report 2022–2023.*
2. **Phair, N.**, *Cybercrime in Australia: 20 years of in-action* (2021).
3. **Coombs, WT**, *Ongoing Crisis Communication: Planning, Managing and Responding* (Sage Publications, 2015).
4. **Barton, L.**, *Crisis in Organisations II* (South-Western College Publishing, 2001).
5. **Duggan, S. J.**, 'Crisis Communication and Social Media: The Crisis Communication Capacity Gap and the Need for Awareness' (2020) 28(2) *Journal of Contingencies and Crisis Management* 149.

6. **Chen, P.**, 'Framing Cybersecurity: Exploring Crisis Frames and Their Influence on Public Perceptions of Cybersecurity' (2019) 54(3) *Australian Journal of Political Science* 377.
7. **Lindgren, M.**, 'Media Literacy and Communication in Times of Crisis: Challenging the Crisis and Resilience Paradigm' (2018) 168(1) *Media International Australia* 63.
8. **Knight, R., and Nurse, J. R. C.**, 'A Framework for Effective Corporate Communication after Cyber Security Incidents' (2020) 99 *Computers & Security*.
9. **Office of the Australian Information Commissioner**, *Data Breach Preparation and Response: A Guide to Managing Data Breaches in Accordance with the Privacy Act 1988 (Cth)* (2021) https://www.oaic.gov.au/privacy/guidance-and-advice/data-breach-preparation-and-response/.
10. **Dybac, S.**, 'Crisis Communication in the Digital Age' (2022) *The PR Hub*.
11. "**Optus Data Breach: A Crisis Mismanaged**," (2022) *Australian Financial Review*.
12. **Matejic, N.**, 'Managing Government Cybersecurity Breaches' (2022) *Crisis Comm*.
13. "**Medicare Data Breach: Government Response Under Scrutiny**," (2022) *Sydney Morning Herald*.
14. **Stilgherrian**, 'Cybersecurity Lessons from Recent Data Breaches' (2022) *Technology Today*.
15. **Office of the Australian Information Commissioner**, *Data Breach Notifications* (2024) https://www.oaic.gov.au/privacy/notifiable-data-breaches/notifiable-data-breaches-publications.

Deb Camden is the Principal of PRISM Communication Architects and Founder of The Communication Dividend, a data and analytics solution supporting communication professionals in proving and improving their value. A seasoned communicator, Deb has built a reputation as a high-performance consultant specialising in strategic communication and managing complex, contentious issues. Her early career as a journalist with the Brisbane Telegraph and The Sunday Mail, combined with her expertise in reputation management, has shaped her strategic approach to handling crises. Deb has been called upon to advise and lead communication responses for various crises, including a passenger train derailment, bomb threat, community outrage from coal seam gas protests, and a potential cyber-attack on critical port infrastructure, all posing significant reputation risks for clients. Deb emphasises that preparedness is crucial for managing all organizational threats, including the increasingly visible cyber crisis management. A Fellow of Communication and Public Relations Australia (CPRA), Deb holds a B Business (Communication) from QUT and an MBA from The University of Queensland. She co-chairs the International Association for the Measurement and Evaluation of Communication (AMEC) Asia Pacific chapter and is a two-time Bronze Award winner in the 2019 AMEC International Awards for Communication Effectiveness.

Conclusion

Dale Stephens, Matthew Stubbs, and Samuel White

This edited collection encapsulates the insights gleaned from the inaugural Research Unit on Military Law and Ethics (RUMLAE) Cyber Resilience Conference, held at the University of Adelaide on September 4, 2023. It draws upon a diverse array of contributors to offer a multifaceted perspective on the promotion of resilience in cyberspace. Spanning government, academia, and industry, the contributions provide a comprehensive examination of the challenges and strategies essential for enhancing cyber resilience.

The imperative for cyber resilience is underscored by the accelerating digitization of the global economy and the concomitant rise in cyberthreats. Projections as of 2023 indicated that 65% of the global GDP would be digitized,[1] emphasizing both the extensive economic opportunities and the critical need for robust cybersecurity measures. This digitization also exposes vulnerabilities inherent in interconnected systems, necessitating resilience strategies to ensure continuity and security.

In their contributions to this volume, Samuel White and Joanna Jarose collectively explored the intersection of international law and legal principles with cybersecurity and resilience. Their analyses emphasized the necessity of adapting existing legal frameworks to confront the unique challenges posed by cyberthreats and warfare. They advocate for international cooperation and robust legal mechanisms to safeguard digital infrastructure and uphold global security.

The chapters by Dale Stephens, Susanne Lloyd-Jones, and Socrates Giatrakos examined the roles of military operations, critical infrastructure security, and intelligence services in cultivating resilience. Their contributions underscore the evolving

D. Stephens · M. Stubbs · S. White (✉)
The University of Adelaide, Adelaide, Australia
e-mail: Samuel.white@adelaide.edu.au

D. Stephens
e-mail: Dale.stephens@adelaide.edu.au

M. Stubbs
e-mail: Matthew.stubbs@adelaide.edu.au

D. Stephens et al. (eds.), *Digital Resilience*,
https://doi.org/10.1007/978-981-97-9746-2_15

nature of warfare in the digital age and the crucial importance of protecting essential systems from cyberthreats.

John Small, Aneta Peretko, and Hamish McNamara delved into the intricate relationship between data protection, disinformation, and digital resilience. Their contributions stress the need for robust data protection laws and innovative legal mechanisms to combat misinformation and bolster trust in digital systems.

Ellie Watford and Beth Nosworthy investigated the legal responsibilities of corporate directors and the role of litigation in fostering resilience. They advocate for legal reforms that integrate cybersecurity duties and emphasize the significance of accountability and transparency in corporate governance.

In their chapter, Sam White and Matthew Stubbs concentrated on non-legal policy responses and the significance of cybersecurity education. Their work underscores the necessity for proactive measures and educational initiatives to empower individuals and organizations to fortify their digital resilience.

The dual frameworks of engineering and ecological resilience presented in this work furnish a robust foundation for comprehending and implementing resilience strategies. Engineering resilience centers on the capacity to endure and recover from disturbances, whereas ecological resilience underscores adaptation and absorption of impacts. These approaches underscore the multifaceted nature of resilience, applicable to both static and dynamic responses to cyberthreats.

Economic resilience is paramount in a digitized global economy, where data access and secure transmission are pivotal. The escalating costs of cybercrime, as evidenced by the financial ramifications on Australian businesses, underscore the need for comprehensive cybersecurity strategies.

On the strategic front, the weaponization of data and cyberoperations poses significant challenges. The evolving nature of these threats mandates a resilient defense strategy that can adapt to and mitigate insidious threats, as elucidated by Australian security officials.

Achieving cyber resilience entails ensuring that systems can recover and adapt in the face of disruptions. By fostering both engineering and ecological resilience, stakeholders can sustain core functions and identities despite challenges. This resilience is indispensable for perpetuating economic growth, national security, and public trust in an interconnected world.

This collection underscores that resilience is a dynamic concept crucial for navigating the complexities of the digital age. As technology advances, resilience principles and practices will become increasingly vital in ensuring that systems, economies, and societies can withstand and thrive amidst evolving cyberthreats. Through a concerted effort to cultivate and sustain resilience, we can forge a secure, trusted, and prosperous digital environment for all.

Note

1. Credit Suisse Research Institute, 'Global Wealth Report' (Report, 15 June 2023) <https://www.ubs.com/global/en/family-office-uhnw/reports/global-wealth-report-2023.html>.

Dale Stephens is a Professor of the faculty of the Adelaide Law School at the University of Adelaide and a Captain in the Royal Australian Navy Reserve who spent over 20 years as a permanent officer in the Royal Australian Navy before taking up his appointment at Adelaide Law School. He has occupied numerous staff officer positions throughout his career in the Australian Defence Force (ADF), including Fleet Legal Officer, Command Legal Officer (Naval Training Command), Chief Legal Officer Strategic Operations Command, Director of Operational and International Law, Deputy Director of the Asia-Pacific Centre for Military Law (a joint venture with Melbourne University Law School), Director Navy Legal and Director of the Military Law Centre. He has deployed twice to East Timor (INTERFET & UNTAET) and twice to Iraq (Baghdad) in senior legal officer positions and has provided extensive advice to Government at the strategic level. He is the recipient of the Conspicuous Service Medal and the (US) Bronze Star as well as ADF and UN commendations for his service.

Matthew Stubbs is a Professor of the faculty of the Adelaide Law School at the University of Adelaide, where he serves as Editor in Chief of the *Adelaide Law Review* and Program Coordinator of Postgraduate Coursework Programs and Military Law Programs. Professor Stubbs is involved with professional bodies in the law and academia, and is a member and former Chair of the Space Law Committee and Human Rights Committee of the Law Society of South Australia and a member of the Law Council of Australia's National Human Rights Committee. Matthew was awarded the Law Society of South Australia President's Medal in 2023.

Samuel White is a Senior Lecturer of the faculty of the Adelaide Law School at the University of Adelaide. He is concurrently a Visiting Fellow at the Australian Defence Force Academy and holds positions as an Adjunct Associate Professor at the University of New England. In 2024, he was made an Associate Fellow of the Royal Historical Society and the first Army Visiting Fellow at the Australian War Memorial. Samuel has also served as both a Royal Australian Infantry Corps and an Australian Army Legal Corps officer in a variety of tactical, operational and strategic level postings. His military experiences focused his doctoral studies, which addressed the constitutional ambit and limitations of responding to foreign interference (both traditional and modern forms) via military responses.

The manufacturer's authorised representative in the EU is Springer Nature Customer Service Centre GmbH, Europaplatz 3, 69115 Heidelberg, Germany. If you have any concerns regarding our products, please contact ProductSafety@springernature.com

Printed and bound by CPI Group (UK) Ltd, Croydon, CR0 4YY
01/10/2026
02225925-0007